Losing the Blanket

Australia and the End of Britain's Empire

David Goldsworthy

MELBOURNE UNIVERSITY PRESS

MELBOURNE UNIVERSITY PRESS
PO Box 278, Carlton South, Victoria 3053, Australia
mup-info@unimelb.edu.au
www.mup.com.au

First published 2002
Text © David Goldsworthy 2002
Design and typography © Melbourne University Press 2002

Typeset in 10 point Meridien
by Syarikat Seng Teik Sdn.Bhd., Malaysia
Printed in Australia by Brown Prior Anderson

National Library of Australia Cataloguing-in-Publication entry

Goldsworthy, David, 1938– .
   Losing the blanket: Australia and the end of Britain's empire.
   Bibliography.
   includes index.
   ISBN 0 522 85028 6.

   1. Decolonization—Great Britain—Colonies—History—20th
   century. 2. Postcolonialism—Great Britain. 3.
   Postcolonialism—Australia. 4. Australia—Foreign relations—
   Great Britain. 5. Great Britain—Foreign relations—Australia.
   6. Australia—Foreign relations. 7. Australia—Politics and
   government—1945–1965. 8. Great Britain—Colonies—
   History—20th century. I. Title.

327.94041

Published with the assistance of the Monash University
Publications Grants Committee

Contents

Acknowledgments

The principal themes and ideas presented in this book were given their first airings at conferences and seminars in Australia, Britain and Canada. I am grateful to the many participants in these gatherings who offered comments. I owe thanks to Stuart Macintyre, who read the manuscript for Melbourne University Press, and Pierre Hutton, who commented on Chapter 4. I thank also Sally Nicholls and Jean Dunn for their fine editing and Margot Jones for steering the work through the production process. Responsibility for the content of the finished work remains mine alone.

Most of the research was done in the National Archives of Australia, the National Library of Australia, the Matheson Library at Monash University and the Public Record Office in London. I am happy to acknowledge the efficient and courteous help provided by the staffs of these institutions. Thanks are also due to Monash University for awarding me an ARC Small Grant, which helped fund my research in London.

Earlier versions of Chapters 2, 3, 5 and 6 have been published as follows: Chapter 2 under the title 'The British colonial order, 1948–60', in David Lowe (ed.), *Australia and the End of Empires: The Impact of Decolonisation in Australia's Near North, 1945–65*, Deakin University Press, Geelong, 1996, pp. 137–59; Chapter 3 under the title 'British territories and Australian mini-imperialism in the 1950s', in *Australian Journal of Politics and History*, vol. 41, 1995, pp. 356–72; Chapter 5 under the title 'Menzies, Britain and the Commonwealth: the old order changeth', in Frank Cain (ed.), *Menzies in War and Peace*, Allen & Unwin, Sydney, 1997, pp. 99–115; and Chapter 6 under the title 'Menzies, Macmillan and Europe', in *Australian Journal of International Affairs*, vol. 51, 1997, pp. 157–69. I thank the respective editors for consenting to the republication of these writings in revised form.

And I thank Jo for her love and support through the years of this book's preparation.

David Goldsworthy

Abbreviations

ANZAM	Australia, New Zealand and Malaya (area)
ANZUS	Australia, New Zealand and the United States (security treaty)
CENTO	Central Treaty Organisation (Britain, Iran, Iraq, Pakistan, Turkey)
EEC	European Economic Community
EFTA	European Free Trade Association
GATT	General Agreement on Tariffs and Trade
NATO	North Atlantic Treaty Organisation
SCAAP	Special Commonwealth African Assistance Plan
SEATO	South-East Asia Treaty Organisation

Introduction

'AUSTRALIANS NO LONGER think of themselves as a British country', John Howard declared to journalists during Australia's Centenary of Federation celebrations in July 2000.[1] This, it might be noted, was not the same as saying that the link with Britain no longer held any special meaning for Australians, or at least those Australians—still the majority of the population in 2000—who were of British Isles descent. Certainly the link remained special enough for large numbers of Australians, including Howard, to feel no contradiction between their Australian nationalism and their monarchism, as had been demonstrated in the republic referendum in the previous year. Their attitude in this respect was a legacy of imperial history, standing in recognisable line of descent from the attitude of those earlier generations of Australians who had stoutly affirmed their dual loyalty to Australia and empire.

In itself, however, Howard's remark was broadly accurate. A great deal had changed during the federal century. At its outset Australia was heavily dependent, in both material and psychological terms, on Britain. At its end, this was no longer the case. Very naturally, the long journey out of Britishness has taken a prominent place among the themes of twentieth-century Australian historiography. The titles or subtitles of various works looking back from the vantage point of the century's later decades make the essential theme quite explicit: *Going it Alone*; *Out of Empire*; *The Demise of the Imperial Ideal*.[2] The various official enactments and measures designed to dispose of what the Whitlam Government in its day called 'colonial relics'[3] have commonly been represented as milestones in the journey: the adoption of the Statute of Westminster in 1942; the *Nationality Act* of 1948; the delimiting of judicial appeals to the Privy Council in 1968; the alteration of the monarch's Australian title to 'Queen of Australia' in 1973; the *Australia Act* of 1986.

There might seem to be a risk of whiggishness in such discourse, but it is clear enough that most writers in the field are well aware of that danger and do their best to guard against it. The common currency of the literature is that change was never a smooth, even or unilinear process, and that the narrative thread cannot be presented as a single-stranded one. It has been stressed, for example, that the notion of initial Australian dependence needs to be qualified by the evidence that Australian assertiveness was part of the interplay from the very outset—though whether or not this was 'thwarted nationalism' at work has been much debated.[4]

Within the literature generally, three broad sub-themes have predominated. The first is the decline of Australia's political and strategic dependence on Britain in international affairs; or, more exactly, the transfer of Australia's primary security relationship from Britain to the United States of America. This process is generally said to have begun during World War II and to have been effectively completed by the 1960s.[5] The second is the relative decline of economic linkages in much the same period. Here the story is one of an Australian transition from loyal membership of the sterling area and an overwhelming reliance on Britain for both trade and investment to a complex worldwide pattern of trading and investment relationships, with Japan and the United States becoming firmly established within this context as Australia's most important economic partners.[6] And the third is the decline of Anglocentric attitudes and general cultural and psychological dependence on Britain. Studies in this realm have typically concentrated on issues of national and personal identity, on the interplay between derivative and nativist cultural impulses in Australia, on issues of sentiment, and not least on the phenomenon of British race patriotism, which arguably was still a determining factor in Australian political culture and external policy in the 1950s—but which faded away in the 1960s.[7] Connections have been posited between these three aspects of decline, although there has not been a consensus on the main directions of influence. For example, on one hand, Stuart Ward proposes that 'the disentangling of Australian and British cultural identities was directly informed by the disentangling of their political and economic interests'.[8] On the other, June Connors speculates: 'Might not the weakening of cultural ties, whether through non-Anglo-Celtic migration, post-colonial consciousness, burgeoning radicalism or any number of other factors, have predisposed Australian politicians and negotiators to accept the British decision to sign up for the EEC?'[9] There is a chicken-or-egg problem here, possibly an inescapable one.

The literature has become very large, as literatures usually do. A glance at Stuart Macintyre's historiographical essay, 'Australia and the Empire',[10] or at the bibliography in Arnold, Spearritt and Walker's *Out of Empire* will be quite enough to establish the point. All in all, it must be said, the 'decline of Britishness' genre has become rather well worn. There have been signs of weariness among some of the writers themselves. Chicken-or-egg problems may have something to do with it. 'Explanations', as Connors puts it, 'have circled back on themselves to the point where many historians have withdrawn from the fray'.[11] When the journal *Australian Historical Studies* put together in 2001 a symposium of essays on the theme of Britishness and Australian identity, the first reaction of one of the contributors, John Rickard, was one of *déjà vu*: 'We have all been there, done that, so many times—or so it seems—and where has it got us?'[12]

However, Rickard went on to join issue with other contributors, thus demonstrating by example that there was life in the old discourse yet. And that brings us to the purpose of this book.

The book stands at a slight distance from the mainstream literature. By and large, it does not seek to dispute the major conventional wisdoms that have been built up over the years on the subject of Australia's journey out of empire. Nor is it concerned to buy into the debate on the main issue that (to judge by the *AHS* symposium) remains in contention, namely the 'thwarted nationalism' thesis already alluded to. What it does seek to do is to bring a different perspective to bear on the matter of Australia and empire by bringing empire more fully into the story.

One of the interesting things about the literature on 'Australia and the empire'—and this point extends to Macintyre's historiographical overview, which uses that phrase as its title—is that by and large the actually existing empire intrudes upon the discourse only in marginal or tangential ways. The real concern of the historical works cited here is usually with the bilateral relationship between Britain and Australia: that is to say, the hub of empire and one of the spokes. Of course there is a large literature on multilateral relationships, especially relationships among the old dominions within the Commonwealth. But that is a different point. The point here is that the literature on the role of the wider empire as a factor in the bilateral Anglo-Australian relationship, especially in the post-war period, is anything but substantial.

This study, then, aims to incorporate the formal empire, and to consider Anglo-Australian interactions with explicit reference to this entity. The word 'formal' needs to be stressed, since it signifies the book's particular interest in the colonial empire, a subject all but untreated in the Australian literature. Jim Davidson is one of the very few to have remarked on the more or less simultaneous processes of the 'decolonisation' of formal empire and the 'de-dominionisation' of Australia in the post-war era; but even he treats these processes as if there were few significant connections between them.[13] This book rests on the premise that there were indeed connections; connections that are well worth drawing out.

The book focuses on the relatively compact period of the 1950s and 1960s. In the 1950s, even after the transfer of power on the Indian subcontinent, Britain still controlled the world's largest empire. In the 1960s, that empire was almost completely dissolved. These were major facts of international politics: key elements, indeed, within the general process of Western decolonisation in the post-war era, which was itself a manifestation, some have argued, of a yet larger phenomenon, 'the dis-europeanisation of the world'.[14] Given the scale of the events, it is not surprising that decolonisation, too, has generated a massive literature. And yet many of the impacts and effects of decolonisation in world politics remain unexplored. In his contribution to David Lowe's edited volume *Australia and the End of Empires*, John Darwin writes that although decolonisation has its 'own' literature, it still forms

> a huge gap in the modern literature of international politics, especially for the period after 1945. The academic cringe towards the 'super powers', combined with Amerocentric or Eurocentric blinkers, has turned the international history of most of the world into a regional sideshow in the great drama of East–West struggle. We would be wiser to recognise that decolonisation—the decay and fall of classical imperialism—has actually been *the* central political fact for much of the world since the 1940s, and that much that is bafflingly treated as 'regional conflict' has been part of its chaotic fall-out.[15]

Darwin's observation effectively lays down a challenge: to give decolonisation its proper due as an explanatory paradigm in post-war international politics, so that it matches, or in some areas even outranks, the East–West conflict in explanatory power. The task would entail tracing the impacts and effects of post-war European decolonisation wherever in the world they might lead—even to third-party countries that on the face of it had little direct involvement in the process. The challenge thus conceived far exceeds in scope the ambit of this book, but it does furnish the book with its central proposition: that the winding down of Britain's formal empire had important implications for the sovereign state of Australia. This is a proposition that in some ways has been illustrated already in Lowe's volume. This book, however, seeks to take the argument a good deal further. In essence, the book aims to respond to Darwin's challenge by pursuing at some length the ramifications of the central question: what was the significance of the ending of Britain's empire for Australia's relationship with Britain, and more broadly for Australia's evolution as a foreign policy actor? To explore this question is to focus on a 'different' variable, or, to put the matter another way, to reconsider a familiar story from a less familiar angle; and thus, potentially, to add a dimension to themes already well established in historical scholarship. In short, the objective is not to supplant, but rather to supplement, existing understandings of the development of Australia's relations with its own former imperial power, and the development of its foreign policy more generally, in an era of significant global change.

Part I of the book focuses on the given question within the time frame of the 1950s, the last full decade of British imperial power, and into the early 1960s. The Indian subcontinent and the Palestine Mandate might have left the fold but Britain's empire in the 1950s still patched the maps of Asia, Africa, the Middle East, the Caribbean and Latin America, and also the Pacific, Indian and Atlantic oceans and the Mediterranean Sea. The fact of empire still enhanced, rather than detracted from, Britain's prestige in the eyes of those who ruled Australia. Pride in the red swathes lingered on, reinforcing these leaders' sense of their own Britishness and influencing the way they understood the world. The existence of empire helped both to express and to underwrite Britain's larger world role, something Australia still valued highly even as it looked increasingly to the United States for global leadership. More tangibly, the existence of Britain's empire still had considerable relevance to specific Australian interests. This was especially true of security interests in Southeast Asia. To a lesser extent it was also true of economic interests. Having material stakes in Britain's empire helped to create in Australia a mindset that was strongly supportive of the imperial status quo. In addition, questions to do with the practical management of empire entered into the exchanges between Britain and Australia. To take one example, the British model of colonial administration provided something of a template for Australia's. To take another, the two countries negotiated periodically on issues affecting British dependent territories, and even discussed, from time to time, the possibility of transferring responsibility for particular territories from Britain to Australia; surely one of the more remarkable illustrations of just how familial the Anglo-Australian relationship could be. In sum: Canberra's perception of Britain's formal empire was mediated by the Anglo-Australian relationship, and for reasons of both sentiment and self-interest, Canberra placed value on the formal empire's existence. Canberra knew of course that imperialism was under siege in assorted ways and would come to an end, but until the later 1950s simply did not anticipate—any more than London did—that the unravelling would prove to be so rapid.

The great wave of decolonisation—Darwin's 'central political fact for much of the world'—reached its climax with the numerous transfers of sovereignty in the 1960s, especially the first half of that decade. It was of course not just a British imperial phenomenon. The 1960s saw also the contraction or complete dissolution of the empires of France, Belgium, the Netherlands and Italy, with only the authoritarian states—Spain, Portugal and the Soviet Union—still grimly hanging on. The most dramatically visible consequence of this simultaneous ending of five empires was a rapid expansion of international society, with the universe of independent states almost trebling in number. In the diplomatic sphere, decolonisation thus meant that countries towards which existing states had felt little need to form detailed policies, precisely because they were 'non-self-governing' (in United Nations parlance), now loomed as independent actors, most of them neutralist in the Cold War context, and hence as necessary objects of foreign policy; a consequence felt by Australia as by all other UN members. This study, however, is concerned less with generalities than with the specific impact on Australia of Britain's movement from imperialism to post-imperialism. Of all the European decolonisations Britain's was by far the most significant from Australia's point of view, and by far the most direct in its impact.

In order to develop this theme, it is first necessary to see decolonisation in the wider context of British national policy. In London's perspective, decolonisation was not a discrete phenomenon but an element inseparable from other elements in what amounted to a sweeping attempt to reconfigure Britain's 'world role'. Several interlinked processes were in train. First, beginning in 1957 there was Britain's movement towards a more nuclear-based defence strategy, which pointed towards large reductions in conventional forces including those based in Australia's Southeast Asian neighbourhood. The ending of empire was intimately associated with this process of defence restructuring. Second, and also dating from 1957, there was the effort to restore and consolidate the political and strategic relationship with the United States, a relationship that had become a good deal less than 'special' during the trauma of Suez. In this effort colonialism was seen by the British as a liability. Third, there was the commercial approach to Europe, which gained significant momentum in 1961. In this context too colonialism was seen by London as something of a hindrance. And fourth, there was the attempt in the early 1960s to fashion the rapidly growing Commonwealth (its growth a direct consequence of decolonisation) into what Britain hoped, for a time, would be a vehicle for a continuing British role in the wider world; the conversion, in other words, of formal empire into informal spheres of influence.

For Australia, therefore, coping with the British retreat from empire in the 1960s merged into the task of coping with the general post-imperial order that Britain was trying to create for itself. Australia had few problems with the second of the four processes that have just been noted. In general, the more Britain and the United States agreed, especially on issues of Cold War strategy, the happier Australia was. But the other three processes were cause for some alarm; not just in themselves, but because they seemed likely to have flow-on effects with the potential to reshape Australia's policy environment in uncongenial ways. The central aim of Part II of the book, then, is to review some of these less congenial implications of Britain's transition to post-imperialism as perceived and experienced by Australia, and to assess Australian responses.

Stuart Ward has argued that the beginning of the end of the sense of a 'special' British connection as a factor in Australian external policy can be dated with remarkable precision. The critical year was 1961–62. This was the year in which Britain's strenuous first attempt to join the European Economic Community generated in Australia a feeling that it was, quite simply, being abandoned: that a relationship which Australian leaders had thought of as uniquely intimate was being sacrificed on the altar of British post-imperial ambitions, with the result that Australia had suddenly to adapt to a much more exposed position in the tough world of international commerce. This Australia managed to do, and quite quickly, but at the expense of a considerable change in the nature of its attachment to Britain.[16]

Ward is right to stress the pivotal character of the early 1960s in the unfolding of the Anglo-Australian story. But a comprehensive understanding of the changes that were taking place at that time requires that the European issue be contextualised. The approach to Europe was just one of a complex of changes in British policy associated with the shedding of the imperial past and the quest for a different kind of future. The implications of Britain's movement from imperialism to post-imperialism for Australia's defence interests, for Australia's position in the Commonwealth, for its policies in the United Nations, and for such appurtenances of Australia's British heritage as the right of immigration into Britain itself were all causes of concern for the Australian Government. Robert Menzies had reportedly concluded by about March 1961 that Australia no longer counted for 'a row of beans' in British eyes.[17] So palpable was Australian disenchantment with Britain in this period that the Commonwealth Relations Office in London mounted a detailed review of the whole relationship (without telling the Australians) to see what might be done to restore it to good order. It concluded that there was little it could do.

The consequences of Britain's dissolution of empire for Australia continued to unfold for some time beyond the pivotal early 1960s. Through the decade British hopes for a sustained or even an enhanced world role were severely undercut by a series of economic crises, with the result that Britain's ambitions and plans increasingly became confined to its northern neighbourhood. In these circumstances Britain's decolonisation came to appear not so much a way of maintaining influence by other means as the concomitant of what was after all a contracting world role, a yielding of spheres of influence to other players, notably the United States. The tide of influence did not flow out altogether smoothly, however. There were eddies and backswirls, one of which took place in Southeast Asia and was of the liveliest concern to Australia. For a time in the mid-1960s, in fact, Britain's military commitment in Southeast Asia, almost as far from the northern world as it was possible to get, actually increased. This was the consequence of a chain of events that began with Britain's formation of the Federation of Malaysia in 1963 as a framework for expediting its decolonisation in the region. Indonesia's military harassment of Malaysia ensued, and Britain was obliged to defend the state it had created. For Australia, this situation gave rise to the most testing of all the foreign policy problems deriving from the manner of British decolonisation. Even as Australia sought to build a stable relationship with Indonesia it was drawn into military collaboration with Britain in defence of Malaysia against Indonesia's policy of Confrontation. It was an episode of critical importance for the development of Australia's policies and diplomacy in the region.

The last of the major post-imperial problems for Australia followed soon afterwards. With Confrontation over and Malaysia evidently secured, Britain began moving towards its decision to withdraw militarily from Southeast Asia; as Australia saw it, to remove the final remnants of the old protective imperial power from Australia's region. For Britain, grasping this nettle was no easy matter. Among other things it required more than three years of negotiation with other parties, a good deal of it with Australia. Most of the detailed negotiation with Australia took place during the first two years after Robert Menzies' departure from the prime ministership. His successor, Harold Holt, was less Anglophile than Menzies and looked unequivocally to Washington for his main foreign policy alliance. But this did not mean that he was willing to see the British forces depart. Rather, he opposed Britain's plans from beginning to end. Australian representations ceased only with the British Cabinet's irrevocable decision of January 1968 to pull out the forces from everywhere east of Suez except Hong Kong and Brunei. Following hard as it did upon the devaluation of sterling, this decision, more than any other single event, signified the quietus of empire. In a still broader conspectus, it was uniquely emblematic of the demise of Britain's world role; for as Robert Holland has argued, 'the very visibility and traditional "feel" of the East of Suez policy had become almost synonymous with the nation's determination to maintain its prestige in the world generally'.[18] Canberra's perspective was more parochial. What it perceived was the final stage of Britain's post-imperial abandonment of Australia.

The winding down of British imperial power, then, had wide-ranging effects and after-effects from the point of view of the policy makers who governed Australia up until the later 1960s. This was especially true of those individual leaders who had grown to maturity during the zenith of empire; leaders representing the last Australian generation for whom the sense of having a higher identity as Britons was still personally and politically important. Although they accepted the inevitability of the ending of empire, such individuals found it extremely difficult to come fully to terms with some of the broader policy changes with which this process was associated. Yet so too did many of their less Anglophile colleagues; changes to the Commonwealth, to trade relationships and to regional security, for example, affected all of them, in ways that most of them felt to be unfavourable. Indeed, it would take several years before it could credibly be said that Australia had fully adjusted to the post-imperial order.

For all these reasons, both the last full decade of British formal imperialism—the 1950s—and the decade of dissolution and its aftermaths—the 1960s—are ripe for reconsideration from an Australian perspective. While there are other accounts of some of the episodes discussed here, this book is the first to consider the subject whole, and to offer an integrated account based on research in the primary sources which, under the majestic workings of the thirty-year rule, can now be accessed in both Britain and Australia.

PART I

Living with Britain's empire

In the 1950s the declared goal of Britain's colonial policy was to transfer power to the dependent territories, or at least to those deemed capable of sustaining independence. But first they had to be adequately 'prepared'. In practice, preparation was a piecemeal and uneven process that did not always reflect any great sense of urgency. The colonial empire remained virtually as far flung at the end of the decade as it had been at the beginning; indeed, between mid-1948 and mid-1960 only three territories—the Anglo-Egyptian condominium of the Sudan, and the colonies of Ghana and Malaya—attained independence. In the early 1960s, however, the rate of political devolution accelerated markedly, and within a few years the management of formal empire ceased to be a significant area of British government business.

In the 1950s and early 1960s Britain's relationship with Australia was similarly a blend of continuity and change. On the one hand, what had once been a formal imperial relationship was still in various constitutional, legal, customary and cultural ways a quasi-imperial one, legitimised by Australia's continued acceptance thereof. Australia was led by Robert Menzies, the 'last of the full-scale Australian political royalists', and many Australians still self-identified as in some sense British.[1] Economic ties were still strong, with Australia a member of the sterling area, Britain the leading source of foreign investment in Australia, and the British market the preferred destination of most Australian exporters. Strong too were certain strategic and diplomatic links. Australia collaborated in Britain's nuclear weapons program, provided support for the British anti-guerrilla campaign in Malaya, and sometimes sided with Britain rather than the United States when these two major powers differed on key issues, such as how best to handle the crises in Indochina in 1954 and Suez in 1956.

On the other hand, the process of de-dominionisation was visibly at work in Australia. The non-British proportion of the Australian population was increasing, and so were non-British cultural influences. At the political level Australia was sometimes assertively independent of Britain, especially in the politics of its own region, and there were significant moves in train involving alternative partners in the realms of strategy and economy. That Australia's primary strategic association was with the United States became progressively more evident during the decade following the ANZUS treaty negotiations of 1950–51; while by the later 1950s the Imperial Preference scheme had been renegotiated and Australia was actively pursuing a closer trade relationship with Japan, as Britain was with Europe.

These two themes—the management of Britain's formal empire in the 1950s and early 1960s, and the relationship between Britain and Australia in the same period—have been discussed in substantial but largely separate literatures. The aim of Part 1 of this book is to bring out some of the many connections between them. Australian interests and involvements in the British colonial empire affected both Australia's relationship with Britain and Australian external policy more generally. One good illustration of this is that Australia sought for several years to enhance its economic and security interests by taking over responsibility for various British island territories in the Indian and South Pacific oceans. Another is that the region of Sub-Saharan Africa, in which Australia had shown negligible interest until the mid-1950s, became perforce an object of Australian foreign policy precisely because of the accelerating movement by Britain (and other powers) towards decolonisation. The approach of decolonisation signalled the emergence of new states that, among other things, appeared likely to become arenas of Cold War competition. Australia, a Cold War partisan, interpreted Africa's emergence largely in this light, and sought to develop strategic and economic policies towards the African region accordingly. In this respect Australia's approach may be seen as representative of its policies towards the late colonial world fairly generally.

1

Empire: the view from Canberra

WINSTON CHURCHILL, we know, did not become Prime Minister of Great Britain in 1940, or for that matter in 1951, to preside over the liquidation of the British Empire. It might equally be said that Robert Menzies did not become Prime Minister of Australia in 1939, or for that matter in 1949, to support any such project. Britain's empire was liquidated nevertheless, mainly in the twenty years or so from the late 1940s to the late 1960s. And in much the same period the ties between Australia and Britain loosened considerably. There were links between these phenomena.

Australia and Britishness

It can of course be argued that the decline in Australia's British connection had been set in motion well before the period embraced by this study, beginning perhaps with the fall of Singapore to the Japanese and the subsequent well-documented anti-British feelings in Australia in the dark days of 1942. Just before Singapore fell, John Curtin had issued his celebrated 'call' to the United States, 'free of any pangs as to our traditional links or kinship with the United Kingdom'. It is clear enough, however, that Curtin did not expect a formal ongoing alliance with the United States, and neither did the United States give him any reason to hope for one. General Douglas MacArthur bluntly told him in June 1942 that the United States would not undertake to guarantee Australia's security; Washington saw Australia only as a temporary base and 'had no sovereign interest in the integrity of Australia'. Rather, MacArthur said, it was Britain that still had responsibilities to Australia through 'ties of blood, sentiment and allegiance to the Crown'.[1] Hence the argument that has sometimes been put, that at the end of the war 'No longer was Australia an imperial Antipodes, but the New Frontier down under',[2] seems to be a case of antedating. Curtin as wartime leader certainly did not wish to be thought disloyal to Britain; in public he declared Australia's attachment to the mother country, and in private he conferred closely with London on matters of defence and foreign policy.[3] So too in the later 1940s did Prime Minister Ben Chifley and his External Affairs Minister H. V. Evatt. Chifley was deeply concerned with maintaining the sterling area, and was capable of proclaiming Australia's Britishness to an extent that the British themselves found both embarrassing and politically inconvenient (their concern was that displays of white-empire bonding might deter the new Commonwealth states in South Asia from joining in plans for Middle East defence).[4] It is true that certain issues were strongly disputed between the Australian and British governments, but this was no new thing and does not alter the general point.

It is also true that Evatt 'turned to America' in so far as he floated the idea of a multilateral Pacific pact. This needs to be seen as a variation on a long-running theme. The problem of finding a way to ensure Pacific security had not simply arisen in the crisis of 1941–42; it had long been an Australian preoccupation. Indeed, as Neville Meaney notes, 'From Federation all Australian governments refused to join in imperial defence schemes which did not provide adequately for their security in the Pacific'.[5] The United States, however, had never shown interest in a formal multilateral pact, any more than it had felt itself to have a 'sovereign interest in the integrity of Australia'. Not until the deepening of the Cold War and the emergence of the People's Republic of China at the century's mid-point did Washington begin to take a closer interest in the idea of a formal alliance focused upon the Pacific region. It was this closer interest that made possible the significant development of Australia's American relationship after mid-century, that is, during the period of the Menzies Government.

This, it should be said, was far from being Menzies' only foray outside the imperial fold. Carl Bridge has referred to the way in which Menzies is 'so often portrayed these days as an obscurantist stick-in-the-mud who hankered vainly to put the British imperial Humpty Dumpty back together again in the 1950s and 1960s'.[6] Rather, as Bridge observes, Menzies

> saw more clearly than most the implications of the new world order of his time. It was Menzies who presided over most of the new and massive migrant intake from Europe. He approved the ANZUS treaty with the new superpower and began freeing up the economy to American penetration. And he saw as early as 1957 that Japanese trade was vital and, despite the still raw wounds of war, pushed through a crucial trade treaty that helped make possible our trading relationship now.[7]

Bridge is right to stress this theme. Nevertheless it is worth making the point that Menzies saw (or more exactly, in some cases, came to see) such policy developments as a matter of pragmatic necessity, which is rather different from saying that he was invariably enthusiastic about them. The best way of developing this point is by way of a dialectical argument, bringing out first some indications of his lack of enthusiasm and second some indications of his acceptance of necessity; with the synthesis of the argument lying in the conclusion that although the United States (and later Japan) increasingly mattered to Australia, Britain still mattered a great deal as well.

On the security agreement with the United States, for which his External Affairs Minister Percy Spender pushed hard during 1950–51, Menzies was for a time less than convinced that it was a good or feasible idea. In mid-1950 he famously told British representatives in London and Ottawa that the proposed treaty was a superstructure 'on a foundation of jelly'.[8] (This undermining remark was quickly relayed, by other people, back to Spender.[9]) Writing home from Washington in August, Menzies opined to the Deputy Prime Minister Arthur Fadden that since the Americans were 'already overwhelmingly friendly to us', Australia did not need a pact with America.[10] Meanwhile even Spender maintained until at least October that if there were to be a pact, British membership would be 'essential . . . on account of their interests in the Pacific'.[11] Washington firmly rejected this idea, largely because it had no wish to become involved in the defence of British colonialism. Richard Casey, who succeeded Spender as Minister for External Affairs in April 1951, continued to worry lest Australia's closer association with the United States 'drift into less close and confident relations with Britain', and in August 1952 he tried to persuade the Americans to let British liaison officers attend meetings of the ANZUS Council. But even this diluted form of British representation was unacceptable to the Americans.[12]

On another security issue of the time, the war between North and South Korea which broke out in mid-1950, Menzies initially overruled Spender's urging that Australian troops (as well as ships and planes) be committed to the American-led United Nations force, partly for the reason that Britain would not be sending ground forces and in that case neither should Australia. This decision was reversed by Spender and Fadden in Menzies' absence after they learned that the British Government had changed its mind.[13]

As for the Japanese trade treaty, it was not Menzies but John McEwen, Minister for Trade and Commerce, who 'pushed through' the agreement, and who recalled later that no one else was keen to share the task with him. According to Malcolm Fraser, 'Menzies wouldn't give him [McEwen] the authority to negotiate in the name of the government because he regarded the political risk as being too great'. Menzies stayed out of the negotiations and did not attend the Cabinet committee meeting which made the key final decisions for Australia, perhaps so that he could retain the option of dissociating himself from them should McEwen's political judgment prove wrong.[14]

In all these cases of decision-making, however, Menzies eventually swung his weight behind the ministers concerned. For example, in February 1951 he authorised Spender to send an extremely forthright message to London rejecting all of the Attlee Government's objections to the ANZUS treaty.[15] Further, the overall trends in Australian policy that found expression in these decisions were evident enough. Interests were interests, and any regret or reluctance Menzies might have felt was no more than a qualification to the main theme. Thus in security matters, ANZUS was followed in 1955–57 by developments in Australian defence doctrine that decisively confirmed the United States as Australia's principal military ally in Southeast Asia and the Southwest Pacific.[16] Given the relative strengths of the United States and other countries' military forces in the Asia-Pacific region during the Cold War, this was hardly to be wondered at. By a similar token, from the early 1950s the Menzies Government scouted well beyond the sterling area and the Commonwealth preference system in its search for export markets. It also made strenuous attempts to obtain American dollar loans for national development, resulting in clashes with the British Government whose overwhelming concern was to reduce rather than increase sterling's indebtedness against the dollar.[17] But given the high degree to which Australia's post-war economic prosperity depended upon both successful trade performance and the attracting of investment capital, these policies too could not have caused much surprise (as distinct from ire) in London.

In short, it could not be said that the British connection constituted some kind of all-consuming obsession on Menzies' part, let alone an all-determining factor in his policy making. To make this general point, however, is not to argue that as of the 1950s Australia's relations with Britain were, or were thought to be, in absolute decline. In particular, the evident fact that the United States was becoming Australia's most important strategic ally did not preclude ongoing, close and substantial connections with Britain across a very wide range of issues and policy areas. For example: in the commercial realm Britain remained Australia's largest trading partner by far. In the sphere of immigration, people from the British Isles continued to provide the largest single component in Australia's annual intake. There was Anglo-Australian military collaboration in Malaya, and a broader regional pattern of imperial defence planning that involved Australia with both Britain and New Zealand. There was a continuing Asia-focused association in the Colombo Plan. There was a shared understanding of many major international problems, leading Australia to provide diplomatic support for Britain rather than the United States when the two powers differed over Indochina in 1954, and leading Menzies to support a beleaguered Britain, again contra the United States, over Suez in 1956. And there was a history going back to the 1940s of close cooperation with Britain in the development of nuclear weaponry.

It is worth amplifying a little on the last three of these examples—on Indochina, Suez and the bomb—since they provide particularly vivid illustrations of the point. In 1954, as defeat loomed for the French army besieged at Dien Bien Phu by the Viet Minh forces, the United States sought its allies' support for 'united action', in effect a military intervention to rescue the French. Menzies and Casey would have none of this, and in a cable to Spender, by now Australian Ambassador in Washington, explicitly rejected the proposition that Australia's destiny was 'so wrapped up with the United States that we should support them even if we believe the course of action proposed by them is wrong'. Menzies and Casey noted that Britain and other Commonwealth countries were also refusing to heed the American call for united action, and argued, in emphatic terms, that this fact in itself made participation in an intervention 'a completely impossible proposition for Australia to promote for it would be the first cleavage in Commonwealth unity . . . we can conceive of nothing more destructive to Commonwealth unity than for Australia to be neutral in a United Kingdom war or the United Kingdom neutral in an Australian war'. In London an appreciative Anthony Eden circulated a copy of this message to his Cabinet colleagues.[18]

Menzies' role in the Suez crisis has been analysed at book length elsewhere and there is no need here to rehearse the details. But what deserves still to be highlighted is the thoroughness of his commitment to Eden's cause. Even after the catastrophic failure of the Anglo-French military assault on Egypt, Menzies remained as one with senior British leaders in his conviction that Britain's Suez policy had been fully justified. For him, Britain had been 'practical and courageous' and 'immeasurably wise'.[19] As for the British view: 'What fools the Americans were', Lord Home, the Commonwealth Secretary, wrote to Menzies six days after Harold Macmillan had succeeded Eden in the prime ministership. 'A blind eye for a week and the world of the free would have been immeasurably stronger. Here Harold is full of determination. There is to be no retreat or excuse for our previous actions. Selwyn's retention is a public mark of that.'[20] In April 1957, six months after Suez, Menzies was still decreeing that 'we must stick with Britain'.[21] His stand on Suez was not merely a case of 'blind loyalty'; it reflected also a conception (which Casey did not altogether share) of Australian self-interest; but the point is that for Menzies, the loyalty and the self-interest led to the same conclusion.

As for the Anglo-Australian interactions on nuclear issues, it was not simply that Australia provided its deserts for the testing of British weaponry.[22] From time to time Australia raised the question of whether Britain might help Australia to become a nuclear power itself, one that would work in close collaboration with Britain. Wayne Reynolds, the historian of Australia's nuclear ambitions, has traced a pattern of close cooperation in which the possibility of Australia itself 'going nuclear' seemed often to be on the cards—at least until 1957. This was the year of the Bermuda conference between Eisenhower and Macmillan at which America agreed to supply nuclear knowhow and technology to Britain, a prize that Britain had long sought and one that greatly diminished the significance of Australia in Britain's nuclear program.[23] Yet as late as June 1961 Menzies sought an assurance from Macmillan that Australia could acquire from Britain 'nuclear means of self-protection if Australia ever judged it necessary in the future'. Macmillan suggested to Home, by this time Foreign Secretary, that Britain should give Australia 'as much as we can', for at least three reasons: to maintain the Anglo-Australian relationship in good order; to head off any similar request from Canberra to Washington; and (presciently) to mitigate the impact on Australia of British entry into Europe and a possible reduction of the British military commitment in Southeast Asia. Others in Whitehall were less enthusiastic and in due course the matter was shelved out of a larger concern not to upset the Americans, a motive that Menzies understood and accepted.[24] But the fact of the request and the nature of Macmillan's initial response both say a great deal about the intimacy on strategic issues that both sides still seemed to take for granted at that time.

Indicative too was Canberra's administrative arrangement for dealing with London. Throughout his long prime ministership Menzies maintained the 'old-dominion' system by which the major responsibility for Australia's conduct of relations with Britain lay in—and was jealously guarded by—the Prime Minister's Department. London, as a retired External Affairs official later sardonically put it, was 'Menzies' sacred preserve'.[25] External Affairs did not always see this disposition of the diplomatic channels as satisfactory, but for Menzies the arrangement was wholly appropriate and in keeping with the particular spirit of the Anglo-Australian connection. (It would survive until 1972.)

Further reinforcing the whole relationship at the Australian end was the continuing reservoir of pro-British sentiment among both the political elite and the general public. Even more powerful in its effect was what might be called a psycho-cultural factor: the belief among many that their own higher identity was British. As the historian Russel Ward put it: 'For most, but not all people, national and imperial patriotism were complementary, not contradictory'.[26] In 1949 Richard Casey, who had the distinction of having served as a minister in both the Australian and British governments, referred to 'the fact that we are a member of a great cooperative society: the British race, of which the senior partner is our mother country'.[27] At the end of 1956 Paul Hasluck, who was undoubtedly an Australian patriot and who possessed the very un-British middle names of Meernaa Caedwalla, could nonetheless, in a letter to Menzies, refer to himself as British, and to Australia as 'a British community and a British democracy'.[28] In an era when (for example) royal tours generated huge popular enthusiasm, and Australian passports were still designated British, few would have found these self-perceptions unusual or remarkable. Casey's and Hasluck's attitudes could be seen as typical expressions of British race patriotism, as some scholars have styled it;[29] a sentiment which not only permeated Australia's domestic political culture but still had an important influence on aspects of Australian external policy. And no one exemplified this attitude better than Menzies. 'You must never entertain any doubt', he wrote to Eden shortly before the British troops went into Suez, 'about the British quality of this country'.[30]

Australia and empire

Matters of empire were an element in the Anglo-Australian nexus right up until the 1960s. For Robert Menzies, the roots of this attitude went back to the jingoism instilled into his generation—born and brought up during the 'high' noon of empire—perhaps more than into any other. David Lowe, in discussing the work of Judith Brett, has expressed what amounts to the scholarly consensus on this matter:

> Menzies' idealised conception of the British empire underpinned his notion of the sources of stability and cohesion in human affairs—not only domestic affairs, but in the ordering of those parts of the world that the empire had touched. In this organic model, to disturb the centre, to disturb Britain's hold on its empire, was to threaten the periphery, which included Australia.[31]

This was a conceptual world that Menzies clearly shared with many of his closest colleagues, almost all of whom were men of the high noon generation.

Yet if Menzies and others conceived of empire in more or less organic terms, it could not be said that they applied the organic idea with equal force to all parts of the empire. For roughly the first two-thirds of the twentieth century, the period that encompassed the political careers of Menzies and most of his colleagues, the British Empire comprised various components, and Australian organicist sentiments applied strongly to only one of them.

This was the empire of Britain and the old dominions—Australia, New Zealand, Canada and South Africa. The Statute of Westminster had officially introduced the designation 'British Commonwealth of Nations', and by the later 1940s the old dominions had been joined as members of that Commonwealth by India, Pakistan and Ceylon. Yet the idea of a special imperial affinity among the old dominions, or perhaps more exactly the sense of a common British descent and a shared allegiance to the Crown, still retained its potency among many who lived in these countries. Loyalty to empire in this sense was fused with loyalty to Britain itself, the seat of the monarchy. Indicatively, in later years Menzies would sometimes refer to the old-dominion group of states as the 'Crown Commonwealth', in order to distinguish them from the ranks of the Commonwealth republics.

The other major component of empire was that congeries of dependent, and mainly tropical, territories still administered (or in the case of 'informal empire', overwhelmingly influenced) by Britain. It was never a secret that Menzies felt little or no sense of familial attachment to the leaders and peoples of the British dependent territories in Asia, Africa, the Caribbean and elsewhere. They had next to nothing to do with what he called in 1955 'the old intimate association'.[32] He saw them as located a long way below the old dominions in the imperial hierarchy, which was also, rather clearly, a racial hierarchy. But, that having been said, Menzies certainly approved of the fact of imperial control in these regions. It was good that they were under British sway, and it could be hoped that British influence would rub off on them. There is a telling entry in Menzies' diary for 12 March 1935, when he visited Colombo on his way to London:

> Here is a golf course, there a soccer football ground (in this climate!), there a cricket ground. The town is clean. A few hundreds of Englishmen rule it and clean it and water it. The more I see of such people the more satisfied I am that while doctrinaires and theorists speculate about self-government for natives (who are chiefly experts in idleness and the demanding of baksheesh), the British calmly go on their way giving to these peoples what they could never give themselves.[33]

More broadly, all the main European empires, with the obvious exception of the Russian, seemed to him to be worthy of support, since all, in their varying ways, could be seen as bearers of European influence in the non-Western parts of the globe. Hence in Australia's own neighbourhood the reinstatement in 1945 of British rule in Southeast Asia, French rule in Indochina and Dutch rule in the East Indies all provided relief and re-assurance, for these were islands of European power in an otherwise alien Asian world. All this made Menzies pro-imperial in a very full sense; his imperial sympathies applied not just to Australia's place in the world, but also, as Gregory Pemberton has put it, 'to the place of other territories in the world'.[34]

The discussion in this book must necessarily take account of all the main senses of empire—the old dominions, the Commonwealth more broadly understood, and the colonial empire—for these senses were interconnected; it was after all the dissolution of the colonial empire that destroyed the 'organic' character of the Commonwealth. Indeed the various senses of the term will sometimes need to be elided. But much has already been written about Australia as an old dominion and as a member of the broader Commonwealth, and relatively little about Australia and the colonial empire. This study focuses mainly on the less familiar of the terrains: that is to say, on the ways in which Australian policy makers approached the issues raised by the existence, the ending and the after-effects of British colonialism.

The colonial question after 1945

Menzies' support for imperialism in all its senses was distinctive only in the force and clarity with which he articulated it. In the 1950s pride in the Empire/Commonwealth was still the norm in Australia, a function of the pride in the British heritage itself. At the political level, pro-imperialism had pervaded the world view of the Liberal Party and its variously labelled predecessors since Federation. Until mid-century Labor too was in many ways a party of empire.

However, the parties' positions were not identical. What made the difference was that Labor's historically derived traditions embraced also an anti-imperial strand, and this emerged from time to time in response to touchstone issues. In World War I conscription provided a case in point. And after 1945, some of the key issues of the day elicited what might be described as differing degrees of adherence to the imperial cause. One was the issue of whether Australia should focus its post-war defence policy on the needs of imperial defence in the Middle East or concentrate rather on its own regional defence. Labor favoured the latter course whereas Menzies accepted the case for the former, at least until the early to middle 1950s when developments in the imperial division of labour resulted in a British-endorsed concentration of Australia's defence effort in Southeast Asia. The other major issue was the future of the colonial empires themselves. For most of the 1940s and 1950s the parties differed on the colonial question. Labor tended to predicate its policies on the right of colonies to self-determination; other factors, such as security considerations, might qualify this goal for some time to come, but self-determination remained fundamental. In office in the 1940s the party pressed the cause of trustee-ship under the United Nations system as the most progressive and humane way of preparing colonial peoples for eventual self-determination while also serving the cause of international peace.[35] While not opposing the 'ultimate' goal of self-determination, Liberal leaders had less faith in United Nations supervision and tended to support the indefinite maintenance of colonial rule by the European powers—especially British rule, but also Dutch and French—on the sorts of grounds noted above, with security, stability and the preservation of Western influence seen as primary, rather than qualifying, considerations. Menzies himself continued robustly to endorse the virtues of empire in all its senses, and this marked him out as a major exemplar of the pro-imperial tradition.

From the mid-1940s, however, there were signs that the European colonial powers might find it a good deal more difficult to hold the line in Asia than observers on either side of Australian politics had been expecting. Nationalism was emerging as a significant political force; the European colonial powers had been gravely weakened by war; and the new super-powers, the United States and the Soviet Union, were both, if for different reasons, strongly opposed to the prolongation of imperial rule. In the swirl of events ideas of trusteeship soon went by the board, and Australia had, for the first time, to begin thinking seriously about the prospect of dealing with post-colonial states in its neighbourhood. No one expressed Australian concern more vividly than Menzies. 'The very arguments used for throwing the Dutch out of the East Indies', he told a Liberal Party convention in 1945, 'are the arguments which will be used to throw the British out of Malaya, to throw the British out of Burma, India, for throwing the Australians out of New Guinea'.[36] The prospect of decolonisation at some stage in the future seemed to presage the replacement of the known and orderly with the unknown, the unreliable, the alien—all the characteristics of 'Asia' as it then featured in Australian imagery. In 1947 Menzies declared that India was not ready for independence, an assertion that helped sow the seeds of his career-long poor relationship with Nehru.[37] And he especially deplored the Chifley Government's support for the Indonesian nationalists, whom he referred to as 'the rebels'. It was 'the very ecstasy of suicide', he argued,

> That we, a country isolated in the world, with a handful of people, a white man's country with all the traditions of our race, should want to set ourselves apart, by saying to our friends here and there, as in the case of the Dutch, who have been great colonists and our friends, 'out with you, we cannot support you'.[38]

His return to office in 1949 coincided closely with Mao's assumption of power in China and with the deepening of the Cold War. In these circumstances the prospect of decolonisation became linked in the minds of Menzies and his senior colleagues with the threat of Asian communism. Complexities such as the interweaving of communism with nationalism, and the possibility that colonial rule might itself be a stimulant to the spread of communist influence (which was how the Americans tended to see it), did not feature largely in the Government's view. The prime task was to check communist expansion, and in this cause colonial power was an asset. At the least it could be seen as a supplement to American power. Thus, although India, Pakistan, Ceylon, Burma, Indonesia and the Philippines had all become independent in the 1940s, the Government could take comfort from the fact that in the 1950s there were still several outposts of European empire in Australia's region—the British in Malaya, Singapore, Borneo, Hong Kong and the Pacific; the French in Indochina and the Pacific; the Dutch in West New Guinea; even the Portuguese in Timor. The collapse of French power in Indochina in 1954 was a severe blow, but at least French involvement, of a kind, could be retained through SEATO. The Dutch position in West New Guinea was strongly supported by the Menzies Government throughout the 1950s notwithstanding America's lack of enthusiasm for it. But the key desideratum for Australia was to keep Britain itself in the region.

Australia's interests

Leaving aside Australia's and Britain's shared involvement in Nauru, the pattern of interests that informed their attitudes and interactions on colonial issues was essentially one of Australian interests in British territories, and not vice versa. This was hardly surprising, in view of the very great differences of scale between Britain's colonial empire and Australia's.

Australia did try to some extent to involve the British in Papua and New Guinea, but with little result. For example, in 1948 Chifley floated the idea that Britain's newly established Overseas Food Corporation might extend its activities to these territories, in association with the Australian Government. The British Minister of Food, John Strachey, was unmoved.[39] In 1952 the Acting British High Commissioner in Canberra reported to London that a good deal of investment from extra-Australian sources would be needed for the development of Australia's territories, and that 'The present Government are anxious to see British companies with experience of large scale development in tropical and sub-tropical countries interest themselves in [Australia's territories] . . . and are prepared to give them the assistance they require'.[40] But there seems to have been no great rush. Eight years later Hasluck, as Minister for Territories, considered appointing a liaison officer in Australia House to recruit soon to be redundant British Colonial Civil Servants for service in Papua and New Guinea. But the Colonial Office frankly doubted whether many, if any, would apply.[41]

By contrast, Australian interests in British territories were of some consequence. They fell into three main categories: security, economy and migration. By far the most important was the security interest. This provided the main reason for Australia's desire that Britain should maintain its imperial presence in the region for as long as possible. It was well understood in Australia that Britain was not the power it once had been. Singapore 1942 lived in the national memory. And yet Britain in the 1950s was still the world's third-ranking power. Outside the superpowers it was the only country with nuclear capacity. In the realm of trade and finance it controlled the sterling area, which in the early 1950s covered a quarter of the world's people and a quarter of its trade. These two attributes, nuclear weaponry and the sterling area, were the essential underpinnings of its major power status. Generally speaking, with overseas commitments and responsibilities that far exceeded those of any other European state, Britain continued to pursue a 'world role' well beyond the American-dominated bounds of NATO. Colonialism was one element in that world role, helping both to signify Britain's status and to underwrite its position through the control of key territories and the provision of a string of garrisons from Gibraltar to Hong Kong. Australia, self-identifying as a British country, was no less keen than Britain itself to see the unilateral British role maintained. In Southeast Asia especially, Britain's global concerns and Australia's local ones overlapped in ways that Australia was much concerned to develop. Anglo-Australian collaboration was central, for example, to the establishment of the Colombo Plan in 1950; the Plan's role in boosting British and Commonwealth influence in Cold War circumstances was, for Australia, one of its essential aspects. And for all Australia's acknowledged dependence on the United States for security purposes, the British and Gurkha forces stationed in Britain's Southeast Asian colonies still weighed heavily in Australia's military calculations.

Indeed, the most significant of all Australian involvements in British colonial territory was its military commitment in Malaya. The ANZAM agreement of 1948 provided a framework for coordination of British, Australian and New Zealand service planning in and around Southeast Asia, and from 1955 Australian troops operated jointly with British and New Zealand troops in the purpose-designed Commonwealth Strategic Reserve in Malaya. From Canberra's point of view these arrangements served both to help crush subversion in a British territory and to give substance to the Australian security doctrine of forward defence.[42]

For the Australian Government the main issue in Malaya was communism, not colonialism. But the issues were intertwined. The Labor Opposition in Canberra criticised the Australian military commitment as intervention in a colonial war, and this, in a literal sense, it was. Even for those who looked on the war as purely an anti-communist struggle colonial policy was relevant, since it was available for use as a weapon—especially in the form of constitutional change favouring the political forces that the British wished to favour. In this way Britain's colonial presence could be seen as stabilising in a political as well as a military sense. The question here, as always in colonial constitutional change, was how far, how fast. The British High Commission in Canberra reported to Malcolm MacDonald, the British Commissioner-General in Southeast Asia, that 'one or two Australian Ministers' privately felt that the British were not moving fast enough on the constitutional front to counteract 'the ideological attraction of Communism for many Asian minds'. This view the High Commission regarded as 'rather ill-considered',[43] and there can be no doubt that Menzies himself took the view that Malayan constitutional progress was quite fast enough—perhaps too fast. The British knew where he stood on such matters; hence it is of some interest that in February 1955, when they were seeking to persuade him to commit forces to the Commonwealth Strategic Reserve unconditionally (that is, without some kind of guarantee of American backing), they offered the encouraging assurance that Malayan constitutional advance was 'bound to be slow'.[44] As it turned out, the rate of constitutional change accelerated markedly quite soon after the Australian military commitment was made, to Canberra's consternation.

The notion of colonialism as reinforcing both military and political security applied also in Singapore. Canberra saw Britain's imperial tenure of Singapore and its naval base not only as vital for regional strategic purposes but also as helping to insure against the rise to power in Singapore politics of radical Chinese aiming at association with China. When in April 1956 constitutional talks between Britain and Singapore headed towards breakdown, Menzies was concerned that the British might seek to resolve the difficulty by expediting Singapore's advance towards independence. As he saw it, the preservation of fundamental security interests was intimately bound up with the maintenance of colonial authority. Thus he sought to stiffen London's spine, signalling his view that 'it would be contrary to Commonwealth interests to grant complete independence to Singapore at this stage . . . No doubt you will seek to avoid the charge being made that the situation is a base [*sic*: case] of colonialism versus self-government'.[45]

To a degree, however, London did see the situation in these terms. By the end of the decade Singapore had internal self-government and was clearly on the path to independence. Fortunately (from Canberra's point of view), Britain still held responsibility for external affairs and defence. Australia found itself playing a complex late-colonial game: even as it sought cautiously to develop political relations with Lee Kuan Yew's new government, it was seeking the closest possible security relationship with the British in Singapore almost as if nothing was going to change in the arena of defence arrangements. As the official directive for the new Australian Commissioner in Singapore in October 1960 pointed out, Australia's defence planning strategy in Southeast Asia relied upon the continuation of existing arrangements in both Malaya (now independent, but party to a post-colonial security treaty with Britain) and Singapore. The Commissioner's principal tasks would therefore include acting as Australian representative in the regional defence planning machinery that Britain had established, specifically the British Defence Coordination Committee (Far East), the Joint Planning Committee (Far East), and the Joint Intelligence Committee (Far East). In addition he would be expected to maintain 'continuous and frank contact' with the United Kingdom Commissioner, the Commanders-in-Chief, and members of their staffs. 'It may be possible', said the Department of External Affairs, 'to influence British policy in Singapore and the Commissioner should, wherever possible, whether directly or after reference in [*sic*] Canberra, seek to inject Australian views'.[46] For a political representative there was a considerable load of security-related duties contained within the position description; and this may be seen as providing a fair indication of Australia's regional priorities at that time.

Defence and security concerns pervaded Australia's view of British colonialism in oceanic areas as well. British Indian Ocean territories, such as the Cocos Islands and Christmas Island, and South Pacific territories, such as the Anglo-French condominium of the New Hebrides and the British Solomon Islands Protectorate, were seen by Australia as part of its security perimeter. Between the late 1940s and the middle 1950s Australia actively explored the possibility of taking over responsibility for these territories from Britain. Security concerns provided much of the incentive for seeking transfer of the two Indian Ocean territories in particular—transfers that were eventually effected.

In the more distant realm of colonial Africa there was at first minimal Australian interest. But in the middle and later 1950s, as Africa 'emerged', the Australian Government developed a broad set of policy ideas with a considerable emphasis on security issues. In 1959 Australia's High Commissioner in Ghana, Stewart Jamieson, described Australian interests in Africa as, first, resisting the possible spread of Soviet influence; second, preventing the proliferation of small states which might come to dominate the UN General Assembly; and third, maintaining military access to air and sea bases in East Africa.[47]

The second broad area of Australian interest was economic. In a very general sense Australia was associated economically with the colonies through their common membership of the sterling area, which in the early 1950s served in some ways as a closed economic system centred upon London. Like the British colonies, Australia held substantial sterling credits in London; like them it was subject to exchange controls and other regulations designed to defend sterling against the greater economic might of the dollar.[48] But although these arrangements had considerable effects on Australia's economic relations with the metropole, their significance for Australia's lateral dealings with colonies was not great in any quantitative sense. Simply, dealings with colonies formed only a small proportion of Australia's economic linkages overseas. The principal connections can be quickly tabulated. Nauru, an Australian-British-New Zealand trust territory, was the major source of phosphate fertiliser for both Australian and New Zealand agriculture. In the Indian Ocean, Christmas Island was another supplier of phosphate. In colonial Southeast Asia interests were still relatively small in scale, but showing signs of growth. The value of Australian private investment in Malayan tin mining was estimated at £6 million in 1948; there were also Australian investments in the Malayan rubber and gold-mining industries.[49] By the end of the 1950s there was a growing trade interest in Singapore, with the trade balance in Australia's favour, along with a 'substantial' volume of private investment.[50] Australian economic interests were evident too in Britain's South Pacific territories. In Fiji Australian-owned multinationals, of which Colonial Sugar Refining and Burns Philp were the best known, were entrenched in the economy. So dominant were they in fact that the British Governor in 1960 actively welcomed the possibility of greater New Zealand economic interest to offset 'the almost complete control' enjoyed by Australian firms; one of his officials concluded that the Australian economic stranglehold 'contributes to the high cost of living in Fiji and to the general distortion of our economy'.[51] In the British Solomon Islands Protectorate, the main air and shipping connections were Australian-owned, most foreign capital was Australian, and the Australian pound served as legal tender along with the British pound. In the New Hebrides, Australian currency circulated alongside French Pacific currency, the Australian Government owned some 40 000 acres of land, and most 'British' residents (including planters) were in fact Australian nationals. In addition there were branches of the Commonwealth Bank throughout the region. All the British South Pacific territories traded with Australia; from Australia's point of view the trade volumes were small, but in every case the trading balances were in Australia's favour. Elsewhere Australian economic interests were much slighter, although by 1955 there were Australian trade commissioners in Trinidad, Hong Kong and the Central African Federation, and by 1960 there was another in Kenya. Modest though it was by comparison with Australian economic interests in Europe, North America and increasingly Japan, this pattern of interests gave Australia a further stake in the British colonial system. Among other things the system provided an administrative and legal framework for trade and investment which to Australians appeared both stable and familiar.

The third category of Australian interest was migration. From time to time British colonial events raised issues for Australia as a country of immigration open to people of European extraction. For example in 1960, 'Africa year', increasing numbers of Britons in British African colonies began inquiring about emigration to Australia. It was British policy to discourage any white exodus from Africa. 'We should therefore be seriously embarrassed', wrote a Colonial Office official, 'if the Australian Government began making great efforts to induce the waverers to quit'. But the Australian Government was not uninterested. In London Australia House pursued the issue, suggesting to the Commonwealth Relations Office that the Australian Trade Commissioner in Nairobi might actively publicise the assisted passage scheme 'with a view to showing a way out to Europeans who have decided to leave the territory'. And Whitehall officials fairly quickly decided that if Europeans had to leave, Australia was a suitable destination. To some extent their hand was forced by South Africa, which had already opened a migration office in Nairobi—'a measure about which we do not seem to have been consulted'; given this, 'we can hardly object to the Australians more or less following suit'.[52] Replying to Australia House, the Colonial Office requested only that Australian officials proceed discreetly, and keep the Governor informed.

Otherwise, the White Australia policy all but ruled out migration to Australia from most British colonial territories; only from the Mediterranean colonies of Malta and Cyprus was there any significant flow. Yet upon occasion colonial problems did arise that tested the limits of the White Australia policy. Such cases had the potential to cause embarrassment for the Australian Government not only domestically but also in the context of Anglo-Australian relations. This proved to be the case, for example, when the possible transfer of the Cocos Islands to Australian jurisdiction came under consideration in the early 1950s.

Britain's world role was important to Australia; so then was that role's colonial component, seen as an expression, and part of the underpinning, of Britain's major power status. Menzies' endorsement of Britain's action at

Suez was of a piece with his support for the British colonial presence, especially in Australia's Asian and Pacific neighbourhood. Of course Australia increasingly looked across the Pacific for its principal defence alliance. Yet in various ways issues of Australian defence were still intermeshed with colonial issues. This was shown above all by Australia's commitment of forces within Britain's Southeast Asian colonial sphere of influence.

The diverse and wide-ranging pattern of Australian interests in the British colonial empire helped to reinforce the pro-imperial mindset that characterised the generation of leaders who ruled Australia in the 1950s. From their point of view, a commitment to colonial empire was both a matter of direct Australian self-interest and an intrinsic element of the larger Anglo-Australian relationship. Canberra knew of course that imperial devolution was going to come eventually. But Canberra was in no hurry to contemplate the necessary policy adjustments. Indeed, until quite late in the decade Canberra simply did not anticipate any pressing need to do so.

2

Australia and Britain as colonial powers

The governor who never was

In May 1950, shortly before the British Commonwealth Relations Secretary, Patrick Gordon Walker, was due to make an Australian tour, a suggestion was put to him (the Commonwealth Relations Office files do not say by whom) 'that it might be a good thing for Commonwealth relations to ask an Australian to become Governor of one of our Colonies in the Pacific area'. Gordon Walker was quite taken with the idea. In December 1950 he sounded out a number of senior British officials including Malcolm MacDonald (Commissioner-General in Southeast Asia), Lord Gowrie (Governor-General of Australia), and E. J. (Ted) Williams (High Commissioner to Australia). His arguments for the proposal were as follows. First, 'the Australians would very much appreciate it': it would help to reduce their 'general touchiness'. Second, it might 'weaken the demand for Australian Governors'—that is, governors within Australia—and 'make them more inclined to appoint British Governors'. Third, 'it is the right way to run the Commonwealth'. Gordon Walker had in mind a territory such as Fiji, or perhaps Malta or Cyprus 'which do not raise the racial issue but present problems of their own to which it might repay us to bring a fresh mind'. The idea was not, of course, to be mentioned to any Australians.[1]

Replying early in 1951, Williams expressed, as did other correspondents, tactful support for the minister's idea. But he also pointed out the most obvious flaw in the minister's reasoning: 'I do not think that it would follow that such an appointment would be likely to weaken the demand for Australian Governors—it might very well have quite the opposite effect and encourage the conviction that Australians can be found to perform the duties equally as well as outsiders'. He also warned that the appointment of an Australian as governor of a territory in the Far East or the Pacific might well encourage Australia's '"territorial ambitions" in respect of British colonial territory'. Nevertheless he produced a list of seventeen possible candidates, with evaluative remarks. Among the minority upon whom his comments were not disparaging were Richard Boyer, Roden Cutler, Alexander Downer, Sir Edmund Herring and Lieutenant-General Sydney Rowell. He thought it questionable, however, whether such men would have any great interest in stepping aside from their Australian careers.[2]

Williams's arguments against the proposal carried weight in Whitehall, the more so since officialdom there was already negatively disposed. The Commonwealth Relations Office feared that notwithstanding the precedent of Richard Casey's success as Governor of Bengal, an Australian governor might run into political trouble that would do more harm than good to Commonwealth relations. The Colonial Office saw 'political appointments' as discouraging to the Colonial Service, and also pointed to the complicating factor of Australia's claim to be involved in determining the future of Dutch New Guinea. This claim was tending to arouse suspicion in the region

> that the Australians are wishing to expand their influence too widely and too rapidly. In such an atmosphere the appointment of an Australian Governor might not be too popular among our colonial population, especially in view of the impression created some time ago by the late Australian Minister of Immigration's tactless way of enforcing the White Australia policy.[3]

Gordon Walker was irked by all this bureaucratic resistance ('The objections to any good idea are always formidable', he minuted on 18 September 1950[4]), but by about April 1951 he had ceased to pursue the idea.

It was an episode of interest primarily for the light it throws on British perceptions of Australia. We may extract three themes. First, there was a sense of familial closeness to Australia, in that the idea was considered at all. It does not seem to have been considered for any other country. Indeed the Colonial Office feared a demonstration effect: what if 'other Commonwealth countries'—a euphemism for South Africa—were moved by the Australian precedent to request a colonial governorship or two? Second, a sense of metropolis contemplating satellite, *de haut en bas*, comes through strongly in some of the arguments put up both for and against the idea: the view, for example, even among the idea's proponents, that Australians should not be allowed to think themselves capable of filling their own governorships. And third, there was concern at the more problematic aspects of dealing with the Australians, created for example by their regional adventurism, their racially discriminatory policies, and their 'general touchiness'. In these three themes can be seen a miniature of a larger picture of the relationship. Their implications in the field of colonial policy are worth teasing out, with reference now to both ends of the relationship, and to the interplay of Australian 'deference' and Australian 'assertiveness' that gave the relationship much of its dynamic, in this policy field as in others.

Intimacy and divergence

The familial intimacy of Britain and Australia (the first theme) was a product of their blood ties, their shared language, their cultural affinities, their economic complementarities, their history of armed alliance. Colonialism was another thing they had in common. Britain and Australia stood in the 1950s as two of the world's few colonial powers. Their incumbent conservative governments experienced alike the international unpopularity of colonialism, variously criticised as it was by overseas foes and friends including the United States, by colonial nationalists, and in some respects by opposition parties at home. But neither government doubted the rightness of its colonial policy. Ideologically, the Australian Government conceived of policy in very much the same way as did the British, albeit with a time-lag effect in so far as Australia's territories were considered (by both countries) to be much less advanced than British colonies. Thus Australia's policy objectives in the early 1950s distinctly resembled Britain's of the 1930s:

> In the administration of its island territories the Australian Government adheres consistently to the view that it has a special trust to discharge towards the indigenous peoples . . . The Government's broad administrative policy . . . has sought among other things to foster the economic and cultural progress of the indigenous peoples with the least possible disturbance of their local customs and mode of life.[5]

As late as 1958 the British High Commissioner in Canberra, Lord Carrington, could inform London that 'their policy, if I am not mistaken, is somewhat akin to British colonial policy between the wars in concentrating more on preserving the native's way of life than on creating for him fresh economic opportunities'.[6] In subsequent years, however, the Australian bedrock notions of 'trusteeship', 'economic and cultural progress' and 'least possible disturbance' were increasingly replaced in Australian policy discourse by talk of preparation, training, political development and constitutional change, indicating a degree of ideological catching-up with Britain.

Paul Hasluck, Australia's long-serving Minister for Territories, disputed the comparability of the British and Australian colonial situations. His belief, as he told Parliament in August 1960, was that the 'New Guinea situation is unique and comparisons with Africa and Asia are inapplicable'. Indeed there were situational differences. But underlying these, colonialism was still colonialism: a system in which a sovereign state ruled over, and made policy for, dependent territories. One of the observers who noted the family resemblances between the colonial orders constructed by different powers was Charles Rowley, for twenty years principal of the Australian School of Pacific Administration. In 1964 Rowley wrote that what Australia was doing in Papua and New Guinea 'is very like what other colonial powers did in their colonies: and the reactions of the people may be broadly similar'.[7]

Another dimension of the familial relationship could be seen in the British Colonial Service's practice of employing Australians under the Dominions Selection Scheme. First applied to Canada in 1923, this scheme was extended to Australia and New Zealand in 1928–29. In 1946–47 eighteen District Officer vacancies were reserved for Australians, seven of them in Malaya and the rest in various African territories. Between 1945 and 1955 eighty Australians were recruited. Their presence became increasingly marked in Britain's Pacific Ocean colonies in particular. 'It would be unusual', notes Anthony Kirk-Greene, the historian of the British service, 'for British Colonial Service officers recruited after 1945 not to be able to name half a dozen Antipodean or South African colleagues'. Several Australians reached fairly senior positions, although in this respect they were outdone by New Zealand which provided ninety-five recruits in 1945–55 with two of them attaining governorships.[8] They did so uncontroversially; for unlike Gordon Walker's mooted Australian governor, they were career appointees, not political ones.

But the factor of colonialism also highlighted the distinction between 'metropolitan' Britain and 'peripheral' Australia (the second theme). The disparities in their power and their spheres of responsibility were at least as great in colonial matters as in any others. Britain was the world's major colonial power, Australia one of the smallest. Britain's imperial perspective was global, Australia's parochial. The flow of influence and precept was one-way. Thus the structure of Australian colonial administration, ascending hierarchically from the District Officer in the field to the Administrator (Governor) in the capital, was broadly patterned upon the British model. Upon occasion Australia explicitly sought guidance. In 1951 the Menzies Cabinet decided to ask the British Government 'to lend to the Australian Government a senior officer of its Colonial Service experienced in matters of organisation who might act as a consultant in relation to organisational problems' in Australian territories.[9] And in 1960 Hasluck, notwithstanding his views on the *sui generis* character of Australian New Guinea, visited the Colonial Office to solicit its thoughts on a breathtakingly comprehensive colonial agenda: '(1) Problems of communication with primitive native peoples speaking a diversity of languages; (2) the drift of native peoples to town and the problems of detribalised urban natives; (3) land tenure;

(4) the early stages of political development in a dependent territory'.[10] The Colonial Office's response to this approach was to ply Hasluck with copies of appropriate reports and to offer to provide places for Australians at the British Government's community development courses for Colonial Service officials.

Privately, British officials were none too flattering in their assessment of the Australian colonial administrative effort. In 1955 W. A. C. Mathieson, who had visited Australian New Guinea as a member of a United Nations Trusteeship Council visiting mission, itemised for his Colonial Office colleagues 'defects in the Australian administrative machine' that included

> extraordinary arrogance, complacency and determination to retain control on the part of senior officers in the Department of Territories . . . An overweight headquarters staff . . . at Port Moresby with a lot of deadwood at the top . . . Lack of clarity in the chain of command from headquarters to districts . . . A cumbersome system of financial control . . . Gross inefficiency in the field of public works.[11]

Four years later another British official was comparably unimpressed with Canberra's administrative methods: 'Australian territories suffer from very detailed control from Canberra [and] it is doubtful if this can be regarded as a benefit. The present system of control in detail from Canberra has indeed provoked intense resentment in Papua/New Guinea in the context of the recent introduction of income tax'.[12] As for race relations, W. H. Formoy of the Colonial Office declared crisply: 'Australians as a rule lack finesse in their dealings with the native population'.[13]

But here it needs to be said that some Australian officials were no less critical of the British colonial style. W. R. Crocker, who worked in the British Colonial Service in the early 1930s, disliked the experience so intensely that he resigned and twice penned critiques, first in his book *Nigeria: A Critique of British Colonial Administration*, published in 1936, and then again in his autobiography *Travelling Back*, published fifty years later. Crocker depicted a demoralised service and deplored, among other things, 'lack of planning', a 'thread of inferior quality' running through the higher ranks, and a general 'drift towards literalism and clerkliness'.[14] A second critic was the senior diplomat Alan Watt. Serving in Singapore from 1954 to 1956 as Australian Commissioner in Southeast Asia, Watt found the atmospherics of the British colonial presence in the region both 'unpleasant' and 'irritating':

> The constant attitude of 'father knows best'; of treating the local population as children; of playing up to the unjustified pretensions of Sultans; of senior and junior British staff treating High Commissioner or Governor as the Queen herself—all this, against the background of the irrevocable loss of imperial prestige during the Second World War seemed to me a form of rather unsuccessful play-acting.

Had he been born in British Southeast Asia, Watt wrote, 'I have no doubt that I would have been working for removal of the imperial umbrella in the shortest practicable time'.[15]

There were also some in Canberra who felt that the proper course for Australia was to concentrate on building links with the emerging post-colonial states of the region, rather than allowing itself to appear too closely associated with a colonial system that was visibly unpopular among local nationalist movements and among states already independent. John Burton, appointed by Evatt as Secretary of the Department of External Affairs, was one such. Burton had been centrally involved in fashioning Australia's policy of support for the Indonesian nationalists against the Dutch in the late 1940s. Still Secretary in the early months of the Menzies Government, he argued against the commitment of Australian troops to support the British against insurgents in Malaya partly on the grounds that newly in-dependent countries such as India, Pakistan, Ceylon and the Philippines would construe such an action as supporting colonialism; his implication was that this was a charge Australia would do well to avoid.[16] Evatt as Leader of the Opposition used a similar argument when in 1955 the troops were in fact committed.

At prime ministerial level in the 1950s, however, such arguments cut no ice. For Menzies, Britain's continuing imperial presence in the region was very much in Australia's strategic, political and economic interest. Indeed the issue transcended mere self-interest; as Menzies put it some years later, Australia felt an 'almost instinctive obligation . . . to help Britain' in Southeast Asia.[17]

Even so there were occasional differences between the Australian and British governments on colonial issues, and this brings us to the third theme: the moments of divergence and diplomatic difficulty. The common factor was usually an Australian departure from deference: in other words, an independent Australian initiative that caused concern in the metropole. In matters imperial, this aspect of the Anglo-Australian pattern had a tradition, of a kind, that went back to Australia's nineteenth-century would-be expansionism in Melanesia,[18] being most vividly exemplified by Queens-land's attempted annexation of New Guinea in 1883. In the 1950s, the tradition of Australian assertiveness showed itself in, for example, the Aus-tralian Government's plans for the future of Nauru (which Britain had doubts about); its hard-line legalist approach to colonial questions in the United Nations (which by the late 1950s Britain saw as insensitive and indeed as threatening to the common colonial position); its support for Dutch colonialism in West New Guinea (which Britain considered ill-advised); and its plan to take over the Cocos Islands on a racially discrimi-natory basis (which provoked not only alarm in Whitehall but also strong criticism in the House of Commons).

Nauru: a colonial microcosm

The relevance of the Anglo-Australian interaction relating to the tiny, but by no means unimportant, territory of Nauru is threefold. First, it was the only territory in which Britain and Australia, along with New Zealand, actually shared colonial responsibility. Second, since we are talking about colonialism it is salutary to have a reminder of what colonialism often entailed, namely the serving of metropolitan interests at the expense of local; a phenomenon illustrated with exceptional clarity in this instance. And third, the case of Nauru is of interest because it introduces into the discussion the United Nations, an important player in colonial affairs in the 1950s.

The legal position was that Nauru was a United Nations trust territory in which Britain, Australia and New Zealand were jointly responsible for administration. In practice, and with the consent of the other trustees, Australia acted as sole administrator, as it had done since the original tripartite agreement of 1919. Through the British Phosphates Commission, the three powers jointly mined the island's phosphate deposits. Virtually all of the output was marketed to Australian and New Zealand farmers in processed form as superphosphate fertiliser. Prices were low, thanks in large measure to the relatively low rate of royalty paid to the Nauruans by the Commission. This was in fact much lower than the rate paid by the same Commission for the same product in Ocean Island, which was a purely British administrative responsibility. Advising a Colonial Office minister in 1960, British officials felt that there was 'some foundation' for the charge that the Nauruans were being exploited.[19] But for Britain's antipodean partners the principle of cheap superphosphate was embedded in the political and economic order, and threats to it were not to be countenanced. Thus Britain generally stayed quiet, and Nauruan issues were not often raised.

In the late 1950s, however, Nauru suddenly became a matter for hard discussion between the three governments. There were various stimuli for this. First, New Zealand began suggesting that with its forthcoming divestment of Western Samoa it might seek also to pull out of the Nauru agreement, so that it would be free to leave the United Nations Trusteeship Council where, along with all other trustee powers, it came under repeated attack.[20] Second, Britain was considering an increase in the phosphate royalty paid in Ocean Island, which would have the side-effect of further highlighting the low rate paid in Nauru. And third, there was a growing realisation that sooner or later, as the phosphate deposits dwindled, alternative arrangements would have to be made for the Nauruan people. This last was politically the most sensitive issue, for the Trusteeship Council was beginning to take a close interest. A briefing paper for Julian Amery, the Colonial Office Minister charged with negotiating the issue with the Australians and New Zealanders, argued that

> From the United Nations point of view it is very desirable that some definite plan should be produced within the next year; otherwise a determined attempt will be made to put the Australians into the dock at the next session of the Trusteeship Council and we and the New Zealanders will find our position embarrassing . . . While this problem is a tiny one by international standards it does contain awkward political possibilities.[21]

All three governments believed that it was a question of settling the Nauruans elsewhere, and that this was essentially Australia's problem. Sir Andrew Cohen, Britain's representative on the Trusteeship Council, told Whitehall officials that in his view the Australians should move to resettle the Nauruans 'in the next four or five years in order that the Nauruan Trusteeship Agreement might be terminated', after which the phosphate could continue to be mined by imported labour as at present, but without the attentions of the Council.[22] In ministerial talks in London in May 1960, Menzies and Hasluck accepted that Australia was the obvious place for resettlement. They insisted however that the Nauruans would have to be settled as individuals. The Australian Government would not permit them to settle as a community and establish 'an enclave'. With some reluctance the British gave way on this point, while privately anticipating 'difficulties in the United Nations over this'.[23]

What seemed to bulk largest in governmental minds was not the human aspect of resettlement, but the financial. This at any rate was the question on which the governments disagreed most sharply. The British initially felt that since Australia derived most of the benefit from the phosphate mining, it should meet most of the cost of resettlement. The most equitable solution, in the British view, was that the price of the phosphate should be raised so that antipodean farmers would ultimately bear the greater part of the cost on a user-pays basis. To Hasluck this was politically unacceptable. His disingenuous counter-proposal was that the three governments should share the cost equally out of their exchequers. Tough negotiations in Wellington in September 1960 led to a compromise proposed by New Zealand: there should be both a phosphate levy and governmental contributions, in proportions to be determined.[24]

In the end there was no resettlement. By 1963 an independence movement had emerged in Nauru, and in 1964 the idea of resettlement was dropped. Australia was reluctant to accede to Nauruan demands for self-rule, but eventually, under pressure from both Britain and New Zealand, did so. Full independence came in 1968. The dealings of 1959–60, then, do not provide a guide to the historical outcome. What they do provide is a revealing illustration of imperial priorities. Australia, along with the other powers, was in Nauru because of its economic significance. The future of the Nauruans themselves was a contingent, not a primary, consideration. When the powers turned their minds to this issue the Australian decision, in which Britain and New Zealand acquiesced, was simple: the Nauruan community, *qua* community, would have to cease to exist. It did not seem to occur to any of the powers to consult the Nauruans before arriving at this decision. Rather, the head of New Zealand's Department of External Affairs 'deprecated in this connection any recourse to a plebiscite for Nauru'.[25] Certainly the powers agreed that the consent of the Nauruan population would need to be gained prior to actual relocation. But this was after the decision in principle had been taken. In this respect, the Nauruan case did not differ from the cases of transfer or potential transfer of sovereignty that will be discussed in the next chapter. In none of them was it thought necessary, at the level of high politics, to consult the populations concerned.

What is also of interest in the Nauruan case is that the administering powers entered into the negotiations of 1959–60 partly in order to head off pressures from the United Nations. Because Nauru was a trust territory, the United Nations had power to examine its affairs through the Trusteeship Council. This was a real factor in metropolitan thinking. So, if more diffusely, was sensitivity to the United Nations in general about colonialism in general. And this takes us back up to a broader level of discussion of the colonial variable in Anglo-Australian relations. This time, however, the context is a multilateral one.

The United Nations factor

From the 1940s to the 1960s the institutions of the United Nations structured much of the international debate on colonialism. The key forums were the Trusteeship Council, on which administering and non-administering powers had parity of numbers, and the Fourth Committee, a committee of the whole which received and debated reports on colonial matters. The temper of the United Nations was unequivocally anti-colonial, and this gave Britain and Australia plenty of incentive to collaborate. Yet relations were not always easy.

Early in the 1950s, British officials were inclined to see the Australians as of little account in Trusteeship Council and Fourth Committee matters. 'Australia and her policies are, if the truth must be stated, of no great interest to the anti-colonials'.[26] 'Denmark, New Zealand and Australia are very small beer. Australia is only likely to excite the [Fourth] Cttee's [*sic*] passion if she runs foul of Indonesia over Dutch New Guinea'.[27] But during the decade the British attitude changed to one of concern as a rift developed between British and Australian approaches. Essentially, Britain's strategy was to exercise a certain flexibility, to cooperate by providing detailed technical information to the Fourth Committee, to make occasional concessions to General Assembly opinion; all in the cause of preserving Britain's fundamental interest, which was to prevent the establishment in UN doctrine of any principle of formal 'accountability' to the United Nations for colonial policy in general. The Australian approach was more hardline. It was marked by a reluctance to be conciliatory; a preference for going down fighting on an issue and then 'reserving Australia's position' on juridical grounds, rather than making tactical concessions.

This was the broad observable difference. But there were underlying complexities, for neither government was wholly of one mind on UN strategy. In Whitehall the Colonial Office, which carried the direct responsibility for colonies, tended to be more hardline on colonial issues in UN forums than the Foreign Office and Commonwealth Relations Office with their wider diplomatic concerns. The influential Andrew Cohen, although a Colonial Office man by background, had an internationalist perspective; and as a Commonwealth Relations Office official remarked, 'our own more flexible policy [than that of the Australians] is more that of Sir Andrew Cohen himself than of the reluctantly acquiescent CO'.[28] In Canberra, at least by the later 1950s, there was evidence of a comparable difference between the hardline Department of Territories and a more flexible Department of External Affairs.

Australia's central concern at the United Nations was the question of New Guinea. In the 1950s one of the forms this concern took was collaboration with the Dutch in an effort to block Indonesian manoeuvres for acquisition of the island's western half. At the United Nations, the Australians' tactic was to oppose Indonesia's efforts to have the West Irian issue inscribed on the General Assembly agenda, and to support the Dutch in their insistence that the issue was one of Dutch domestic jurisdiction under Article 2(7) of the United Nations Charter. Britain felt it unwise to side with Australia and the Netherlands in this dispute, seeing inscription as unpreventable. West Irian was duly inscribed. The Australians were similarly unsuccessful with other initiatives—on disarmament, and on the question of membership for Laos and Cambodia—which could be attributed to the same root cause as their New Guinea policy, namely their security worries. All this, M. S. Williams of the Foreign Office reported back to London, made the Australians 'more than usually difficult to deal with since they tend to ascribe their lack of success to lack of United Kingdom support to which they feel entitled'.[29]

They were difficult to deal with at a personal level as well. In the opinion of M. E. Allen, a member of the British delegation, his Australian opposite number was 'thin-skinned, even for an Australian'. The most problematic individual, in the British view, was Percy Spender, Ambassador to the United States and also chairman of Australia's UN delegation. Spender was 'erratic', and dominated by personal feelings: 'From what we hear', Allen wrote, 'the unfortunate Australian-Dutch manoeuvre over Western New Guinea was originally his idea. And you probably know that he went so far as to complain to the Americans about our attitude over Western New Guinea (shocking them to the core by this display of Commonwealth non-solidarity)'.[30]

The desire for support in fact worked both ways. As bolsters to its major power status, Britain wished so far as possible to maintain the solidarity both of the independent Commonwealth countries and of the colonial powers. Australia fell into both categories. In 1956 Australia began a two-year term as a member of the Security Council, which increased Britain's keenness to be able to count on Australia's support on issues that mattered to Britain, including imperial issues.[31] But by 1956 the Australian tendency to go its own way on such issues at the United Nations seemed if anything to be increasing. In discussion with the British, Brian Hill of the Australian delegation wondered whether, in order to protect Australian interests in New Guinea, 'it was really necessary to give automatic support to British, French and Belgian interests over colonial possessions'. To stifle such thoughts, a British official wrote, it was necessary 'to mention Australia's strategic interest in the preservation of Malaya'.[32] But the key difference of the time, which related to the inscription of items for General Assembly debate, was not readily resolvable. Both countries maintained that colonial affairs were legally a matter of domestic jurisdiction. By 1957, however, Britain had ceased to contest the inscription even of its own most politically sensitive territory, Cyprus. The Australians continued to oppose the inscription of Cyprus (and for that matter Algeria, regardless of French intentions) in the foreknowledge of defeat but in the cause of resisting every possible precedent for an undermining of the domestic jurisdiction clause.[33] In short, the middle 1950s marked something of a low point in Anglo-Australian relations at the United Nations, with each side somewhat aggrieved at the other's unwillingness to provide the support to which it felt 'entitled', on colonial questions in particular.

Personal relationships were still of considerable importance. By 1957 there was some improvement at this level. In the British view, 'Spender is noticeably mellower than in previous years. This is said by some of his delegation to be due to the better functioning of his gastric juices'.[34] And the arrival of James Plimsoll at the United Nations in 1959 as Australia's

Permanent Representative was much welcomed by the British. Plimsoll was seen as sensible and realistic, with the potential ability to steer the Australians towards a more flexible policy on colonial problems.[35] In British eyes the stumbling block now was Kevin Kelly, the Australian representative on the Trusteeship Council and the Fourth Committee, who was very much in the inflexible Australian tradition. Cohen understood why the Australians had to be cautious: 'They have a very backward area on which they are spending a great deal of money; it is very important to them strategically; and it is going increasingly to be the object of criticism in the United Nations'.[36] But Kelly's 'narrow and legalistic' approach would eventually, in Cohen's view, prove counter-productive; damaging to the Australian position 'and our own as well'.[37]

In these circumstances Whitehall began thinking about ways and means of exerting 'our influence over her' (Australia) to induce change in the Australian approach to Trusteeship Council matters.[38] Cohen decided to visit Canberra for 'a frank and friendly talk'.[39] Preparing papers for his visit, Whitehall officials perceived an opportunity for playing upon bureaucratic differences in Canberra, believing that Plimsoll, 'and perhaps the Department of External Affairs, are more sympathetic to our policies than are the Department of Territories, which . . . have so far dictated policy on these Colonial issues at the U.N.'.[40] Plimsoll and Cohen both attended a Colonial Office meeting on UN issues on 15 January 1960. One of the British officials present reported to the High Commission in Canberra that Plimsoll evidently hoped for some significant change in Australian policy as a result of the forthcoming Canberra talks.[41]

Three weeks later Cohen flew to Canberra. He had three days of discussions with External Affairs and Territories officials, and as a guest of the Territories Department went on to tour Australian New Guinea. In the British judgment, the visit was a considerable success. It appeared that key officials in Canberra were in a mood to make changes, and the talks with Cohen probably helped this process along. As Cohen himself saw it, the Australians, partly because of prodding from Plimsoll in New York, 'have looked at their [United Nations] policy again [and] I think that they have realised the need for greater flexibility and a more constructive approach. This view seems to be shared by the Department of Territories'.[42] Kelly's term at the United Nations was coming to its end and he would be replaced by John Forsythe who had attended the Cohen talks. A few weeks later Cohen's assessment of Australian thinking was borne out by events. The senior External Affairs officials Arthur Tange and Ralph Harry recommended to Menzies that External Affairs rather than Territories should now take responsibility for trusteeship issues at the United Nations. Menzies agreed to this.[43] They further recommended that Australia should henceforth adopt 'a less rigid and legalistic approach (unless a real Australian interest is at stake) ... We feel that such a revision of our tactics may prove useful in getting a better reception for Australia's policies and performance' in the world body. This recommendation was approved by the Acting Minister, Sir Garfield Barwick, on Menzies' behalf.[44]

Australian colonial policy: the zephyr of change

That Canberra was willing to make these tactical changes suggests a somewhat broader matter for consideration. The first half of 1960 was a time of remarkable change in colonial policy. Britain was visibly accelerating its rate of colonial devolution. It was not alone among the European powers in doing so. France in Sub-Saharan Africa, Belgium in Equatorial Africa and Italy in the Horn of Africa were also stepping up the pace, indeed overtaking Britain in their rate of divestment. The Dutch in West New Guinea were proposing a ten-year plan for independence. Spain in Western Sahara and Portugal in its African and Asian territories had not yet begun to move, but like all the colonial powers they had to contend with a strongly anti-colonial international climate which made itself felt especially in the United Nations. The question of interest here is whether signs of change could be detected in Australia's own colonial policy in response to the temper of these times—policy on the ground, as distinct from tactical manoeuvres in the Trusteeship Council—and if so, whether it is plausible to see British influence as playing some part.

It is useful to return to the Cohen talks. The transcript shows that there was considerable discussion not just of United Nations matters but of broader issues affecting preparation for colonial self-rule. As it happened, the talks were held just a few days after Harold Macmillan delivered his 'wind of change' speech in South Africa. The speech was comprehensively reported in Australia as elsewhere, with an *Age* editorial offering the pertinent comment: 'in the past Mr Macmillan's thinking has had some effect on the attitude of the Commonwealth Government, and members of Cabinet and all parties would be well advised to study his South African speech and ask themselves how Australia's performance measures against it'.[45] The Territories and External Affairs officials who attended the Cohen talks would have been well aware of the speech, and especially the concept of wind of change that gave the speech its immediate public impact.

So far as Australian colonial policy went, British officials in Canberra felt that Cohen 'made a deep and important impact upon the Territories Department',[46] both in the talks and in his subsequent tour of Australian

New Guinea. They sensed that Territories' policy was in any case beginning to acquire a certain momentum; or at least that C. R. Lambert, Secretary of the Department, seemed to appreciate 'the necessity for more speed in measures for training and preparing the people for the future'.[47] The degree to which this was the case cannot be readily checked. But importantly, the Department's Minister was himself willing to move ahead on the constitutional front at this time. Hasluck had decided that there should be a major constitutional advance, namely the first election of islander representatives (by assemblies of delegates, not universal franchise) to the Papua and New Guinea Legislative Council. In April 1960 he secured Cabinet's agreement that in a new Council to be elected in 1961, the indigenous ranks should be increased from three nominated members in a house of twenty-seven to six nominated and six elected in a house of thirty-seven. Hasluck usually maintained that his initiatives on Papua and New Guinea owed little or nothing to external influences, but on this occasion his Cabinet submission did refer to the 'constant' pressure in the United Nations.[48] The wind of change blew strongly indeed at Lake Success, and Canberra had no option but to register what was being said since Australian New Guinea was a UN trust territory.

A further step came in May 1960 when Menzies and Hasluck visited London for a Commonwealth Prime Ministers Meeting. A major purpose of this meeting, at least as far as the British were concerned, was to get Commonwealth leaders used to the idea that change was afoot in colonial policy and would not be halted. Menzies took the point, acknowledging in a meeting with three other Crown Commonwealth Prime Ministers—John Diefenbaker of Canada, Keith Holyoake of New Zealand and Macmillan— that 'political independence is arriving or about to arrive in many States. It is a fact of life that they must be given their independence'.[49] While in London Hasluck, as noted earlier, discussed the future of Australian policy in Papua and New Guinea with Colonial Office officials.[50] Menzies and Hasluck also talked with Iain Macleod, Britain's Colonial Secretary, about current developments in British policy. Macleod believed strongly that it was better to depart sooner, in good grace, than later, almost certainly under duress. Menzies appears to have become increasingly accepting of this point of view. On his return to Australia a few weeks later, he stated at a Sydney airport press conference:

> Whereas at one time many of us might have thought that it was better to go slowly in granting independence so that all the conditions existed for a wise exercise of self-government, I think the prevailing school of thought today is that if in doubt you should go sooner, not later. I belong to that school of thought myself now, though I didn't once.

Asked if he would apply that view to New Guinea, he responded: 'I would apply that to any country'. [51] These remarks were widely noted and regarded as significant.[52] And while it would be naive to suppose that they had any immediate or direct effect on Australia's policy towards Papua and New Guinea, it is reasonable to suppose that they strengthened the hands of those policy makers and administrators who favoured more rapid change against those who opposed it.

Britain, or more exactly a Briton, did have a further impact on policy for Australian New Guinea after the new Legislative Council had taken office. The Briton was Sir Hugh Foot, Cohen's successor as British representative on the Trusteeship Council, and like Cohen a former colonial governor known for his liberal views. Foot led a UN visiting mission to Australian New Guinea in April–May 1962. In talks in Canberra before the mission began its work, Foot argued that 'it was urgently necessary for Australia to decide what it was doing in New Guinea; to re-examine the reasons for its being there . . . and, in general, to re-examine the fundamental principles on which Australia was working'.[53] His mission went on to produce a report stressing the need for more rapid constitutional and educational change along with the removal of racial discrimination. This was in line with Foot's view, expressed in a letter to an Australian diplomat, that 'In political advance what is most important is to be ahead and not behind public opinion—to take and keep the initiative'.[54] In response to Foot's report, Hasluck maintained that under his administration the requisite changes were already in train without any help from outsiders. Foot's blunt reaction was 'Not true'.[55] The issues were no doubt complex and contestable. But as Roger Thompson has pointed out, subsequent scholarship, including the major biography of Hasluck by Robert Porter, has established that Foot's report 'did produce a hastening of the slow pace in both racial discrimination reform and political and educational advances in the territory'.[56] In short, there are grounds for accepting that the new thinking on decolonisation, as mediated through the British connection among other channels, was having an effect on Australia's colonial policy.

Nevertheless it would be misleading to suggest that the Australians felt anything like the British degree of commitment to accelerated decolonisation. Menzies might have accepted its inevitability, but he still put a distinctly leisurely construction on the concept of 'going sooner' in Papua and New Guinea. As Geoffrey Bolton has observed, 'Menzies and Hasluck returned from a conference of Commonwealth prime ministers accepting that Papua New Guinea must move more swiftly towards independence. Even then, the deadline was seen as falling in the late 1980s or 1990s'.[57] Moreover, rather in the manner of President Kennedy, who went along with British plans for decolonisation everywhere except in left-leaning British Guiana (which was too close to the United States for comfort), the Menzies Government at the beginning of the 1960s still felt uneasy about other countries' moves towards decolonisation in Australia's immediate neighbourhood. As of 1961 its preferred dispensation for the North Borneo territories, for example, was 'the indefinite continuation of British rule'.[58] By a similar token, it remained concerned that British influence in the South Pacific should be maintained for as long as possible. In 1962 Tange told the British High Commissioner for the Western Pacific that the rate of constitutional change in Britain's island colonies 'was clearly much faster than the Australians thought proper, or convenient to Australia'.[59]

Most important of all for the Australian Government was the question of whether the Netherlands would be able to maintain its colonial position in West New Guinea against Indonesia's territorial claim.[60] This was of course the closest of all European colonies to Australia, abutting directly as it did upon Australia's own New Guinea territories. Australia in the 1950s placed extremely high importance on supporting the Dutch colonial position, for this was a case where the broad desire to maintain a common colonial front coincided exceptionally closely with Canberra's perception of Australia's security interest.[61] But by the end of the decade Australia was virtually isolated in its support for the Netherlands. 'Basically, we are counting upon the Dutch sweating it out and the Indonesians refraining from force', Tange wrote to Patrick Shaw, the Australian Ambassador in Jakarta, in October 1960. But Tange also felt that 'the trend is clear—we are doing less and less for the Dutch and doing more (perhaps nothing significant yet) for Indonesia'.[62]

In February 1961 Tange, in his own words, 'tried to prepare'[63] Menzies for the likelihood that policy on West New Guinea would need to be reappraised. His advice was that Menzies and the Cabinet should assume that 'Indonesia will pursue the claim persistently', that 'war is a possibility though not an imminent probability', and that 'The Dutch will withdraw'.[64] There is no doubt that in this case Tange sensed the changing wind. But the real turning point came in December 1961 when in the space of a few days a number of new factors came into play. First, on 21 and 22 December, Macmillan met Kennedy in Bermuda, where they discussed, among other issues, the West New Guinea problem. They reached the conclusion that they should do everything possible to prevent military conflict. To this end they would pressure the Dutch to find a way of extricating themselves from the territory, while simultaneously pushing the Australians to accept that the game was up.[65] Second, on 22 December, Barwick took office as Minister for External Affairs. By his biographer's account, Barwick had already decided that of all the items of business that would confront him, West New Guinea was the one that most urgently needed attention; Barwick personally 'had no taste for the Dutch position', and had thought for some time that Australia 'was, at the very least, facing ridicule and enmity for its continued support for the Dutch'.[66] Third, on the very day that Barwick assumed office, New Zealand, evidently in touch with Britain, indicated that it would no longer support the Dutch-Australian position. And fourth, on 27 December, Menzies received from Macmillan a letter which left no room for doubt that Britain and the United States were determined to force the Dutch to hand over the territory to Indonesia.[67] In other words, Australia's isolation from its allies was complete.

Historians have differed on the question of which of these factors tipped the balance among Australia's policy makers. Some, such as David Marr, have cast Barwick in the role of prime mover; others, such as Stuart Doran, have put much greater weight on the factor of international pressure. The two views are not irreconcilable, however, in that Barwick's advocacy and the international pressures could be seen as mutually reinforcing.

On 30 December Barwick gave the first intimation of policy change by referring in a public statement to Australia's 'great interest in the ability of the indigenous people of West New Guinea to have the ultimate choice of their own future whether it be for integration with Indonesia or for independence'.[68] After further talks with Menzies on 4 January 1962 he issued a second statement asserting that there was 'no evidence whatever of any present threat to Australia or to any Australian territorial interest'[69] arising from the West New Guinea situation. It appears that he had in hand a new assessment of the security issue by the Chiefs of Staff; their view was that European control of the territory was no longer vital to Australian defence.[70] Meeting on 11 January, Cabinet reluctantly accepted Barwick's argument that Australia must now withdraw its support for the Dutch. Its conclusion was summarised by Barwick thus: 'we have been obliged to conclude, from the past response of the United States and from our knowledge of the probability that the United States will not give military assistance to the Dutch under attack, that Dutch withdrawal largely on Indonesian terms is inevitable'.[71] Cabinet's acceptance of Barwick's argument did not mean, however, that it endorsed the judgment that there were no implications for Australian or regional security. Quite the reverse. In a subsequent decision, as Thompson records, Cabinet resolved

> to more than double the strength of the locally-raised Pacific Islands Regiment in order to cope with possible future Indonesian subversive actions in Papua New Guinea. This was not only in the interests of the defence of the nearby Australian mainland. Australia's Minister of Defence, Athol Townley, also was concerned that 'eastern New Guinea should not become an area from which unsettling influence could be extended into other Pacific Islands territories'.[72]

David Marr has described the decision of January 1962 as 'the most profound shift in Australian foreign policy since the war'.[73] It might not have been that, but the abandonment of support for an allied colonial presence was certainly an important watershed in the Menzies Government's regional policy. Looking back many years later, Barwick himself offered this judgment: 'I must say, on reflection, that I took a bold course seeing how committed Menzies had been to the then existing policy . . . But the ship of state did change course though perhaps not to the new bearings which I favoured'.[74]

In August 1962, under a face-saving deal brokered by the United States, the Netherlands yielded West New Guinea to a transitional United Nations authority, and in May 1963 Indonesia assumed full control. The broader significance of this transfer of power for Australia and Australians was well brought out by Barwick a year or so later:

> it came as a tremendous psychological shock to many people in Australia when a land frontier with Indonesia developed . . . for Australians living so long surrounded by the predictable the sudden proximity of the less predictable, I am sure, carried and still carries great concern. Yet one of the consequences of our emergence as a nation of great and growing significance and of our increasing international maturity is the problem of living with neighbours, proximate and remote, with all the alarms and anxieties that are so often entailed in the process.[75]

Adaptation to the less predictable was always part of the meaning of the ending of empires. Through the 1950s Australia had resisted rather than adapted, but by the end of the decade the game had changed and there was little option but to think afresh. In a general contextual sense this was because by that time the European powers, among which Britain was by far the most important from Australia's point of view, were visibly moving towards imperial divestment, in Australia's neighbourhood as elsewhere. In a particular and local sense, it was the case of West New Guinea that most dramatically signalled the new realities.

In retrospect, the 1950s can be seen as the last full decade of the British colonial order, in Australia's region of the world as elsewhere. With conservative politicians in power in both countries, and more especially with Menzies at the helm in Australia, it was also the last full decade of the familial style of political intimacy between the two governments. In their dealings on colonial questions the closeness of the relationship was much in evidence. One good indication was that Australia's own colonial ideology and its philosophy of colonial administration, like so many other aspects of Australian national life, closely reflected the British model. Psychologically speaking, the familial relationship retained something of its parent-child character. With reference to the British end of the relationship we have noted, for example, Whitehall passing many a judgment about Australian touchiness, immaturity, and the like; considering, in parental mode, the gift of a colonial governorship to the Australians; still thinking a decade later in terms of 'our influence' over them. At the Australian end the phenomenon of British race patriotism was still plainly operative. And empire, it might be said, still provided Australia with something of a security blanket, in psychological terms and to some degree in military terms as well.

But the analysis of colonial interactions also shows up tensions and divergences of a kind that had long played a part in the relationship. Sometimes British and Australian readings of their own interests in colonial matters led them on different paths. The Australian tradition of regional assertiveness on certain issues where security questions and colonial questions came together, which had aggravated the British in the nineteenth century, aggravated them again in the 1950s in the matter of West New Guinea. Perhaps most indicative was the tactical divergence at the United Nations, for it illustrated so clearly the differing world views of a major power that could afford a certain flexibility and a minor one whose only defence, it felt, was to be inflexible.

In the end, though, the two governments' underlying like-mindedness on colonial affairs was always more important than their divergences on particular questions. For this reason alone it was not surprising that they should have begun to modify their thinking about colonialism along fairly much the same lines at roughly the same time—with Australia lagging a certain distance behind.

3

British islands, Australian ambitions

IN JANUARY 1954 R. N. Hamilton, an official in the South Pacific branch of the Department of External Affairs, spelt out in a memo to James Plimsoll, at that time an Assistant Secretary, the rationale of Australian policy in the arc of islands to the west, north and east of the Australian continent.

1. To exert dominant political influence in the area with a view to maintaining Australian security behind a peripheral screen of islands.
2. To this may be added (independent of the security aspects of each):
   (a) extension of Australian economic interests throughout the region
   (b) fostering of development among the native peoples of the area
   (c) assumption of U.K. obligations in the area.
3. The peripheral screen of islands comprises
   Cocos and Christmas Islands
   Portuguese Timor
   Netherlands New Guinea
   New Guinea and Nauru
   Solomons
   New Hebrides
   New Caledonia
   Norfolk Island

Maximisation of influence may be identified in certain circumstances (i.e. under 2(c) above) with the assumption of sovereignty.[1]

The theme of assumption of sovereignty has so far received little attention in the historiography of Australia's efforts 'to exert dominant political influence in the area'. Yet this strand in the broader story of Australian mini-imperialism is well worth examining, especially in the 1950s when Australian ambitions to acquire sovereignty over British territories both came to a head and came to an end. In 1951 the British High Commissioner in Australia referred in a despatch to Australia's '"territorial ambitions" in respect of British colonial territory'.[2] Five of the territories on Hamilton's list were at that time under British rule (the Cocos Islands, Christmas Island, and the British Solomon Islands Protectorate), British co-dominion (the New Hebrides) or British co-trusteeship (Nauru). At different times and with varying degrees of intensity, Australia showed interest in taking over British responsibilities in all five. Analysis of Australian manoeuvres to this end helps to illuminate an understudied aspect of Australian regional policy.

It also provides a study in Anglo-Australian interaction. Understandings between Australia and Britain on the transfer of territory were not necessarily easy to arrive at. The issue of colonial transfer had the capacity to heighten sensitivities in London and Canberra on, for example, racial questions; or to create complications in domestic bureaucratic politics, for example between External Affairs, Defence, Territories and Immigration in Canberra; or to raise diplomatic problems in relation to third countries, for example Singapore in the Indian Ocean and France in the South Pacific. But at a deeper level, the complex of political, cultural and constitutional ties between Britain and Australia gave their colonial negotiations an essentially intra-familial character, and this was ultimately a facilitating factor; as the Commonwealth Relations Office remarked apropos the Cocos Islands, 'the proposed transfer would not, in the strict legal sense, involve any change of sovereignty since the Islands would remain under the Crown'.[3] And a further enabling factor was the growing complementarity between Australia's regional strategic and economic interests, on one hand, and, on the other, the unfolding logic of empire by which Britain was increasingly willing to consider reducing its colonial responsibilities in Australia's region. Indeed, by the end of the 1950s the wheel had turned; Britain seemed more anxious to transfer certain territories than Australia was to acquire them.

What emerged in the 1950s, in fact, was a dualism in Australian policy. An undiminished interest in acquiring British territories on Australia's Indian Ocean flank went hand in hand with a rapidly diminishing interest in territorial acquisition on the South Pacific flank. Correspondingly there were two separate reasons why Anglo-Australian negotiations, having come to a head, then came to an end. First, Australia was successful in its efforts in the Indian Ocean. Second, it lost interest in taking over territories in the South Pacific.

Nauru

By far the least complex of the five cases, Nauru requires only a brief discussion. As was noted in Chapter 1, this tiny Pacific island was a UN trust territory in which Britain, Australia and New Zealand were jointly responsible for administration. In practice, and with the consent of the other trustees, Australia acted as sole administrator, as it had done since the original tripartite agreement of 1919.

Australia held the lion's share of the economic interest in Nauru. To defend it, Australia was determined to maintain its de facto monopoly of administrative control. In 1947, however, Evatt went further, sounding out the British and New Zealanders on the possibility of Australia becoming de jure sole administrator. New Zealand had its own access to cheap phosphate to consider, and so resisted this ambit claim. Faced with division between their co-trustees, the British supported the status quo. Evatt backed down. But he achieved his political goal nonetheless, by securing shortly afterwards an agreement that there could be no change in Nauru's administration without the consent of all three parties; in other words, an Australian power of veto over any attempt to dilute its de facto administrative monopoly.[4] Accordingly, Australia had no further incentive to seek transfer of the British share of responsibility.

The Cocos Islands

The Cocos Islands case gave rise to a much more protracted and difficult negotiation. Comprising twenty-seven coral islands grouped into two atolls, the Cocos group had long been administered by Britain as part of the Colony of Singapore. In 1945 the RAF built a military airfield there, but used it for only a few months, after which it fell into disrepair. The Clunies Ross family, which dominated Cocos affairs, then proposed turning the airfield into a coconut plantation. But with post-war international tensions increasing, the Chiefs of Staff in London took the view that an airfield in the Cocos group would be 'essential' for the defence of air and sea communications from Britain via the Middle East to the Far East.[5] In 1948 the defence planning arrangement ANZAM was taking shape, with a major role envisaged for Australia: indeed, full strategic partnership with Britain in the ANZAM region. Against this background Britain asked Australia whether it had any interest in rehabilitating and operating the Cocos airfield. The Defence Committee's advice to the Chifley Government in June 1948 was that the airfield should be rehabilitated 'in connection with the defence of vital British Commonwealth sea communications'. To this, the Department of Civil Aviation added the recommendation that the field be used as a staging point on a new civil air route between Australia and South Africa. The Government accepted these recommendations, and in 1949 informed London of its interest in developing the airfield for both military and civil purposes. London's response was that if Australia was prepared to finance and carry out the necessary public works, Britain would concede to Australia, for an agreed period, 'the entire operation and administration of the airfield in time of peace', on the understanding that the islands would continue to be administered by Britain as part of the Colony of Singapore and that Britain reserved the right to resume control of the airfield in an emergency.[6] Late in the year, two events—the first Soviet nuclear test and the communist takeover in China—considerably increased the perceived strategic importance of the islands.

The new Australian Minister for External Affairs, Percy Spender, turned his mind to the Cocos issue in May–June 1950. Spender was less than satisfied with what he found in the files. In a letter to Menzies, he noted that the Cocos Islands 'face a long and vulnerable portion of the Australian coastline', and expressed his concern at 'the very considerable limitation on the rights which Australia would acquire by its initiative and expenditure' under the terms of the British offer. His recommendation was that Australia should press for a full transfer of sovereignty. Spender's advice was supported by other key ministers, notably Richard Casey, Acting Minister for Air, and Philip McBride, Minister for Defence, who referred to the possibility of 'a deterioration in the position' in Indonesia. Menzies soon concurred. In August 1950 he told the British Prime Minister, Clement Attlee, that 'the limited nature of Australian control which you would be willing to concede . . . scarcely corresponds with the substantial nature of this investment . . . the most satisfactory solution from our point of view might well be the transfer of sovereignty'.[7]

The ball was now in London's court. The British Government was aware that India, Pakistan and Ceylon all disliked the prospect of such a transfer, and that Indonesia might be angered by it.[8] But the Chiefs of Staff plumped for transfer, arguing that it would be to the general ANZAM advantage if Australia were to take full strategic and financial responsibility for the islands. So advised, the British Cabinet decided early in 1951 to agree to the Australian request. It would be important to secure the acquiescence of the unofficial members of the Singapore Legislative Council, but no major legal or administrative problems were envisaged. Both sides hoped that the transfer could be effected by the unobtrusive device of a British Order in Council within a matter of months.[9]

It was not to be so simple. The transfer took nearly five more years to bring about, and in the end required legislation in both countries, with full, and to some degree embarrassing, parliamentary scrutiny. The most important delaying factor, in a phrase, was White Australia. Britain and Australia had agreed that the islanders, who were mostly of Malay descent, should become, or have the option of becoming, Australian citizens after the transfer, and this was stated in the public announcement of the transfer decision in June 1951. But what London had not appreciated—or perhaps more accurately, what Canberra had not explained—was the nature of the Australian citizenship that would be conferred. Immediately after the public announcement of the decision, the Secretary of the Australian Department of Immigration, Tasman Heyes, put his Department's position on the record in a letter to his opposite number in External Affairs, Alan Watt: 'although all persons born in the Islands are to become Australian citizens, it is not desired that those not of predominantly European descent should be free to settle in Australia'. Rather they should be Australian citizens in the same sense as were the inhabitants of Papua; that is, they should be subject to Section 3 of the Immigration Act, which empowered the Commonwealth Government to prohibit the immigration into the Commonwealth, defined as mainland Australia and Tasmania, of any persons, including Australian citizens born outside these limits.[10]

It fell to Casey, now Minister for External Affairs, to offer a belated explanation of Section 3 to the British. He did so in August 1951, at a difficult meeting in Singapore with Sir Franklin Gimson, Governor of Singapore, and Malcolm McDonald, Britain's Commissioner-General in Southeast Asia. Accounts of the meeting indicate that the British officials reacted strongly, as subsequently did the Commonwealth Relations Office in London. The matter was seriously embarrassing to the British, who felt that they had been misled; further, it might not now be possible to secure the support of the unofficial members in the Singapore Legislative Council for local legislation.[11]

This was not a happy turn of events for the Department of External Affairs. For the sake of expediting the transfer, External Affairs would have been willing to waive the application of Section 3 in the case of the Cocos Islanders, but felt blocked by Immigration and also by Territories, which maintained that no such precedent should be set.[12] Casey wondered whether it might not be better to abandon the whole scheme, or to limit the request for transfer to the island that contained the airfield (and, as it happened, no permanent population). He believed however that 'the true reason' for any such change of front would be only too well understood by the Asian critics of Australian immigration policy, who would be bound to exploit the issue to Australia's discomfort.[13]

In October Casey sought resolution of the problem in Cabinet, presenting his Department's view that Britain and Singapore should be given assurances that Cocos Islanders would be permitted to enter Australia for permanent residence. Instead, Cabinet backed Immigration and Territories. Thus the hardline view of Section 3 was confirmed as Australian policy. But at the same time Cabinet resolved to continue negotiations for the acquisition of the Cocos.[14]

The problem became one of devising a 'form of words' on the migration question. The British indicated that any formula that satisfied the Singapore unofficials would also be acceptable to them. Over several months, Casey, his officials and British officials collaborated in the search for a formula. In July 1952 the Singapore politicians declared themselves satisfied with a simple assurance from Casey that 'applications from Cocos Islanders after the transfer to enter Australia will receive the most sympathetic consideration'.[15] The problem appeared resolved.

But Canberra's relief proved premature. For the Law Officers in London now advised that transfer by Order in Council could not legally be effected without extending Australia's boundaries to embrace the islands. Since this would give the islanders unrestricted right of entry to the mainland, it was politically unthinkable from the Australian Cabinet's point of view. So legislation it would have to be. This meant another round of discussions, which under the stewardship of the two countries' Law Officers dragged on for two full years. The Australian Government became increasingly anxious that the British Act should be passed while the Singapore politicians who had accepted Casey's assurance were still in office, that is, before the next Singapore election, due in 1955. Even more important for the Australians was the need to achieve the transfer before there was any further devolution of power from Britain to Singapore; there could be no certainty that a self-governing Singapore would prove willing to part with the territory.[16]

In September 1954 the British declared themselves ready to proceed with an enabling Act. But what they first required was an Australian re-affirmation of the immigration rights of the islanders, couched in terms which British ministers could, if necessary, use in parliamentary debate. After due consideration Casey provided in December an assurance adapted from the Singapore formula: 'It is not expected that any substantial number of Cocos Islanders will desire to go to Australia, but the Australian Government has indicated in the course of negotiations that should any such applications be received they would be most sympathetically considered'.[17]

In the British parliamentary debate that followed, early in 1955, the Labour Opposition saw to it that discussion turned very largely on the migration issue. Debate became heated. Ministers made use of the Casey formula; the Opposition nevertheless divided the House on a motion which, by implication, accused the Government of acquiescing in the existence of first-class and second-class Australian citizenship.[18] As their private communications make clear, ministers were all the more aggrieved at this in that it was the British Labour Government which had made the initial agreement without checking the point about White Australia.[19]

And British indignation was soon fuelled further. It was the British understanding that the words 'go to Australia' in the Casey formula would cover any request from the islanders 'to enter and settle in Australia'. But as the Australian High Commission in London explained to British officials, the Australian view was that 'it would be preferable . . . not to refer to permanent settlement' in the published exchange of letters confirming the transfer agreement.[20] It looked as if Canberra was backsliding again. The dispute became very specific. Australia wanted the three words 'and settle in' to be excluded from the published text. But British ministers and the Colonial Office argued that when the letters were tabled in the House of Commons, Opposition attention might focus on the omission of these words leading to 'another troublesome debate. They will therefore be most reluctant to omit them at this late stage'.[21]

The issue had now become a distinctly sensitive one between the governments. In March 1955 the Australian Cabinet reaffirmed its view that the words 'and settle in' should not be included in the letters.[22] Early in April the Prime Minister's Department proposed to London a new form of words that closely reflected the hardline attitude of the Department of Immigration. 'Visits' by Cocos Islanders were not problematic; but 'applications for permanent residence will be dealt with on their merits as they arise and careful consideration will be given to each case in accordance with the broad principles governing Australian immigration policy'.[23] No 'sympathetic consideration' here. Britain's Acting High Commissioner in Canberra reported back to London that both Casey and the Minister for Immigration, Harold Holt, felt that the British ministers' parliamentary statements had gone further than was justified by the Casey formula of December 1954, 'and cannot yet see way clear to accepting compromise'.[24]

In London the mood similarly hardened against compromise. 'For us to have pursued the matter more deeply with Mr Casey at the time', wrote W. A. W. Clark of the Commonwealth Relations Office, 'would have been tantamount to querying the bona fides of the Australian Government . . . We must insist that the assurances that they [British ministers] gave to the U.K. Parliament are honoured'.[25] Instructing British officials in Canberra to approach Casey directly, the Office insisted that any further Australian prevarication would create 'a sorry state of affairs between United Kingdom and Australian Governments'.[26]

Early in May 1955, the Australian position began to shift in the direction the British required. Partly this was because of direct representations from the Acting British High Commissioner to Casey and Holt. But it also reflected the continuing play of bureaucratic politics with senior External Affairs officials, in particular James Plimsoll, working upon their counterparts in the Department of Immigration which had effectively driven

Australian policy up to this point. As the British representative reported back to London, 'I had a meeting with Casey Holt and officials today. Plimsoll had meanwhile been working on Immigration Department with such good effect that I found Holt in a very reasonable frame of mind'.[27] At this point Menzies decided to take the question back to Cabinet once more. 'This is unfortunate', the British representative cabled London, 'but with Holt on our side there should be no complications'.[28] Meeting on 10 May, Cabinet at last backed down. It reinstated Casey's 1954 formula in a subtly modified form: 'The view of the Australian Government is that it is not likely that any appreciable number of Cocos Islanders will desire to come to Australia, but should application for entry be received from any of them, it will be sympathetically considered'. And Cabinet further decided that the British High Commissioner should be informed 'that the Government's interpretation of "sympathetically considered" extended to permanent as well as temporary residence'.[29] There remained only the diplomacy of nego-tiating the subtle modifications with the British: the substitution of 'appreci-able' for 'substantial', and the omission of 'most' before 'sympathetically'. London balked at the first, but accepted the second.[30] And thus, with a couple of carefully turned phrases, the deal was secured. Transfer of the islands followed in November 1955.

The White Australia policy had discomfited Britain when it was first established because it was directed in part against the Japanese at a time of Anglo-Japanese alliance. It returned to discomfit Britain again, and some in Canberra as well, in the context of this colonial negotiation of the 1950s. With hindsight, the Cocos question can be seen as a small yet not insignifi-cant test case for the principle of White Australia. Canberra's hand was forced by its own desire to acquire a strategic asset. The resistance of the Immigration and Territories departments, and of a majority of ministers, was eventually worn down by pressure from London abetted by pressure from the Department of External Affairs, with its more internationalist view of the matter. Holt insisted that no precedent was being set. Never-theless a principle had been breached. In a way that had certainly not been anticipated when the issue first arose, the Cocos negotiations knocked a tiny chip in the walls of White Australia.

Christmas Island

Christmas Island in the Indian Ocean (not to be confused with Christmas Island in the Pacific, a British thermo-nuclear testing site in 1957) provided a further instance of Australian mini-imperialism at work. There were cer-tain resemblances to the Cocos case. Christmas Island too was administered

by Britain as part of the Colony of Singapore. Once again strategic considerations were relevant. Once again the question of the immigration rights of
the islanders, most of whom were Singapore Chinese, lurked in the background. But the most significant factor in this case, as with Nauru, was
Australian interest in the island's phosphate. The Christmas Island deposits,
mined under lease by a commission that was co-owned by Australia and
New Zealand, provided Australia with a quarter of its superphosphate
fertiliser requirements.

The first official Australian proposal for a transfer of authority was
made by the Minister for Territories to the Commonwealth Relations Office
in 1947. London responded negatively. The question lapsed until 1954,
when Canberra's interest was revived partly by the Cocos negotiations and
partly by the prospect of constitutional changes in Singapore. C. R. Lambert,
Secretary of the Department of Territories, pushed for an Australian initiative on the ground that 'after these changes, transfer might prove to be con-
stitutionally more complicated and politically a greater hazard'.[31] The
Defence Committee, under Sir Frederick Shedden, Secretary of the Defence
Department, argued that the island's strategic importance to Australia had
increased in recent years. Bearing in mind that Australia could not rely on
Indonesia for the use of airfields in either war or peace, and also that the
Cocos group, while accessible to Australian transport aircraft, lay beyond
the safe range of the RAAF's fighters, an airstrip on Christmas Island would
provide a valuable defence asset, especially as a staging point for fighters
between Australia and the Malaya-Singapore area. In addition, the island
lay on the line of prolongation of Australian long range missile testing and
so might assume increasing strategic importance as more powerful rockets
were developed.[32]

On the basis of this advice, Cabinet resolved in November 1954 to
request transfer.[33] But neither Menzies nor Casey saw fit to move rapidly.
Through 1955 they engaged in no more than the most informal of sound-
ings-out of British ministers. The Cocos negotiations were clearly a complicating factor in this period. Further, Australian diplomats in Southeast Asia
and London were advising Canberra that the Singapore politicians might
prove 'emotionally resistant'. Well aware that the Cocos deal was being
pushed through before they acquired greater political power, the Singa-
poreans would be more unhappy about Christmas Island because Singapore
earned revenue from phosphate royalties and taxation. And if they resisted,
the Australian High Commission in London felt, the British would be 'most
reluctant to override them'.[34]

But in February 1956, three months after Cocos ceased to be an issue,
Casey decided that Australia must grasp this nettle. In a long letter to
Menzies, he first outlined the difficulties. In his judgment, the British had

no inclination whatever to transfer sovereignty over Christmas Island at present. They feared hostile reactions in Singapore; they did not wish to deprive Singapore of revenue; they did not wish to be accused of 'trading British subjects'. Accordingly the Governor of Singapore had put it to Casey that Australia should postpone any further approach for at least a year. Casey appreciated too the risk of adverse constructions being placed on Australia's motives:

> Australia's desire to have this base would be related to Empire building by Australia, and in publicity this would be related to Australian troops in Malaya and the transfer of Cocos Islands. The Malayan and Singapore Communists would develop this theme, and suggest that as the United Kingdom was moving out Australia was moving in.

These were real problems. But Casey warned that the longer the time that elapsed, the less likelihood there was of Australia ever acquiring Christmas Island. Once Singapore ceased to be under direct British control, 'the possibility exists that it could come under a Government which is either Communist or subject to Communist pressure'. New constitutional talks were scheduled for April 1956. This might be Australia's last opportunity to have its views seriously considered by Britain. 'Hereafter events in Singapore and Malaya may move so swiftly that the United Kingdom will not be in a position, even if it wishes, to alter the sovereignty and administration of Christmas Island'. Casey then proposed a diplomatic ploy. Menzies' letter to Eden should make things easier for the British by suggesting either a direct transfer or, if Britain felt unable to accept this, the detachment of the island from Singapore and its maintenance as a separate British territory. This second course would sufficiently meet Australia's economic interest and also its defence interest, provided Britain gave permission for the building of an airstrip. For the time being, at any rate; it ought to be possible to establish an implicit understanding that detachment from Singapore was simply a first step, with full transfer to follow in due course.[35]

This was an important letter. It persuaded Menzies, who wrote to Eden in March 1956 in the terms Casey had recommended.[36] Britain's response was much delayed however by its Malayan and Singaporean preoccupations (and perhaps also, after July, by the Suez crisis). Turning its attention to Christmas Island in October, Eden's Cabinet was given somewhat conflicting signals. On one hand it was advised by the Chiefs of Staff that the island was of no particular strategic value to Britain but could be of potential value in supporting Australia's role as an ANZAM partner; hence transfer seemed a good idea. On the other, Cabinet was warned by Eden of 'political difficulties' that were 'too great to be faced just now'. This was the cue for Cabinet to make use of the second option that the Australians had suggested: it resolved that the administration of the island should be severed from that of Singapore, and that the question of transfer to Australia should be left for further consideration.[37] But if this was broadly satisfactory to the Australians, they were less pleased with the British view that it would not be politically possible 'in present circumstances' to deprive Singapore of its revenue from phosphate royalties and taxation. The Australian preference was for a clean break and a lump sum compensation payment to Singapore, rather than a continuing arrangement which kept the island in Singapore's consciousness 'and which might afford opportunity in future for Singapore to request revision of agreement'.[38]

The relative salience of Australia's other concerns in Christmas Island —immigration and security—began to shift at about this time. First, the migration problem was quickly defused. Though Holt had declared that the Cocos decision was not to be seen as a precedent, this, in practice, was precisely what it turned out to be. For the conveniently available Cocos formula was now applied directly and without fuss to Christmas Island. A principle breached in one case was no longer a principle, as no doubt both Immigration and External Affairs perceived very clearly. Those who now search for first auguries of the demise of White Australia might do well to give these two cases more attention.

Second, there was a rather abrupt down-grading in Australia's strategic evaluation of the island. In June 1956, a senior Defence official had minuted his agreement with the British Chiefs of Staff's view that the island was not of great strategic importance.[39] The real change came at the end of the year, when the Defence Committee formally revised its earlier assessment. By 1960 the RAAF would have fighters that could reach the Cocos Islands, making a Christmas Island airstrip strategically unnecessary. More broadly, strategic doctrine now held that if Malaya were lost, Australian forward defence would be based on the 'Northwest approaches', specifically Dutch New Guinea, Australian New Guinea, the Admiralty Islands and the Cocos Islands; Christmas Island played no part in the plan. The Defence Committee's conclusion was that the island's only real strategic significance now lay in its possible future role in the missile testing program.[40]

External Affairs was at first startled by this quite drastic reappraisal. Arthur Tange, the Department Secretary, despatched a stiff note to Shedden: 'Those [1954] views played a large part in the formulation by the Government of its policy in respect of Christmas Island and there have been important consequences of that policy. Australian representations to the United Kingdom authorities have to a considerable extent been based upon Defence considerations'. Indeed, London had only just signalled to Canberra its acceptance and understanding of Australia's strategic interest in the island.[41] External Affairs, clearly, sensed diplomatic embarrassment ahead. But however inopportunely the exercise might have been timed, Defence's reassessment appeared on reflection to make sense and so had to be accepted by External Affairs—if not conveyed, in so many words, to London.

Effectively this left the economic interest as Australia's only real concern. Federal Cabinet decided in February 1957 that the economic interest was important enough in itself to merit continuing pressure for full transfer, and that the British idea of continuing the royalty payments to Singapore must be opposed.[42] Once again a colonial factor, namely the prospect of an imminent Singapore constitutional conference, provided a powerful stimulus. In mid-February the Government despatched an official delegation to London to negotiate the royalties problem in particular, and to maintain the pressure in general. And this time it was the British who began to yield. The key factor in Whitehall was probably the advice received from the men on the spot, the Governor of Singapore, Sir Robert Black, and the Commissioner-General in Southeast Asia, Sir Robert Scott. These two supported the Australian view that the break between Singapore and Christmas Island ought to be clearcut, and that a one-off compensation payment was the way to achieve this. They argued further that since 'only' Australia and New Zealand had any real interest in the island, there was no good reason for Britain to go on carrying the island's administration.[43] After this, questions of cost and compensation were quickly resolved, with Australia and New Zealand agreeing to meet the full cost of a lump sum payment. In March 1957 Harold Macmillan's Cabinet saw no need to prolong things, agreeing that 'from the economic and defence viewpoint, and in the general political and Commonwealth interest', the transfer should go ahead.[44]

In all this, the much anticipated hostility of the Singapore politicians quite failed to materialise. When told by the Governor of the British decision, Lim Yew Hock 'said the matter had come as a surprise', and very promptly agreed to 'take the money'.[45]

Both the Cocos and Christmas Island cases show an Australia acting true to its mini-imperialist tradition, acquiring authority over territories along its putative strategic perimeter, and in the latter instance securing an important economic interest. The British High Commissioner who wrote in 1951 of Australia's '"territorial ambitions" in respect of British colonial territory' would not have been surprised. There, however, Australian manoeuvres for territorial acquisition came to their end. On Australia's other flank, the South Pacific, Canberra's territorial ambitions simply petered out in the 1950s. The two principal cases were those of the New Hebrides and the Solomon Islands.

The New Hebrides

The New Hebrides group was administered as an Anglo-French condominium under a protocol of 1914. From the British point of view the
condominium had never worked satisfactorily. London saw the French
Government as continually pursuing 'a policy designed to benefit, often
exclusively, its own nationals, especially its planters'. By contrast, British
interest was waning and a number of British planters had sold their estates.
It was apparent that 'compared to his outlay in other parts of the Colonial
Empire, the United Kingdom taxpayer obtains a very poor return in the New
Hebrides'. At the same time, neither France nor Britain was investing in
social or economic development for the Melanesian population. Nor were
they attempting to foster political advance. By 1950, the manifest inability
of the joint administration to handle effectively 'the greater responsibility
now devolving on Colonial powers for the advancement of native peoples'
was causing concern at Cabinet level in London; 'the possibility of international criticism of the present state of affairs cannot be overlooked'.[46]

So it was not surprising that when, in January 1950, Spender proposed
to London that Australia should take over the British share of the condominium, the British Government had little hesitation in agreeing in principle. Indeed Britain had proposed the same thing as long ago as 1926, and
had approved the idea when Australia aired it at the Imperial Conference of
1937. In 1950 Britain's only stipulation was that transfer should be subject
to negotiation with the French. Consultation with the New Hebrideans was
not envisaged. The British High Commissioner for the Western Pacific did
raise the question of consultation, but only to comment that 'in view of the
very primitive stage of development of the native population, it would be
impossible for them to form an opinion on the question of transfer even if
it were practicable to consult them on the matter; it is not, in any case,
thought that they would raise any objection'.[47]

As Spender outlined them, Australian interests in the New Hebrides
were both strategic and economic. The islands lay in the Australian defence
area (a point conceded, once again, by the British Chiefs of Staff). In addition, the Australian Government wished to implement a plan for the
development of the 40 000 acres of land that it owned in the islands.[48] And
there were further Australian interests to be taken into account. Most of the
British residents, including planters and missionaries, were in fact Australian citizens. Australian currency circulated freely. Australia was the
group's principal trading partner, and by far its most important supplier of
imported foodstuffs and building materials.

Not unlike his predecessor Evatt, Spender was an energetic and sometimes impetuous foreign minister. His proposal to the British was made at
the Colombo Conference, little more than a month after he came to office,

and without the knowledge of important Cabinet colleagues—Richard Casey for one.[49] Spender had an activist vision of Australian policy and he was losing no time in implementing it. As it turned out, however, nothing more could be done on this issue during his term of office. For the next move was up to the French; and it was not until April 1951, the month of Spender's translation to the ambassadorship in Washington, that they informed the British that they were prepared to discuss the Australian proposal. From this time on the story was essentially one of efforts by the Australians, and especially the Department of External Affairs, to retreat from the advanced position to which Spender had led them.

Several factors contributed to Canberra's growing unease over the New Hebrides. First, the French had made plain in their note of April 1951 that in their view any transfer from Britain to Australia should take place on the basis of existing administrative arrangements. This ran counter to the preference that had developed in Canberra, namely that the condominium should be abandoned and replaced by a system of partitioning under which Australia would have exclusive responsibility in the parts of the New Hebrides where its interests were concentrated.

Second, in a way that prefigured its change of mind on Christmas Island, the Defence Committee came up in July 1951 with a notably lukewarm assessment of the New Hebrides group's strategic value to Australia. Certainly the group occupied a strategic position in the 'inner screen of islands', and it was important that its maritime facilities should be denied to any potential enemy. But 'in the light of . . . the accepted probable form and scale of attack against Australia and its Territories there is no important military requirement for an advanced Australian base in the New Hebrides nor is there sufficient justification, from a defence point of view, to acquire territory in the New Hebrides'.[50]

Third, the Department of Territories was voicing concern at the administrative implications of the Spender initiative. It doubted whether a sufficient number of trained administrators could be found to supplant the British administrative staff, especially in view of the need to work in diplomatic tandem with the French, who operated according to very different administrative principles.[51]

By October 1951 the Department of External Affairs was extremely unhappy about the whole idea. Laurence (Jim) McIntyre wrote to Sir Keith Officer, the Australian Ambassador in Paris, asking him 'not to give the French Government too much ground for thinking that we are anxious to press on with the New Hebrides affair . . . We in the Department shudder at the idea of becoming involved in the condominium'. Not only were there the difficulties just noted; McIntyre felt that the whole project could well be complicated by what might happen in respect of the Cocos Islands. If the

Cocos negotiations ran aground on the Cabinet's unwillingness to concede immigration rights, 'the wisdom of our attempting to assume the overlordship of another batch of island natives will be highly debatable'.[52]

The looming problem here was that even as Canberra cooled, London, and in particular the Colonial Office, remained keen to transfer responsibility and was actively pressing Paris to make a further statement. Learning of this, Australian officials sought first to persuade the British to desist, and second to persuade Casey to send an official letter to London designed to get Australia off the hook.[53] A strategy meeting between Casey, the Minister for Territories Paul Hasluck, and the senior External Affairs officials McIntyre and Ralph Harry was held in May 1952. Harry, who had checked staffing and financial questions, spoke of the likely need for at least thirty administrators and of the high cost of setting up new administrative machinery and initiating development projects. Casey affirmed that he could not regard the transfer as a matter of national interest. The Defence Committee's view, noted above, helped clinch the matter.[54] The outcome was a letter from Casey to Oliver Lyttelton, the British Colonial Secretary, in June. Citing uncertainty about the French attitude, and more especially the dearth of experienced officers in the Territories service, Casey concluded 'that we must defer any proposal for assumption of United Kingdom responsibilities in the New Hebrides for at least two years'.[55]

This was not what the British wanted to hear. As internal Whitehall memorandums make plain, the Colonial Office in particular was frankly sceptical about Casey's administrative 'excuse'[56] (though Casey was in fact faithfully following his official advice on this point). The Colonial Office now had to face the unwelcome responsibility of thinking about long-term development planning, while remaining worried that the whole issue of New Hebridean administration was likely to attract international criticism.

In September 1953 the British returned to the charge. Australia's two-year moratorium on further proposals would expire in nine months; was there now 'any likelihood of the Australian Government being willing to take over United Kingdom responsibilities'?[57] Allen Brown, Secretary of the Prime Minister's Department in Canberra, felt that the question should go to full Cabinet,[58] and in February 1954 it did. External Affairs and Territories combined to produce a Cabinet paper of generally negative drift. A Cabinet decision against taking over from Britain

> would not cut across Australia's essential Interests [*sic*]:
> (a) While the New Hebrides are so situated as to fall within the field of close Australian interest, their strategic significance to Australia is less than that of adjacent territories such as the Solomons and Australian defence is not threatened so long as they remain in friendly hands.

(b) Assumption of United Kingdom's responsibilities in the Condominium would not by itself safeguard Australian strategic interests in the Territory to the full and might well involve the Australian Government in administrative and political difficulties.

(c) There is no evidence to suggest that the French Government are now more favourably disposed towards the principle of partition than they were in 1950 ... So long as a Condominium remains in existence, the problems arising out of divided control will persist, and would not in any way be eased by the substitution of Australia for the United Kingdom.

(d) While the United Kingdom retains her responsibilities in the condominium, Australia has the opportunity to see that its interests are protected.[59]

Cabinet was quick to agree that the Spender offer should remain withdrawn 'at present'. Its more immediate worry was that forthcoming Anglo-French discussions on the revision of the condominium agreement might lead to an increase in French influence relative to British, which might undermine the Australians' preferred strategy of using the British presence to protect Australian interests. Cabinet thus resolved to inform London of its concern that the British role be fully maintained, and that Australia be kept fully informed of the progress of the Anglo-French negotiations.[60] The British duly provided assurances, while making it clear that they were willing to resume discussions on transfer at any time.[61] But Australia was now set in its policy of encouraging the British both to remain and to concede nothing to the French. In conversation with a British official in 1956, Hasluck 'expressed some distrust of the reliability of the French, e.g. in regard to defence and the control of Asiatic immigration, and implied that it was for this reason amongst others that they would be glad to see us [the British] remain in the New Hebrides'.[62]

The practical task, Hasluck wrote to Menzies in the same year, lay in finding ways of 'supporting and strengthening the British position' in the condominium. To this end he proposed that Australia might send experts to advise on problems in agriculture, communications and other areas; might provide scholarships in Australian secondary schools for New Hebridean students; and might invite 'a suitable number of prominent New Hebridean natives' to visit Australia 'to see a British democracy and a British community at work', thus counteracting the French practice of 'inviting local chiefs to visit Paris to see the sights'. In the longer term, Hasluck foresaw growing pressures for change among the Melanesian population and the possibility of confusion and instability, which might well occur at a time of waning British effort and increasing French effort. If this were to happen, 'Australia must be prepared to act decisively'.[63] But such an eventuality seemed still a long way off, and called for no immediate contingency planning.

The British Solomons

In the nearby British Solomon Islands Protectorate, Australia's economic presence was long established and overt. The main air and shipping connections were Australian-owned, and Australian interests played major roles in the islands' banking, finance, capital investment and trade. Britain's commitment, by contrast, had never been very deep. Both its administrative provisioning and its developmental expenditure were minimal.

The question of transferring responsibility had been raised intermittently by both sides over quite a long period. Casey, as Federal Treasurer, suggested it to the British in the mid-1930s, but no official approach was made. In 1949 Sir Brian Freeston, Governor of Fiji, sent a despatch to the Colonial Office recommending, on grounds of economy and geography, a comprehensive unloading of British territory: not just the British Solomons to Australia, but Pitcairn to New Zealand and the British share of the New Hebrides to France. (The Office recoiled from such drastic surgery.)[64] In the mid-1950s transfer of the British Solomons came to be advocated in particular by the two most senior officers of the Australian Department of Territories, Lambert and his deputy J. E. Willoughby, and by the Australian Consul in New Caledonia, J. S. Cumpston. Their argument was that a transfer of the British Solomons made obvious sense not only because of Australia's interests there but because of the islands' proximity to Papua and New Guinea, because Australia already administered a portion of the Solomons group (in particular Bougainville), and because the British were doing so little to develop the Protectorate.[65] Unlike in the New Hebrides, the Department of Territories envisaged no great administrative difficulties; Lambert asserted that 'we would have greater confidence in our capacity to organise and staff a successful Administration in the Solomons than in the New Hebrides and, indeed, there might be mutual advantage to the Solomons and New Guinea if both were administered by Australia'.[66]

Hasluck was cautiously receptive to this advocacy, as was indicated by a letter to Casey in February 1954:

> If Australia is to incur heavier responsibilities of this kind [in the South Pacific], I would regard it as being more directly to Australian advantage to accept responsibility in respect of the British Solomon Islands Protectorate and we would have greater confidence in our capacity to undertake the administration of that Territory ... On geographical grounds there would indeed be some arguments in favour of administering the whole of the Solomon Islands as one territory, although any move to that end would, of course, involve the question of our trusteeship agreement with the United Nations.[67]

In January 1956 Hasluck raised the general question of Australian interests in both the Solomons and the New Hebrides in discussion with the

Prime Minister. Menzies decided that the issue should be referred to Cabinet for comprehensive consideration. This meant that External Affairs, Territories and Defence were all required to review their existing assessments and come up with recommendations. Hasluck wrote again to Casey, putting the view that 'if Cabinet should decide that it was desirable for Australia to do more I believe that we would be able to do as much as and probably more than is being done by the United Kingdom at present'.[68] The Department of Territories was by this time in no doubt about the case for transfer of the Solomons, as it made plain not only in its bureaucratic dealings in Canberra but also in its exchanges with the British. Lambert visited Honiara in March 1956 chiefly to discuss cooperation between the British administration in the Solomons and the Australian administration in Papua and New Guinea, but while there he forcefully put to British officials the view that the islanders would be better off materially under his department, which was in a position to outspend the British. This was a sensitive point with the Governor, Sir John Gutch, who was forever lobbying Whitehall for better funding for his backwater protectorate. Gutch put it to the Colonial Office that Australia would indeed provide more money; further, 'how can one deny the Commonwealth Government the right to insist on it when the Solomons are an essential link in her defensive chain of island territories?'[69] At this stage however Gutch opposed transfer and so did the Colonial Office, for a complex of geopolitical and administrative reasons. For one thing, 'claims by other countries on British territories in the Pacific and in other regions might be encouraged'. For another, Australians were not known for their sensitivity in handling native populations 'and would not be welcomed as a governing class'.[70]

Back in Canberra, the bullishness of Territories was offset by scepticism in Defence. It was important that the British Solomons, like the New Hebrides, should be kept out of unfriendly hands. But all that followed from this was that they should remain in friendly hands; it did not follow that Australia should seek to take over their administration. Indeed, in both the British Solomons and the New Hebrides

> there would be certain disadvantages from the defence point of view in assuming such responsibility:
> (i) Australia would be faced with an internal security problem in the territories. Should Service aid in support of the civil power be required, this could not be easily met from existing Service resources.
> (ii) The R.A.N. and R.A.A.F would be faced with a patrol responsibility which it could not meet under present circumstances.[71]

External Affairs did not align itself firmly with either Territories or Defence, at least while the Cabinet paper was being drafted. This document went up to Cabinet in May 1956. It showed External Affairs and Territories agreeing on at least the minimum ground that internal stability in both the British Solomons and the New Hebrides was very much in Australia's interest; and this desideratum pointed to the need 'for Australia to be able to have some effective control over what happens in the islands'. But the lack of bureaucratic consensus on the policy implications of this view meant that the paper made no attempt to urge a particular course of action. Rather, ministers were invited to decide between 'transfer' and 'measures to establish a closer liaison between Australia and the United Kingdom in regard to the administration of these territories and in regard to British policy towards them'.[72] Transfer was clearly the Territories preference, at least for the Solomons. Other evidence shows that the latter course was the External Affairs preference. Two weeks before the Cabinet discussion, Casey had agreed with his officials that a 'positive conclusion by the Government' would be undesirable. And in the Cabinet discussion itself, Casey came out openly against transfers on the basis of a departmental brief which maintained that there would be no significant defence advantage; that Australian economic interests in the islands were not so great as to justify transfer; that administration and development of the islands would be extremely expensive; that 'so far as we are aware there are no strong pressures on the part of Australian communities in the territories for Australia to assume responsibility'; and that 'we should be buying further troubles in the U.N. if we undertook further territorial responsibilities'. Casey's arguments carried the day. In the end Cabinet endorsed only a minimal version of the 'closer liaison' option, inviting Hasluck to submit a paper on the question of ways and means.[73] In April 1959 Hasluck was moved to authorise one more departmental examination of the New Hebrides question, but nothing came of it.

There, in effect, the long tradition of Australian territorial ambition in the South Pacific was given its quietus. Indeed, the passing of the decade saw the Australian and British positions all but reversed. Whereas in earlier times it was usually Australia which approached Britain to discuss questions of transfer, in the late 1950s senior politicians and officials in Britain showed a good deal more interest in off-loading Britain's smaller Pacific territories onto Australia and New Zealand than the antipodean governments did in acquiring them. Macmillan himself came to favour the idea of transfer; it seemed to him 'an obvious way of reducing the colonial burden for Britain'.[74] The influential Cabinet Secretary Sir Norman Brook was also in favour. So too were the Treasury, the Commonwealth Relations Office and the Official Committee on Colonial Policy. Another British advocate of transfer was the Duke of Edinburgh, who after visiting the Southwest Pacific in 1959 pressed the matter in a discussion with Macmillan. The Prime Minister's interest seems to have been further stimulated by this royal intervention; he wrote to the Colonial Secretary, Alan Lennox-Boyd, about the advantages of transfer,[75] and the matter then went to Cabinet where it was resolved that officials should prepare a report.

With reference to the New Hebrides in particular, Lord Home, as Commonwealth Relations Secretary, felt, even at this late stage, 'pretty sure' that Menzies 'would like it if the expense could be swallowed'.[76] Reinforced by this ministerial opinion, the Commonwealth Relations Office persuaded itself that the Australian Government might still be open to the idea. The Colonial Office, however, now took a very different line on the New Hebrides, on four main grounds. First, it believed that Britain still had a moral responsibility for the political and economic advancement of the New Hebridean islanders. Second, it believed that no transfer should take place without consulting the islanders—who would almost certainly be opposed to the idea. Third, it believed that any attempt to pass on responsibility to Australia would create unwanted difficulties in the United Nations. Fourth, it had little doubt that Australia was no longer anxious to acquire territory.[77] On the last point the Colonial Office had clearly got it right. And in mid-1960 the Commonwealth Relations Office finally accepted that the Australians had no interest in taking on such responsibilities 'even as a long-term objective'.[78] The question thereby lapsed, although a formal British decision to preserve the status quo in the New Hebrides was not made until 1964 (after Britain had spent some time agonising over whether to turn the whole territory over to France).

Into the 1960s

With the transfer issue laid to rest, Australia and New Zealand went on to maintain what the Colonial Office described as 'fairly close contact' with Britain on South Pacific problems.[79] In the circumstances of late colonialism, strategic considerations became increasingly salient. In 1959 Britain asked Australia to consider augmenting its modest defence role in the Solomons and the New Hebrides and to join Britain in contingency planning for the islands' defence. As the Australian Joint Planning Committee was well aware, both these island groups lay within the Australian area of the ANZAM region. The Australian Government, however, was reluctant in the extreme to contemplate direct military involvement. The Committee further noted that 'Any serious disorder in one of the territories . . . might touch off trouble in the Australian administered territories'.[80] But the Government refused even to guarantee to provide reinforcements in the event of internal disorder in the British islands. Here there were signs of Australia wanting to have things both ways. Its main goal was to preserve both Australian and British influence in the area for as long as possible, in the cause of helping the islands, as the Joint Planning Committee put it, 'to develop politically along lines consistent with Papua and New Guinea and favourable to Australia';[81] yet it apparently hoped that this could be achieved with minimal demand on Australian resources. The Government did however decide in 1960 to provide fairly extensive educational assistance in Fiji. Meanwhile Britain began to accelerate the rate of constitutional change in its island territories, a development that caused some unease in Canberra. Tange's statement to the senior British representative in the region, that Britain's pace 'was clearly much faster than the Australians thought proper, or convenient to Australia',[82] has already been noted.

Some of the Anglo-Australian interactions on island issues took place in multilateral contexts. One such was the South Pacific Commission, based in French New Caledonia. This organisation dealt primarily with technical and developmental matters, but in 1961 Australian and New Zealand delegates took the opportunity of a Commission meeting in Canberra to air their concern about the Soviet Union's apparent interest in the region. In 1962 another organisation was added, in response to a suggestion aired by Barwick at an ANZUS meeting. This was a 'study group' comprising officials from the three ANZUS partners plus the Pacific colonial powers Britain and France. The aim of the group, which began meeting in Washington at mid-year, was to hold joint discussions on the future of the Pacific dependencies; America's participation was a sign that strategic considerations would feature prominently. The French withdrew at an early stage, 'apparently out of suspicion of what they thought would be predominantly Anglo-Saxon discussions', as Barwick put it. The other four parties held a series of meetings from August to November. One of the main values of the exercise, in Barwick's view, was that the United States was encouraged to define its policy towards the South Pacific, the gist of which was that 'it is essential that no land areas in the Pacific be alienated from effective control by the allies'. The wish to maintain control of the area through and beyond the decolonisation process was manifest in some of the group's guidelines for further study: territories should not be forced into independence 'as a result of outside pressure', while in cases where independence was conferred 'the greatest care should be taken to ensure that the maintenance of security will not be placed in jeopardy'. Barwick commended the group's conclusions to Cabinet in March 1963.[83] But the group did not evolve into a significant forum beyond that point.

Generally, so long as the British colonial system remained in place, Australia and New Zealand on one side and Britain on the other showed a wary understanding of each other's positions. A Colonial Office paper of 1963 captured the flavour:

The Australians and New Zealanders realise that our colonies are of little or no positive value to us, but that they are rather a financial, defence and political burden. We have from time to time assured them that we do not intend to abandon our responsibilities and leave a mess behind, but quite naturally they still watch developments in our territories very closely. They also help in a number of ways which we are glad to acknowledge, particularly over education, external defence, and the exchange of intelligence.

Australia and New Zealand proved unwilling, however, to meet the British wish that they open their markets more widely to islands produce, an attitude that was giving rise to economic difficulties in Fiji in particular. For the British, this, like the Australian refusal to guarantee military reinforcements in the event of security crises, was a matter of continuing regret.[84]

We are left with an intriguing picture of a two-track Australian policy. On its Indian Ocean flank, Australia in the 1950s moved to acquire new territories. In the same period, its historic interest in territorial acquisition in the South Pacific faded away.

Clearly, the Cocos Islands were of defence significance. Christmas Island was not so important in defence planning, but its phosphate made it economically important. There was a strong incentive to acquire these islands in that they might otherwise fall quite soon under the control of an independent Singapore, which, it was felt, might have no great regard for Australian interests. The concession on immigration policy, Cabinet eventually decided, was an acceptable price to pay. Further, these islands were not seen as problematic, even potentially problematic, as possessions. Their populations numbered only in the hundreds; hence there seemed little or no need to think ahead about economic and social development, let alone political change.

By contrast, the Pacific islands were problematic, or potentially so, in several ways. Their populations numbered in the tens of thousands. In the mid-1950s independence was not yet foreseeable, but problems of administrative expense, economic and social development, and political change —and unwelcome international attention to boot—all were. For the Australians, as a British report later put it, 'odium and expense' were powerful deterrents.[85] So, in the New Hebrides, was the prospect of dealing with the French. Australian interests in the islands, though by no means negligible, were of insufficient weight to counter these factors. Simply, Australia preferred that the Pacific islands' problems should be in someone else's basket; while evidently seeing no reason to doubt that Australian interests in the islands would be at least as well served under British administration— increasingly unwilling though that administration might be—as they would have been under Australian.

4

Australia discovers Africa

Until the 1950s Australia had no diplomatic ties with, let alone coherent and thought-out policies towards, any of the countries of tropical Africa. There were longstanding relations with the northern and southern extremities of the continent: Egypt with its Canal, South Africa with its Cape route and its Commonwealth credentials. A High Commission had been established in South Africa in 1946. But Sub-Saharan black Africa, blanketed by European empires and of little apparent relevance to Australia's material interests, barely impinged upon the official mind in Canberra.

In the first half of the 1950s, however, it began to matter to a few officials that some, perhaps most (though surely not all), Sub-Saharan countries would attain independence perhaps within a few decades. Their emergence into sovereign statehood would mean that, however indirectly, they would become objects of Australian external policy. Thus a modicum of preliminary thinking seemed advisable. To trace the process by which ideas began to take shape is to enter into an intriguing case study of the way in which the demise of other nation's empires—in particular the British—impacted upon Australia, effectively obliging Canberra to develop policy towards a large region of the world virtually from scratch, and in the process reconceptualising, to a degree, Australia's own political, economic and military interests. Like decolonisation itself, this policy making was a piecemeal, rather messy and not very well coordinated process. Nevertheless, within a few years it did have a discernible and distinctive shape.

The Central African Federation as crux

If there is one individual who should be credited with setting the process in motion, it is the rather unlikely figure of Sir Thomas (Tommy) White. A businessman, Liberal politician and Minister for Civil Aviation in the post-war Menzies Government, White was appointed Australian High Commissioner in London in 1951. During his first two years in this post he was able to watch the British Government creating the Central African Federation, an exercise in imperial constitution making that yoked together the self-governing settler territory of Southern Rhodesia and the crown colonies of Northern Rhodesia and Nyasaland under a white government based in Salisbury. White took a close interest, partly, it seems, because he had family interests in Southern Rhodesia. Early in 1954 he wrote to Richard Casey recommending the appointment of an Australian high commissioner to the Federation.

Casey's officials noted that Treasury would doubtless oppose the recommendation, on grounds of expense, and that several ministers were against any expansion in overseas posts. Yet they felt that the idea had some merit 'as a means of encouraging the development of Africa along lines that will be friendly to the rest of the British Commonwealth and in a way that would not lead to friction with the outside world'. Their advice to Casey was that the department might make expedient use of a forthcoming visit to London by Paul McGuire, who would be en route to Italy in order to take up his post as Australian Ambassador. Specifically, McGuire, who was known for his literary ability (he had been a journalist for the Catholic press before being recruited to External Affairs), might be asked to prepare a report on 'the problems and opportunities facing the Commonwealth as a result of the rapid advance of African territories to self-government'. He would do this not by visiting Africa but by consulting officials in Whitehall.[1] Evidently it was assumed that the creation of an Australian policy towards Africa would be primarily a function of Australia's relationship with Britain; not a surprising attitude for the time.

Casey followed the advice. On 26 February he wrote to McGuire, mentioning White's initiative and requesting a report that would explore not just the question of the high commissionership in the Federation but the problems of British Africa at large—'for example the Mau Mau question and the chances of racial tension in the continent blowing up into something causing grave international repercussions'—and that might also seek to throw light 'on wider colonial problems extending even to Asia, such as Malaya'.[2]

It was a challenging brief for McGuire, but he seems to have become rather quickly a missionary for the cause that had been thrust upon him. In London on 6 April, accompanied by Jim McIntyre and Colin Moodie from the Australian High Commission, he met Sir Percivale Liesching and A. F. Morley of the Commonwealth Relations Office; two days later, he met Sir William Gorell Barnes of the Colonial Office. As the British reported it,

McGuire pressed the case for a high commissioner and 'talked vaguely' about making Australian expertise available. Whether by accident or design, he failed to explain whether he was acting on instructions or simply pursuing his own interest. The British were in fact somewhat bemused. 'At one stage the Australians said that it would take a great deal to get Mr Casey and the Cabinet generally at Canberra to turn their minds to African problems at all. The three Australians present thought they ought to do so in some way'.[3] But McIntyre and Moodie appeared less committed to this proposition than McGuire.[4] The British formed the impression that 'a small pressure group in Australia House, possibly encouraged by the High Commissioner, who has personal interests in Africa, [was] striving to get the Department in Canberra interested'.[5]

What is most interesting politically is that McGuire's suggestion of an Australian high commissioner in Salisbury caused a considerable flap in the Commonwealth Relations Office, for two reasons. The first was that such an appointment might precipitate a similar request from the Indian Government. This the Federal Government in Salisbury would almost certainly reject, given that Indian Commissioners in East Africa, and especially Abu Pant in Kenya, had been siding with African nationalists against white rule. Such a situation would be 'extremely bad from every point of view', and in particular would create a diplomatic headache for Britain. Liesching conveyed this point to McGuire 'very strongly'.[6] The second reason was that the Federal Government would undoubtedly claim that the appointment of an Australian high commissioner to Salisbury signified that the Federation was, and should be seen to be, an independent foreign policy actor—a claim which at this stage the British had no wish to support.[7] In short, McGuire's proposal seemed to the British officials a rather clumsy intrusion into imperial policy, reflecting Australian ignorance of the issues involved. They insisted therefore that any further ideas about representation in Central Africa must be fully discussed in the first instance with the Commonwealth Relations Office.

McGuire, undaunted, proceeded to Rome and composed his report to Casey. With this document, delivered in mid-June, he clearly hoped to influence Canberra to move beyond what he would later call 'SEATO isolationism'.[8] Over nineteen pages of text he developed three themes: that Africa was of increasing strategic importance ('it seems evident that Communist imperialism has a coherent doctrine for Africa'); that there were going to be 'notable opportunities for the development of economic relations'; and that Africa had much to teach Australia in its administration of Papua and New Guinea, since 'the pressures of the advancing world on primitive peoples produce corresponding phases and problems. Mau-Mau [*sic*] is not unlike the Cargo Cult'). The Central African Federation remained the single best hope for liberal multi-racialism in the continent, and Australia should certainly persist with the idea of a high commissioner. 'Can we keep out of all this unless we are to retreat into the Eastern segment of the world and go indifferent to the great cause of the Commonwealth?'[9]

McGuire would have been disappointed had he been privy to the reaction among senior officials in the Department to his paper—'an exceedingly slim production', 'a magazine article'.[10] The Secretary, Tange, saw fit to commission from Central Branch a quite separate survey of British African policy and its relevance to Australia, though it is not clear whether this was because he judged McGuire's report unsatisfactory or because he simply wanted additional information.[11] The outcome at any rate was a report to Tange by J. E. Oldham, Special Adviser on Commonwealth Affairs, which drew variously upon McGuire's paper, the Central Branch survey and Oldham's own ideas. This document picked up on the theme of representation in the Federation as the key to Australian interests. An appointment there would enable Australia simultaneously to develop trade, to study 'native policies' for application in New Guinea, and to help ensure for itself 'the strategic use of the Federation as a stable African base' in a future war. But there were grander imperial implications:

> If racial co-operation can be made to survive there, it can survive throughout British Africa, the alternative being chaos or an Afrikaans-type of European dictatorship from South Africa to Kenya, with the consequent offence to British West Africa and end of direct British influence in Africa. The survival of the Federation on a basis of racial co-operation would offer for the Commonwealth as a whole a middle way between the extremes of apartheid and of intemperate native nationalisms.[12]

Oldham's paper is of some interest as a summary statement of what a few External Affairs officials now perceived to be the emerging pattern of Australian interests in Africa. It formed one of the bases of a brief prepared for Menzies in advance of the next Commonwealth Prime Ministers Meeting, probably the first significant brief Menzies had received on British Africa and the implications of the movement towards self-government. The brief asserted the increasing importance of Africa for Australia, with particular emphasis on issues of defence and communications. Not only was it important to deny Africa to external enemies, to secure it as an operational base and to retain its resources for the West; from Australia's point of view it also offered an alternative air route to Europe (in continuation of the Cocos Islands route) if ever the Middle East route were interdicted. This was surely of high strategic significance.[13]

There was however another hare running. In a quite separate exercise the Department of Commerce and Agriculture, which had sent a trade mission to the Federation in February 1954, decided to appoint a trade com-

missioner there. This decision was announced in September by the Department's Minister, John McEwen, effectively, if unintentionally, killing off the
idea of a high commissioner. It transpired that Commerce and Agriculture
had not been told of External Affairs' moves on Central Africa. More embar-
rassingly for External Affairs, the Department of Commerce and Agriculture, unaware of the diplomatic protocol, had failed to clear its public
announcement with the Commonwealth Relations Office in London, which
that Office, demonstrating a certain restraint, deemed regrettable. The whole
series of events may have been one of the factors prompting a paternalistic
British judgment in November that Canberra was handicapped by 'a not
very efficient Department of External Affairs'.[14]

Cold War perceptions

In however faltering a manner, External Affairs had now put a few ideas in
place. But it did not build on them. Other issues pressed, and Sub-Saharan
Africa went to the back burner where it simmered along, virtually unnoticed
by Canberra, for some years. One junior diplomat who did take some notice
was Richard Woolcott, who in October 1956 took time off from his duties in
the Australian High Commission in South Africa to make an eighteen-day
visit to British East Africa; his report on developments there ran to twenty
pages.[15] But the official who most systematically followed Sub-Saharan
African events was Hugh Gilchrist, First Secretary in the High Commission
in South Africa. In April 1957 Gilchrist informed Tange of the Commission's
intention to prepare a series of study papers on African-Australian relations,
in view of the increasing pace of African political evolution and the need for
Australia to be in a position to decide (if ever it became necessary) whether
to back 'white' or 'black' forces in the continent.[16]

On returning to Canberra in March 1959 Gilchrist sent Tange a memorandum, 'Australia and Africa', outlining the key issues as he saw them.
On the positive side, the Sudan and Ghana had attained independence, the
latter joining the Commonwealth (and receiving an Australian High Commissioner). On the other side, severe disturbances in Nyasaland presaged
major problems for the Central African Federation. The next year, 1960,
Gilchrist wrote, was going to be to Africa what 1948 had been to Asia: a
year of fundamental change, during which several countries were likely to
become independent or near-independent. As a result, 'power will move
out of the hands of people generally known to us and friendly to us, into
those of people less well-known, whose attitudes to us are uncertain and
unstable, and may be unfriendly'. Gilchrist argued that Australia's thinking
had not evolved far beyond '(a) hope that changes will be peaceful and
orderly, (b) fear of Russia getting footholds, (c) concern at possible increased

external pressure on our trusteeship [that is, colonial] and immigration policies, disinclination to become deeply involved'. This was not good enough. There needed to be a thorough assessment of Australian interests, and further study of several large questions. Gilchrist urged attention to seven issues in particular. First, and encompassing all other concerns, there was the Western strategic interest, which Gilchrist saw as alarmingly ill-served. There was no 'Monroe Doctrine' for Africa; no plan or joint policy for keeping hostile powers out or for keeping Africa aligned with the West. Very little was being done to establish African-European collaboration. There was no security treaty corresponding to SEATO. In regional politics Nasser in Egypt and Nkrumah in Ghana were seizing the initiative, abetted by 'the Asians'. 'Are we happy about this?' The imperative need, surely, was for Britain and the United States to reach agreement on basic objectives, to coordinate their intelligence and policy-making activities, and to bring in the French in due course.

Second, there was the issue of Indian Ocean security: 'With Suez under the UAR, Aden under some pressure, Trincomalee neutralised and Singapore an increasingly risky bet, the defence significance of east and south African ports and airfields is increased. We would want to see them in friendly, or at worst neutral, hands'. Third, there was the matter of the United Nations. As African states gained increasing representation, their attitudes on trusteeship, race relations, immigration, communism, foreign investment and technical assistance would carry increasing weight in the General Assembly—perhaps to the detriment of Australian interests. Fourth, there were potential problems for the Commonwealth, an institution much valued by Australia: 'white/non-white antagonism in Africa might split the Commonwealth. India's objectives in East Africa are obscure'. Fifth, there were the economic links between Australia and Africa: trade and aid. Trade was growing, but could grow faster if promoted. On the aid front, a 'Colombo Plan' for Africa might have the disadvantage of diverting funds from Asia, but could have the advantage of bringing the United States into Africa 'as a co-developer'. Sixth, there was the relevance of African experience for Papua New Guinea: 'Problems at present embryonic in New Guinea are overwhelming in colonial and White-settled Africa. Can we learn anything . . .?' And seventh, there was the issue of colonialism itself. What should Australia's attitude be? 'How do we reconcile our policies in Asia with those in Africa? If Welensky or Mboya asks us for moral support, what is our answer? Do we in principle back the Blacks all along the line, "agree with the United Kingdom", maintain a stony silence? Offer (as in Kashmir) to mediate?'[17]

Gilchrist's paper was firmly realist in tenor. It gave little indication that the new African states might be seen as of interest in their own right.

Rather, Gilchrist focused firmly on Australian self-interest. He did this by interpreting Africa's political evolution in terms of overarching security concerns. Sub-Saharan Africa loomed as a potential new arena in the Cold War, and that was the main reason why Australia—separated from Africa only by the Indian Ocean—had to take notice. And he did it also by arguing that Africa's emergence might threaten Australia's specific position on matters of race, immigration and trusteeship. This had implications not only for Australia's domestic politics and its colonial policy, but also for its diplomacy and its standing in the Asian region. Australia must therefore work to build good relations with the new Africa. Friendly overtures would be needed; so too, probably, would material assistance.

Gilchrist's document made an impression on the Department. This is evident from the many notes scribbled by Tange and others in its margins (for example, opposite the point about Indian Ocean security, the terse annotation 'Get a J.I.C. paper'). Its impact perhaps owed something to its forthright style and its pointed questioning. But in the broader picture, it could be said that Gilchrist's paper caught a tide. By early 1959 African independence was becoming one of the global issues; the stuff of everyday headlines; an idea whose time was coming. The Department needed a thinkpiece, and Gilchrist's paper provided it.

Canberra was still anything but well equipped to run an African policy. In 1959 the Middle East and Africa section of External Affairs had a paper establishment of four desk officers; in practice, almost the entire workload was being carried by a single individual, Barrie Dexter. But some of the more senior officials were now showing some interest, and there were signs of policy beginning to move. Reflecting this, from about this time department officials began to generate a good deal of paper on Africa. Given that there is this documentary material to draw upon, it is appropriate to switch now from a largely narrative approach to a more thematic one. By and large, the main themes adumbrated in Gilchrist's paper were the themes that structured departmental thinking in the next few years. Correspondingly, the most salient ones—Western policy coordination, the strategic imperative, the need to build good relations, the question of material assistance, the pervasive issue of race—will be put to use in structuring the balance of this discussion.

Western policy coordination

The notion that the Western powers should coordinate their policies in Africa struck a chord among the External Affairs officials most centrally involved. Gilchrist's views were echoed and reinforced by Stewart Jamieson, the High Commissioner in Ghana, and Dexter, in his lonely eminence at the Middle East and Africa desk. They argued in various papers that a concerted policy was necessary if the West's problems in Africa were not to become even more acute. They further argued that cooperation among the colonial powers might facilitate organic unions among African countries, which could enhance their prospects of viability while also usefully reducing their numbers in the General Assembly. Dexter noted that there were some potential bases of cooperation. The Commission for Technical Cooperation in Africa was one; the NATO Expert Group on Soviet Penetration of Sub-Saharan Africa (which Australia was not supposed to know about[18]) was another. But the problem, as Dexter saw it, was that the colonial policies of the European powers—Britain, France, Belgium, Portugal, Spain—were pulling in different directions, and the United States, while showing greater interest than in the past, was not keen to intervene in a situation where its European allies were so divided. The issue was further complicated by America's fear of the colonial taint. Pressure would therefore have to come from other sources.[19]

More senior members of the Department, such as Tange, Peter Heydon (a First Assistant Secretary) and F. J. Blakeney (an Assistant Secretary), were generally sceptical about the prospect of reconciling the conflicting interests of the Western powers in Africa. But Heydon did encourage Jamieson, who was due to visit London in May 1959, to sound out the British on the matter.[20] Jamieson accordingly met a group of Foreign Office, Common-wealth Relations Office and Colonial Office officials, to whom he outlined the views he and Dexter had been urging:

> Australia's interest in Africa might be classified under three headings. First, there was the general interest in resisting the possible spread of Russian influ-ence and Communism over the Continent; secondly; [sic] the United Nations interest in preventing a proliferation of small States in the United Nations Organisation which might quite soon create in that body an irresponsible two-thirds majority. Thirdly, a general military interest in developments in East Africa in relation to air and sea bases.

Jamieson also put the case for the creation of African federations, and advo-cated the pooling of information among colonial powers to prevent pan-Africans playing them off against each other.[21]

It was clear from Jamieson's report of this meeting, Blakeney later observed, 'that his reception was rather frigid'. The British officials argued that systemisation of information among the European powers would only lead to leakages, and that coordination in any wider sense 'was impossible because of the French position, particularly in Algeria, and, to a lesser extent, Belgian reluctance'.[22] Dexter and Jamieson nevertheless continued to press their case upon their seniors in Canberra. In June Dexter drafted a brief for Menzies in which he argued once more the case for coordination, and rehearsed once more the argument for organic unions. (It is not clear whether this brief actually reached Menzies.) A few weeks later he went so far as to propose Australia for the mediator role, with the aim of bringing the major Western powers together. For his part, Jamieson wrote to Tange that he could not agree that coordination was 'probably impossible'. Events seemed, he thought, to be forcing coordination upon the West. The key question was whether de Gaulle could resolve the Algerian crisis; if that were done, there would be no major obstacles.[23]

But against the opposition of the Department's senior officers these relative juniors could not prevail, and by the later part of 1959 this would-be initiative in the realm of high-level geopolitics had run into the sand. At least it could be said (and was, in a brief prepared for Menzies in April 1960[24]) that if the Western powers were failing to coordinate their efforts in Africa, so too were the communist powers.

Defence and security issues

As noted earlier, the injunction to 'Get a J.I.C. paper' on the question of military security had been added to the margin of Gilchrist's document. In June 1959 Tange acted on this, asking the Department of Defence to provide 'a brief description of British (and non-British) sea and air bases in Africa South of the Sahara, and discussion as to their importance to Australia in terms of: (a) use by Commonwealth forces, or (b) use by unfriendly or enemy forces, in various kinds of emergency (global war, limited war)'. The Joint Intelligence Committee confirmed in a note in September that if sea and air bases in Africa were controlled by an enemy, Australian communications with Europe could be seriously disrupted, and that tanker traffic from the Persian Gulf might also be threatened. These comments prompted Dexter to assert in March 1960 that Sub-Saharan Africa might 'become for Australia as significant as the Middle East, if not more significant than it'. By February 1961, in the judgment of J. R. Rowland, head of the Europe, Africa and Middle East branch (and an official whose views carried weight), the acceleration of African events, and in particular the Congo crisis, had further heightened the global importance of Africa 'and hence its importance for the defence of Australia'.[25]

The threat to airfields, ports and communications generally was perceived to emanate not so much from the new African governments themselves as from the Soviet Union and China, which were both thought to be mounting major efforts to win Cold War allies in the continent. The Soviet

Union, 'with its new Institute for African Studies, its broadcasts, its publications and its offers of loans and scholarships, clearly regards Africa as a field for penetration of the first importance'. China was making a similar effort, effectively competing with both the Soviet Union and Taiwan (as well as the West) in the quest for friends, and specifically for countries that would support its campaign for admission to the United Nations.[26]

The problem for Australia, with its very limited diplomatic and military resources, was what to do. There seemed no prospect of security agreements with black African states, and provision of weaponry to them was out of the question. All that was really possible was to take part in the general diplomatic effort to create favourable African attitudes towards the Western world. So Australia sought to do this. At an ANZUS meeting in April 1962 the Australian delegation reported to the Americans that notwithstanding 'the need to concentrate its limited resources nearer home . . . Australia plays a modest part in maintaining the links of African countries with countries of Western background and association'. It was doing this through a multidimensional program in which diplomatic representation, United Nations activities, the Commonwealth association, educational assistance, contributions to the international aid effort, a visitors program, and training in Canberra for African foreign service officers all played a part.[27]

Goodwill

The only feasible way of trying to cope with the overriding security problem, in short, was to cultivate African goodwill. And this meshed with Australia's further objective of seeking to defuse potential African hostility towards Australian policies on specific and sensitive issues such as race, immigration and trusteeship. As DEA put it in a message to the Australian missions in Africa in August 1961, 'It seems to us that the creation of a favourable and friendly image of Australia is one of our most important tasks in Africa at present'.[28] All concerned were well aware that the pursuit of this goal had implications for Australia's reputation not just in Africa, but also much closer to home. In Dexter's words,

> To a degree we will be judged on the manner in which we show our interest in and create new ties with the newly independent peoples of Africa. This has implications for us in South East Asia: the more we establish friendly relations with the new African countries, the more are our policies likely to be accepted in South East Asia.[29]

In a sense then Australian policy in Africa was developing into a large-scale public relations effort, with questions of Australia's 'image' coming very much to the fore. Even so, to describe the Australian approach simply as image diplomacy would be insufficient. Necessarily, the task involved an attempt to begin perceiving the African countries not just as pawns in a Great Game, but as countries of significance and interest in their own right. Hence, by degrees, Australian interactions with Africa became progressively more informed by knowledge, sympathy, and a measure of understanding.

The development of the policy of cultivating goodwill can be traced back at least as far as the beginning of 'Africa Year', 1960. A brief for Menzies in preparation for the Commonwealth Prime Ministers Meeting of May 1960 argued that there was no alternative to accepting the new African states and trying to ensure that, non-aligned though they might be, they remained on friendly terms with the West. This meant that they merited 'political support and sympathy', and that something of a deaf ear had to be turned to their anti-colonial rhetoric. Menzies was advised that relationships with African leaders should be well cultivated since 'personal leadership' might be even more important in Africa than in Asia.[30] This was politically astute advice, but it may be doubted that Menzies, as distinct from his officials in External Affairs, went out of his way to follow it; establishing personal links with the new African leaders, let alone cultivating them, was never his forte.

There was also a non-African leader who very much merited cultivation, at least in the view of James Plimsoll, Australia's Permanent Representative at the United Nations. This was the UN Secretary-General Dag Hammarskjold. Africa was Hammarskjold's major cause during 1960–61, and he more than once sounded out Plimsoll on the possibility of Australia contributing to the UN's work in the continent. Plimsoll advised External Affairs that Australia would do well to support Hammarskjold as far as possible. One reason was that this might help to bring about the evolution of Africa in a way that would not be 'too harmful or dangerous' to the democratic world. The other was that Australia would stand to gain if Hammarskjold came to regard Australia 'as a liberal and constructive influence'. In particular, it would be useful to have his support in the difficulties that Australia might experience over Papua and New Guinea once African states had become independent.[31] It is not clear how far Canberra followed up Plimsoll's recommendation; attempts to cultivate Hammarskjold would in any event have been cut short by his death in Africa in 1961.

Apart from cultivating key leaders, External Affairs officials argued, Australia should exploit to the hilt the Commonwealth connection, for this was arguably Australia's greatest diplomatic asset in Africa. This theme was heavily stressed in a paper prepared for an Australian heads of mission meeting in Geneva:

The Commonwealth association is virtually Australia's only direct link with Africa and the sole foundation on which to build up future relations with African countries. Without it, we would have poor access to Africa and little scope for seeking support on issues such as New Guinea. It is, therefore, very much in our interests to work for the strengthening of the Commonwealth in Africa, through which we would hope to develop a relationship with the rest of the Continent.[32]

In keeping with this objective, the Australian High Commission in Accra, Ghana, was supplemented by one in Lagos when Nigeria became independent in October 1960. High Commissions in Tanganyika and Kenya (where Australia already had a Trade Commissioner) followed on behind. All these posts had what External Affairs called 'visiting and reporting responsibilities' in several other countries, allowing for at least minimal diplomatic contacts across the region, including contacts with countries that were formerly French and Belgian colonies.

External Affairs continued to generate 'goodwill' plans. Advised by Jamieson of 'the importance attributed to gifts in Africa generally', the Department, through J. P. Quinn, an Assistant Secretary, devised a gifts policy. Gifts should be presented at independence to countries that had actual or potential significance for Australia, and/or were members of the Commonwealth, and/or were large and influential and therefore in a position to affect Australia's relations with the continent at large. Quinn suggested that a set of *Commonwealth Law Reports* (costing £267 if bound in legal buckram, £312 in half calf) would be suitable for important countries such as Nigeria; for less important countries, the *Australian Encyclopaedia* (costing £50) might suffice. As a personal gift for an incoming prime minister or president, a shortwave radio might be appropriate. In addition the Prime Minister's Department in Canberra had some Heysen watercolours awaiting disposal. One of these was presented, it appears, to the new, and possibly mystified, government of Cameroun.[33]

Another idea, recommended by Tange to Menzies, was to establish a program of visits to Australia (and Australian New Guinea) by prominent African leaders. 'Favourable reports from a Ghanaian or Nigerian High Commissioner on his own treatment', Tange argued, 'will carry far more conviction than anything we can do. Leaders like Mboya, Kenneth Kaunda, Nyerere or even the Prime Minister of Nigeria are the type of guest who could be a good investment'. Menzies' response is not recorded, but several African leaders (including Mboya and Nyerere from Tange's short list) did indeed visit Australia in subsequent years.[34]

It would also be a good idea, the Department decided in 1961, to send a high level Australian official on an extended tour of Sub-Saharan Africa, both to enhance the Department's own knowledge of the region and to 'help to establish a friendly picture of Australia among African leaders and, in particular, to counter any possible false impressions of our attitude towards racial matters'.[35] Menzies approved, and in October–November 1961, K. C. O. (Mick) Shann, the senior External Affairs officer in London, made the tour, visiting the Sudan, Ethiopia, Kenya, Tanganyika, Uganda, Ruanda Urundi, Congo (Leopoldville) and Mauritius. The most prolonged African journey yet undertaken by an Australian diplomat, it resulted in a correspondingly marathon report, 122 pages in length. Fortunately Shann was a very readable writer; indeed he was known for his 'picturesque reporting' (designed, apparently, to 'capture Menzies' attention').[36] A passage from his covering letter will serve to illustrate:

> As is always the case, I suppose, the reality of Africa was completely contrary to the expectation. One does not get the classical impression of the greasy Limpopo River set about with fever trees, although I did see a few fever trees in Ethiopia, and have no intention of planting any in my garden in Canberra. One gets an impression of enormous fertility and potential behind the poverty of the vast majority of the people, who are on the whole extremely friendly and pleasant.

The report was full of acute observations on contemporary politics in the countries Shann visited, and presumably these made a useful contribution to the Department's still fairly meagre stock of institutional knowledge about Africa. But here it must suffice simply to note his perceptions on two of the questions that most exercised Australian officialdom. The first was the question of Africa's relevance as a model, or otherwise, for the administration of Papua and New Guinea. Shann plumped firmly for the French model, which focused on the training of a sophisticated political and administrative elite, rather than the Belgian, which concentrated on the development of physical infrastructure, or the British, which fell somewhere between. Drawing a contrast between the chaos of the Congo and the racial tensions of Kenya, on one hand, and the situation in francophone Africa on the other—'The French territories are a model of order and good relations between the new countries and the colonial power'—Shann reached the conclusion that Australia's vital need was 'to do some solid pressure-cooking of technically and administratively competent Papuans'. And the second question was the one that External Affairs was perhaps keenest to have answered: that of Australia's image. Shann concluded:

> There is a remarkable unanimity throughout the countries I visited in the view which is held of Australia. They think about us very little; when they do they regard us as rich, self-satisfied, isolationist, and not interested in anyone else's problems. They identify us with the United Kingdom and its conservative and legalistic policies in the United Nations. They know about our migration policy,

but for the time being it does not engender much heat. They have also heard of, and are critical of, our attitude towards aboriginals. The image of Australia is basically an inaccurate one, but there is a good deal we can do about this through representation in the area, visits and printed material.

It seemed a fairly tall order. But as Shann pointed out there was also a certain amount Australia could do in a more practical sense, especially through technical assistance programs. Such programs 'need not be expensive, but they are much more likely to make an impact and improve our relations with the Africans than large and grandiose schemes financed from directions which the Africans suspect politically'.[37]

Canberra was in fact already attuned to the potential benefits of an aid program—benefits for the African countries, for Australia, for the Commonwealth, and for the broader Western interest. From External Affairs' point of view aid also had the advantage of being a concrete issue that would need to go to Cabinet for decision, thus requiring ministers to turn their minds to African issues.

Aid

For policy makers in London, the speeding up of decolonisation brought a new urgency to the issue of foreign aid, and especially aid to Africa. In the early months of 1960 the idea of a 'Colombo Plan for Africa', which had been mooted from time to time over the years, was dusted off, and in April the Commonwealth Relations Office came up with a concrete proposal for a multilateral assistance plan in which recipients and donors alike would be Commonwealth countries. The Office hoped that its scheme would help convince newly independent African states of the value of the Commonwealth, while also reducing Britain's share of the load. It perceived that the key to success would lie with the two wealthiest dominions, Canada and Australia; without them a Commonwealth assistance plan would not be sustainable. It realised that Australia would have to give priority to its own region, with its actually existing Colombo Plan. But it hoped that Canberra would be not unresponsive to an 'Africa Year' proposal couched in terms of Commonwealth solidarity. The Commonwealth Prime Ministers Meeting scheduled for May would provide a suitable opportunity for the diplomatic spadework. Not all of Whitehall was convinced of the merits of the Commonwealth Relations Office's plan, however. The Foreign Office thought the exclusion of foreign countries a mistake. Treasury doubted that much support would be forthcoming from the dominions. Even the Colonial Office had doubts, seeing the plan as largely window dressing. With the

Prime Ministers Meeting approaching, the British Government did not yet have an agreed position.[38]

As it turned out Britain's hand was forced by the fact that Nkrumah of Ghana coincidentally put forward a similar idea. To London it suddenly seemed, as Ronald Hyam notes, 'that if Britain did not take a lead, Ghana, or even Canada, might make proposals prejudicial to British freedom of action'.[39] Thus the Commonwealth Relations Office idea, with some modifications, was put into circulation. Persuading the old dominions proved in the event to be a straightforward task; Diefenbaker was enthusiastic and Menzies expressed his support not only in the meeting but in comments to the media.[40] A conference of Commonwealth finance ministers in September put the scheme into final form as the Special Commonwealth African Assistance Plan (SCAAP), with the emphasis on technical and educational assistance.

Menzies' agreement to the British proposal could well have been anticipated, since it was of a piece with the key ideas about aid to Africa that the relevant policy makers in Canberra had been developing over the preceding year or two. The clearest summary of these ideas came in February 1961, when as Minister for External Affairs Menzies sought Cabinet approval for Australia's contribution to SCAAP. The case he outlined to his colleagues rested on seven main points. First, Australia could not stand aloof from the general Western effort aimed at preventing economic deterioration, and consequent political aggravation, in post-independence Africa. Second, African countries were becoming increasingly influential in world affairs, especially at the UN; it was desirable therefore to cultivate their goodwill. Third, the aid program would help to strengthen the Commonwealth association. Fourth, the involvement of Commonwealth countries in African aid might encourage the United States to become more involved. Fifth, aid would help to provide a counterweight to Soviet and Chinese influence. Sixth, it should improve Australia's prospects of persuading African countries to 'buy Australian'. And seventh, it might help to secure the friendship of Eastern and Southern African countries that were of importance in the defence of the Indian Ocean and in the provision of alternative routes to Europe.

Australia could not, however, give very much. Australian expertise and equipment were in limited supply. Large amounts of capital were needed for the development of Australia's dependent territories and Australia itself. Moreover, the priority of aid to South and Southeast Asia had to be maintained. Hence Menzies' proposal was, as he himself described it, a modest one: Australia should commit up to £200 000 a year to African aid, provided that this did not prejudice Colombo Plan aid or other existing commitments. Aid should be channelled through SCAAP but would take a bilateral form, providing experts, training and equipment on the model of Australia's contribution to the Colombo Plan's Technical Cooperation Scheme.[41]

Cabinet agreed, and so the scheme was launched. Certainly it was modest, but on reviewing it in December 1964 External Affairs officials judged it to have been effective, not least in political terms: 'even in small quantities, aid is a useful instrument of our diplomacy in Africa'. The same officials judged that Australia's broad policy concerns had become more urgent than ever: to ensure that African regimes 'do not fall into Communist hands'; to encourage Africans to refrain from taking anti-Australian stands at the United Nations; and to assist in the Western effort to prevent racial conflict breaking out in Africa, for Australia was 'peculiarly vulnerable to the effects of racial conflict anywhere'. Largely for these reasons they were prepared to recommend an expansion of the aid program, offering aid in small volumes to some non-Commonwealth countries and raising the annual allocation to around £500 000.[42]

Here, then, was an incipient aid policy motivated by broad geopolitical considerations, narrow Australian self-interest, and a concern to help in the consolidation of African independence; a microcosm of Australian policy overall.

Race

There is one more theme to be extracted. To judge by their numerous uneasy references to the issue of race, officials felt that here, if anywhere, was Australia's Achilles heel. The point is illustrated nicely by a Tange despatch of February 1961 which, having raised the question of whether it would be a good idea to invite African journalists to visit Australia, went on immediately to raise the spectre of counter-productive results: 'might they, in coming to Australia, look for the wrong things and concentrate on finding evidence of discrimination?'[43]

Gilchrist had posed the race question bluntly. What would Australia do if ever confronted with the need to choose between white and black in Africa—between 'Welensky' and 'Mboya'? Certainly it could be argued that this was a highly unlikely contingency. It could further be argued that even if racial tensions became severe Australia did not necessarily have to take sides. As one serving Ambassador wrote, the function of diplomacy was surely 'to straddle situations without unnecessarily alienating either side'.[44] But many officials feared that Australia was already in danger of being perceived as aligned with one side, namely 'white' Africa—and most specifically South Africa—on race issues. Plimsoll, who visited Nigeria in July

1959, looked forward to the appointment of an Australian High Commissioner in Lagos partly on the grounds that 'the presence of an accredited Australian representative makes it more easy for us to differentiate ourselves from South Africa in the minds of coloured people and particularly of Africans'. He reminded the department that this was also important 'in our Australian relations with Asia'.[45] And by June 1961 Tange was worried enough about the risk of guilt by association with South Africa to write a substantial memorandum to Menzies on the subject: 'Mr Ballard [the High Commissioner in Accra] has found an impression in Ghana that Australia has sought to defend South Africa and that we are birds of a feather, because of our aborigine (and no doubt immigration) policies. He comments that this impression may be more or less beyond the reach of rational argument'. Furthermore, Australian diplomats in Africa had encountered fears among African diplomats that if they came to Australia they would be subjected to racial discrimination. Tange argued that 'racial discrimination will be a major international issue henceforth', with the new African countries leading the fight and the communist powers exploiting the situation. Australia could no longer assume that it was safe from concerted international action against its policies on race-related matters. The first and most important way of diverting any such threat would be to 'give careful attention to the light in which our relations with South Africa appear'; there must be no misunderstanding of Australia's opposition to apartheid and its support for a liberal solution to South Africa's problems. To supplement this defence, Australia must work to ensure that the basis of its own race policies was properly understood. But this would have to be done very carefully, 'for protesting too much may bring about the very things we seek to avoid'.[46]

There is a strong sense of tightrope-walking in this document. Tange was proposing to Menzies a public relations exercise rather than actual change in Australia's policies, but the clear implication of his proposal was that Australia might find itself not only on the defensive, but with a real case to answer. This was not a message that Menzies was likely to find congenial. That Tange phrased his submission with such tactful care reflected the fact that he was advising a Prime Minister (and Minister for External Affairs) who only three months earlier had fought hard to keep South Africa as a member of the Commonwealth, against the bitter opposition of the African and Asian members; and who only two months earlier had resisted to the last ditch the pressure on Australia to join the UN majority in censuring apartheid.[47]

It was never going to be an easy task, then, for External Affairs to persuade Menzies that the time had come for liberalisation of the Australian position; and even less easy to do so just to accommodate the views of the

'Afro-Asians'. In even hinting at the merits of liberalisation, the Department had to contend with the instincts not only of Menzies but of most of his ministers, to say nothing of the generally conservative policy advice issuing from his other department, Prime Minister's. In addition, some External Affairs officials would have tended towards the Menzies view. J. C. G. Kevin, Australian Ambassador to South Africa and a strong supporter of South African government policies,[48] wrote to Tange that 'The acquisition of African goodwill should not have to depend upon our adopting too positive an attitude of opposition to South Africa'. The Ambassador further wondered 'what precisely we expect of a friendly relationship with the African States, beyond their complaisance in United Nations voting'—which could not be assured anyway.[49]

For the most part, however, External Affairs opinion favoured maintaining the goodwill policy in Sub-Saharan Africa and putting a clear distance between Australia and apartheid. Thus the operational lines presumably became clearer for the Department in late 1961 when Barwick succeeded Menzies as Minister for External Affairs, for Barwick's position on South Africa was closer to the Department's than Menzies' had been. Even so, when Barwick argued in Cabinet in September 1963 for a toughening of Australia's anti-apartheid stance at the United Nations, he offered reasons for doing so that were more instrumental than substantive; they were 'to safeguard Australia's general international standing and to improve our tactical position in the Eighteenth General Assembly'. But Menzies remained reluctant to change his position even on tactical grounds, and in Cabinet the majority of ministers continued to back the Menzies line. Cabinet's conclusion in the 1963 debate was that it 'did not feel that Australia's position, including in relation to its own domestic policies, would in the long run be assisted by concessions to United Nations or African pressures over South Africa, nor that it would be in keeping with its policy towards, and relationship with, South Africa to make such concessions'.[50] No amount of urging from External Affairs, it seemed, would budge Menzies and his colleagues on this issue.

Barwick also diverged from Menzies on another test case for Australia's African policy. This was the problem of the future of Southern Rhodesia. Given that the Central African Federation seemed unlikely to survive, the question was whether Southern Rhodesia should be allowed to become fully independent and a member of the Commonwealth while still under white minority rule. Seeking to plumb Australian views on this question in 1962, British officials received different answers from different quarters. Plimsoll of External Affairs felt that the Australian Government would not support Rhodesian independence and Commonwealth membership prior to majority rule. By contrast, Bunting of the Prime Minister's Department described Menzies as feeling that Rhodesia should be given independence 'at an appropriate moment', for example when Nyasaland was given it, and should be seen as eligible for Commonwealth membership. N. E. Costar of the British High Commission in Canberra reported that these disparities were typical of the general difference between the two departmental cultures, and that Prime Minister's was the department more closely attuned to the majority view in Cabinet:

> The views expressed to you by Plimsoll about the grant of independence to Southern Rhodesia do not necessarily represent the attitude of the Australian Government, although they are exactly what we have come to expect from the Department of External Affairs . . . The question is, therefore, which way the balance of opinion would go within the Australian Government machine. On the one hand there is the Department of External Affairs view, preoccupied with Australia's position at the United Nations, at times it seems to me almost pathologically keen to take a line independent of British leads, and unhappy at seeing Australia lined up in world opinion (which, in fact, seems to mean Afro-Asian opinion) with the unrepentant colonial powers . . . On the other, there is the feeling, more typical of Ministers, which instinctively welcomes the prospect of an additional voice in the Commonwealth sympathetic to Australia's policies in such matters as New Guinea, immigration, etc., unlikely to criticise her and willing to play her part to defend the West against Communism.[51]

Costar at this stage was not altogether sure of Barwick's attitude, but the British were not left in doubt for long: Barwick was an External Affairs man, convinced that independence and Commonwealth membership for Rhodesia 'on her present basis . . . would lead to appalling trouble'.[52]

There remained, then, a certain ambiguity in Australia's position on the Rhodesian issue. And this emerged into view when Rhodesia's unilateral declaration of independence in November 1965 brought the issue to crisis point. On one hand the Australian Government agreed with Britain and the United Nations that the declaration was illegal and illegitimate; on the other it appeared anything but wholehearted about imposing the economic sanctions sought by Britain and mandated by the United Nations. 'We are not entirely satisfied with the Australian attitude towards sanctions', Foreign Office officials reported to their Minister, Michael Stewart, in June 1966, 'and their collaboration with us, e.g. at the United Nations, has been less close than we would have expected'. The British attributed this to 'brotherly interest for the white Rhodesians, among many elements of the Australian population'.[53] By this time Menzies was gone from the scene, yet his successor Harold Holt seemed not to differ much from him on this issue at least. Indeed, when he visited London for talks in July 1966, Holt's attitude rather confirmed the Foreign Office judgment. 'There was no doubting Mr Holt's sympathy for the Smith regime', a Whitehall official noted; Holt had said that 'if he were a Rhodesian he would feel that he was committing racial suicide by conceding majority rule'. On which the recipient of this note, Harold Wilson's private secretary Michael Palliser, commented: 'He sounds pretty old-fashioned!'[54]

This account of the origins of Australia's African policy both begins and ends with Central Africa. In 1954 the creation of the Federation stimulated Canberra's first uncertain steps towards devising a policy. A dozen years later the response to the Rhodesian Unilateral Declaration of Independence demonstrated that Australian policy still had its uncertainties. These in turn reflected the complexities of Australia's own situation as a Western country proximate to Asia, as a country obsessed with its strategic lines of communication, as a colonial power itself. It reflected too the divide within the Australian Government between those who sought to adapt to the sweeping reconfiguration of the geopolitical landscape brought about by the ending of empires and those for whom this reconfiguration reinforced their desire to cling to older verities wherever they could. One of the many consequences of Britain's imperial retreat, from Africa as elsewhere, was that it forced some hard, and to a degree fresh, thinking in Australia about these problems. As of the mid-1960s Australia had not yet fully resolved them, not least because the older verities still carried some weight among senior policy makers. This showed up rather clearly in Australia's African policy, despite the earnest endeavours of External Affairs to bring about attitudinal change.

Change did come, eventually. The Australian governments of the 1970s were liberal on racial issues and outspokenly hostile towards apartheid; and in 1979 an Australian Prime Minister, Malcolm Fraser, played an important part in the Commonwealth's brokering of the transition from Rhodesia to Zimbabwe. But that is another story.[55]

Coping with the end of empire

THE ISSUES DISCUSSED in Part I were not the weightiest in Anglo-Australian relations in the 1950s. They did not rank in importance with Anglo-Australian military cooperation in ANZAM, SEATO and the Commonwealth Strategic Reserve; with the crisis in French Indochina; with the Suez crisis; or with collaboration on nuclear issues. They were nevertheless strands in the geopolitical tapestry, interweaving with other strands. Indeed, many of the Anglo-Australian interactions bearing upon the problems of late colonialism bore also upon Britain's and Australia's wider geopolitical concerns. Thus the study of these interactions in Part 1 provided a perspective on the larger relationship.

Part II concentrates on the 1960s, the decade in which what had been the greatest of the European formal empires—the British and the French—along with the Belgian and the remnants of the Dutch and the Italian (though not yet the Spanish or the Portuguese), all but disappeared from the world map. This was historical change on a colossal scale; indeed, in Darwin's view,

> The most profound change in world politics in the fifty years since the end of the Second World War . . . For most of the world's population this great transformation has been more immediate, more lasting and more fundamental in its effects than the events that dominate the Western view of post-war international politics, above all the Cold War.[1]

In Britain's case, the sheer scale and speed of the change cannot be overemphasised. The first great wave of British divestment had rolled through South Asia and the Palestine Mandate in 1947–48. In the next dozen years only three territories under British purview attained independence: the Anglo-Egyptian condominium of the Sudan, and the colonies of Ghana and Malaya. But then a second great wave began. From 1960 the

British Government began to accelerate the pace of change, providing places in the decolonisation queue even for territories previously seen as considerably less than 'viable'. The result was that almost all the British territories in Africa, the Caribbean, South America, the Pacific, Southeast Asia, the Middle East and the Mediterranean—some twenty-eight countries— became independent in the space of eight years.

Decolonisation and associated changes had consequences not just for the parties principal—the metropolitan powers and their ex-dependencies —but for third parties as well. One point is self-evident: for Australia as for other third parties, international relations became more varied and challenging as the universe of independent states rapidly expanded. This had obvious implications for Australia's security in its own region in a time of Cold War hostilities, intermittent armed conflicts in nearby states, and Asian neutralism. It seemed of growing importance to court the favours of new states lest they be swayed by Soviet and Chinese blandishments. Given Australia's geographical location at so great a distance from its major allies, it seemed especially important that the security of supply and communications routes not be jeopardised by decolonisation. Australia wanted also to guard against the risk that post-colonial states in Asia and Africa would take to attacking Australia's race and immigration policies in international bodies. And, as has already been discussed, the rapidity and scope of decolonisation by all the main Western European imperial powers raised very directly the question of what form Australia's own colonial policy should now take.

In addition to these considerations, the ending of formal empire was typically bound up with a revisioning by the metropolitan power of its international role, and this too had implications for third parties. Such a development was markedly apparent in the Anglo-Australian relationship. In essence: for Australia, coping with Britain's retreat from empire necessarily meant trying to cope also with the post-imperial order that Britain was simultaneously seeking to fashion for itself.

It is necessary first to comment on some of the factors that generated the process of British decolonisation, and more particularly the second wave. There is now a substantial literature devoted to this subject.[2] Much of it focuses explicitly or implicitly on the question of whether the second wave is better understood as a 'retreat' or as a 'rationalisation' on Britain's part.[3] Commonly it has been interpreted in grand-sweep terms as a function of the relative decline in British power since World War II; as David Percox summarises this view, 'the financial and material strains of the Second World War made it inevitable that the British Empire's days were numbered'.[4] The decline in power was made cruelly evident by—above all other events—the fiasco of Suez in 1956. Decolonisation followed soon after. In turn there followed Dean Acheson's jibe: Britain had lost an empire and not yet found a role.

This declinist view of events has much explanatory power, but in the nature of big-picture explanations it seems rather mechanistic and misses a good deal of the complexity of the story. The supposedly focal event—Suez —certainly brought a huge loss of prestige and certainly demonstrated that Britain lacked the economic or military might to act unilaterally if the United States was determined to block what it was doing. The fact that Britain was a great deal less powerful than the United States did not of itself, however, spell the end of Britain's world role. As Gordon Martel has put it, in the aftermath of Suez Britain did not cease looking for ways 'to exploit the opportunities that the world beyond Europe offered [it]',[5] while in the broad context of the West's Cold War strategy Britain maintained a strong belief in its distinctive global role beyond the bounds of NATO. One way and another, British unilateralism continued for at least another decade.

The wave of decolonisation that began to gather momentum after the British election of 1959—some three years after the Suez crisis—was propelled by many factors that were not necessarily associated with decline. Among them was the internal dynamic of colonial policy itself, premised on a teleology (the goal of independence) and informed by continuous dialogue within the imperial system (between metropolis and satellites). From the late 1950s the rate at which this dynamic worked itself out was much boosted by the unexpectedly rapid growth of colonial nationalism. Another factor was the belief, engendered by crises such as those in Cyprus, Kenya and Nyasaland in the 1950s, that prolongation of colonial rule would probably entail growing repression and hence loss of life. As Matthew Jones argues, ministers and officials became increasingly apprehensive 'that repressive action could carry heavy domestic and international costs, just when Britain was trying to shed the negative image of its colonial past';[6] prolongation did not seem worth such costs. Another was the fading of optimistic assumptions about colonial economic development, which in turn meant that the 'viability' precondition for independence looked increasingly unrealistic; if viability were to be achieved at all, the expenses 'would obviously have to be met by the UK Government',[7] and this was not an attractive prospect. There were also external pressures from the United Nations and to some degree from Washington. There were chain reaction effects generated by other imperial divestments, such as de Gaulle's in Francophone Africa. And there was the wish to head off Soviet and Chinese influence in British territories. Some would argue that in the historical moment of 1959–60 British economic weakness was itself a major precipitating factor. Darwin has plausibly argued, however, that this explanation should not be pushed too far; the British policy makers of 1959–60 generally believed, on the evidence available, that the economy had recovered from wartime setbacks, that continuing industrial expansion was likely, and that the prospects for the sterling area were bright. Not until a few years later did a series of economic and financial crises bring into full view the structural weaknesses of the economy. On this view, the factors pushing Britain into accelerated decolonisation should be seen as primarily political and strategic rather than economic.[8]

Along with the 'push' factors went a good deal of cool political calculation by the British leadership on how Britain's global interests might best be advanced. Harold Macmillan made it plain that his view of empire was based firmly on an unsentimental reading of national interest. Soon after succeeding to the prime ministership in 1957 he called for his now famous profit and loss accounting of empire, which would take all relevant economic, political and strategic factors into the account. The significance of this accounting exercise has perhaps been rather overstated in the literature—in fact Whitehall's response to Macmillan's call was to generate some carefully ambiguous findings[9]—but what still deserves close attention is Macmillan's underlying reasoning: 'There are presumably places where it is of vital interest to us that we should maintain our influence, and others where there is no United Kingdom interest in resisting constitutional change'.[10] Clearly he saw little point in hanging on to territories that were marginal to British interests. 'Our external policy', he argued in December 1958, 'should in principle be directed to reducing our colonial commitments'.[11] To use the terminology of Martel's argument, this was an approach that can be understood in terms of 'rationalisation' as well as in terms of 'retreat'. In the event, the approach (however described) acquired a kind of self-fulfilling momentum, such that within an unexpectedly short time British interest required that the imperial decks be cleared more or less completely.

The key question here is what is meant by British interest. Consideration of this question requires that decolonisation be seen in the context of a larger policy framework. Whatever Acheson's perception of the matter, the British policy makers of the late 1950s and early 1960s did not lack ambitions for the national future. The central point is that the winding down of empire was bound up with a large-scale effort by Britain to maintain its unilateral world role by reconstructing it. As Macmillan explained in a letter to the Queen: 'The Conservative Party are being asked, and I think will agree, to turn their minds from the old Imperialism which no longer has its old power, to a new concept of Britain's ability to influence the world'.[12]

The first essential was a major rethinking of British defence doctrine. If Britain wished to maintain and indeed extend its influence both inside and outside NATO, as Robert Holland has argued, 'it was vital to possess a credible nuclear deterrent in a constant state of modernization'. Accordingly, within just a few months of the Suez crisis Macmillan had overseen a defence review that 'secured a switch of resources from conventional to nuclear programmes on a scale not contemplated by Churchill or Eden'. There were some side-effects for colonialism. For one thing, the scaling down of conventional forces clearly meant that Britain 'was not going to fight any large-scale anti-insurgency campaigns of an imperial type in the foreseeable future'. For another, the development of Britain's nuclear capacity (with considerable help from Presidents Eisenhower and Kennedy) gave Britain an unprecedented sense of strategic security to which the old imperialism, and even the so-called garrison colonies, were simply irrelevant. As Holland puts it, 'The almost brazen confidence with which British officials went through the motions of successive decolonizations at Lancaster House undoubtedly bore some relationship to the prospect, and final achievement, of this nuclear apotheosis'.[13] The point to be stressed here is that in Canberra's perspective, the close association between British decolonisation and the new direction in British defence thinking, with its clear signalling of cuts in conventional forces, had distinctly unsettling implications for Australia's own defence strategy.

The reconstructing of Britain's global role required also the further development of its relationships with both the Western and the non-aligned (or ex-colonial) world. For this effort, what might be seen as a resuscitated version of Churchill's 'three circles' provided a conceptual base. There was first the revival and consolidation of the special relationship with the United States, a project to which Macmillan devoted assiduous attention in the years following the nadir of Suez. In this endeavour, prolongation of formal empire could only be 'a liability'.[14] Macmillan's efforts in this respect were generally successful, as evidenced by the American assistance for Britain's nuclear program. Second, there was the approach to Europe. This was a particular expression of Britain's general attempt in this period to strengthen its political and economic engagement with the industrialised powers of the global north. Menzies was alive to the link between decolonisation and the European bid: 'I do suspect', he wrote to Walter Crocker in July 1961, 'that the present Government in London is withdrawing somewhat precipitately from its African and other responsibilities so that it may achieve in the latter part of the twentieth century a new and European phase of its history'.[15] In this context, however, it should be stressed that the British policy makers of the late 1950s and early 1960s did not envisage decolonisation as somehow weakening the Commonwealth. Rather, the new Commonwealth, much augmented by decolonisation, would constitute the third circle: an array of states which would, Britain hoped, be a vehicle for continuing British influence in large areas of the world beyond NATO. Seen in this perspective, decolonisation was effectively 'the pursuit of imperialism by other means'.[16]

Supposedly, the three circles would form a kind of Venn diagram in which Britain would constitute the shaded sector of triple overlap. Or, as a senior Foreign Office official put it in October 1959: 'United Kingdom power will thus be founded on United States partnership, buttressed by Western European solidarity (we hope), and usable through the instrument of the Commonwealth'.[17]

For Australia, then, coping with the multilateral consequences of British decolonisation—such as the need to deal with new states and to accommodate new defence scenarios—was bound up with the specific task of coping with the general post-imperial role that Britain was aiming to create for itself. Australia had few problems with the first of Britain's three diplomatic endeavours. Although Britain's increasingly close nuclear partnership with the United States after 1957 entailed the downgrading of Australia in Britain's nuclear development program, it could still be said that, in general, the more Britain and the United States agreed on issues of international strategy, the happier Australia was. But the other endeavours were cause for some alarm, since they—or at least their potential flow-on effects—seemed likely to affect Australia's political, strategic and economic interests in unwished for ways. In short, the changes in British policy towards the Commonwealth and Europe made the early 1960s very much a watershed period in the Anglo-Australian relationship.

To describe it thus is not simply to offer a retrospective construction of events. Those who were involved at the time were well aware that significant changes were in train. In this respect a brief prepared by officials in the British High Commission in Canberra in March 1962, for British eyes only, provides instructive reading. 'Anglo-Australian relations', according to the brief, 'have begun to change fundamentally during the past two years'. In part this could be attributed to the 'growing maturity and realism' of Australia itself; but in larger part it was because British policy was moving in ways whose impact upon Australia was generally experienced by the Australians as adverse. As the High Commission saw it, three issues in particular were fuelling the Australians' sense of grievance. The first, a direct consequence of decolonisation, was the changing character of the Commonwealth, an association in which, it seemed to the Australians, Britain had become 'chiefly concerned with appeasing the Afro-Asian members'. The second, another after-effect of empire, was Britain's move towards a restrictive policy on Commonwealth immigration. If indeed the effect of Britain's new immigration legislation turned out to be discrimination equally against Australians and non-white immigrants, not only would a major link between Britain and Australia be harmed, but the resentment caused in Australia would 'magnify the damage many times over'. The third was Britain's declared intention to link itself more closely, both economically and politically, with Europe. This carried drastic implications for Australia's trade; furthermore, as the High Commission saw it, 'our role as a European power must increasingly affect our policies outside Europe ... and will often not necessarily accord with Australian interests'.[18]

What then could Britain do to maintain the relationship in good order? Seeking to turn back the clock was not an option; that would be 'unrealistic sentimentalism on our part'.[19] Rather, it was necessary to prepare for a change in the very nature of the relationship:

> Australia is still (with New Zealand) Britain's best friend in the world. The bond of attachment runs deep. But ... Australians are no longer content, largely because of bitter experience, to rely on gentlemen's agreements and broad assurances from Britain, and it is perhaps best that relations should in future follow the pattern rather of close and friendly business associates who will, while protecting their own interests, deal honestly with each other ... If we fail to readjust our thinking to these changes, then Britain and Australia will drift into different camps.[20]

As the decade wore on, there were continuing developments in British post-imperial policy that had palpable repercussions for Australia. Two were of particular significance. The first was Britain's creation of federal Malaysia in 1963, as a framework within which to complete formal decolonisation in Southeast Asia. Since one of the consequences was Indonesia's launching of an armed campaign against this act of *nekolim* (neo-colonial imperialism), Australia was caught in a particularly awkward dilemma: how to help defend Malaysia while simultaneously trying to build a stable relationship with Indonesia. And the second was Britain's 1968 decision to withdraw the military forces that it had established in Southeast Asia in imperial times and maintained through the first few post-imperial years—a decision deeply alarming to Australia, which felt anything but secure in what seemed an increasingly turbulent region.

Not that the second decision was unexpected. Whether or not Britain would remain in Southeast Asia militarily once formal imperial rule was ended was already a matter for discussion in the early 1960s. At that time, however, it was different in kind from the other issues between Australia and Britain in the sense that it was not yet a matter for open Australian grievance. It was Australia, after all, that had made the decision to construct its major security alliance with the United States, not with Britain, and it was Britain that had had to make the decision not to 'oppose or appear to dislike the trend towards an ANZUS grouping because it excludes Britain'.[21] Meanwhile Britain's declared position as of 1962 was that its forces would remain in Southeast Asia indefinitely. But there was a passage in the High Commission brief which, had the Australians been permitted to see it, would have brought them no comfort: 'nor should we, for reasons of sentiment, still less of prestige . . . try to reassure them [the Australians] by undertaking commitments, particularly in the military field, from which we may have to withdraw in the near future and which we shall not, in the event, be able to honour'.[22] And in fact, once the die had been cast on the major issues of the early 1960s, the issue of the durability of Britain's post-imperial military presence in Southeast Asia became the most salient matter of difficulty between Australia and Britain.

This is, by and large, a well-known story. Indeed, several of these issues and events have generated substantial literatures based at least in part on primary sources. This account differs from earlier ones, however, in that it seeks to bring all the key episodes into a single narrative; a narrative ordered by the theme of the British transition to post-imperialism as perceived, interpreted and acted upon by policy makers in Australia.

5

Things falling apart: Menzies, Britain and the new Commonwealth

Soot on the statues

During a session of the Commonwealth Prime Ministers Meeting in London in March 1961, Harold Macmillan, in the chair, was called away temporarily on some other matter of state. To replace him in the chair, he chose Jawaharlal Nehru.

Robert Menzies was shocked. There was little love lost between him and Nehru, but that was not the issue. Menzies knew himself to be the Commonwealth's senior statesman. He had first become a Commonwealth Prime Minister in 1939, many years earlier than anyone else at the meeting, and had never faltered in his devotion to the Commonwealth and to the monarch as its head. Moreover he believed himself to be personally close to Macmillan—indeed, a good deal closer than any other Commonwealth leader. The two of them shared, after all, their Scottish descent, their year of birth (1894), their political conservatism, their Cold War partisanship, and perhaps most significantly their conviction that the English-speaking peoples were the central force for civilisation and sanity in a difficult and dangerous world. And there was Nehru, a republican, a neutralist, an underminer of the British world role. Yet it was to Nehru that Macmillan gave the nod.

Was Macmillan's gesture meant to be of little account, at most perhaps an acknowledgment that Nehru had the longest unbroken period of prime ministerial service in the Commonwealth? Or was Macmillan signalling something quite significant, and with full premeditation: that in his view it had become more important for Britain to accommodate the new Commonwealth than to placate the old?

We know about this incident, and also that the matter preyed on Menzies' mind, because three months later his High Commissioner in

London, Sir Eric Harrison, called on Duncan Sandys, the Secretary of State for Commonwealth Relations, with a number of complaints about Britain's recent mistreatment of Australia, of which this was one example. According to an official's record of the meeting, Menzies was said by Harrison to be 'much put out by Mr Macmillan's apparent preference for a brown face'. He 'had now got the idea firmly fixed in his head that compared with the "brown" Commonwealth countries, Australia did not "count for a row of beans"'.[1] Another official reported Harrison as expressing, very forcefully, the view that 'the sooty faces on the statues round the quadrangle [of the Commonwealth Relations Office] was an omen of where our friendships now lay ... he thought it improbable that Mr Menzies would attend another meeting'.[2]

Harrison did not say so, but the Nehru incident must have been all the more painful to Menzies because of a public defeat he had suffered at Nehru's hands in the previous year, in circumstances which led him to feel that he had been badly let down by Macmillan. Nehru had tabled a motion for discussion in the UN General Assembly session of October 1960, calling for a summit meeting between Eisenhower and Khrushchev in the wake of the U2 spy-plane affair. Eisenhower was totally opposed to the idea of a bilateral meeting with Khrushchev, but was willing to accept a suggestion, which Menzies put to him and Macmillan when the three of them met in Washington, that an amendment be moved proposing a meeting of the Big Four instead. The three men decided that Menzies would take the responsibility for presenting the amendment to the Assembly. This he did—only to find himself subjected to an angry personal attack by Nehru. In the subsequent vote the Australian amendment was overwhelmingly defeated, with only Britain, the United States, Canada and New Zealand in support. Howard Beale, Australia's Ambassador in Washington, later remembered this occasion as 'a bad experience' for his Prime Minister, not just because of Nehru's attack but because 'The British apparently did not do anything to try and get votes from those countries where they had influence', and neither did the Americans.[3] The incident at the Prime Ministers Meeting some five months later would undoubtedly have brought back sour memories, while also falling into place as an element in a larger pattern: what Harrison, at his meeting with Sandys, called a British 'sloughing off' of Australia.

Were Menzies and Harrison right about this? It would be difficult to sustain an argument that the sloughing off of Australia was a deliberate act of British policy. Rather, Britain in the early 1960s was making a major effort to reconstruct its world role, chiefly in relation to the United States and Europe, but also in matters of empire and Commonwealth, and the weakening of various links with Australia was essentially one of the by-products of this process. But for Menzies, Harrison and a good many other

Australians, it made little difference how far the weakening was intended or unintended. For them the process was painful not just because certain Australian interests were being undermined, but because the British connection was central to their very notion of Australian identity. In other words, the changes that Britain was engineering cut to the core of their sense of self.

For Menzies personally, the period from the Prime Ministers Meeting of March 1961 to its successor in September 1962 appears to have been the nadir. Though he kept his disillusionment with the British reasonably well hidden from public view, insiders perceived it well enough. He was 'clearly still somewhat *froissé* with the UK', a Commonwealth Relations Office official wrote in September 1961.[4] 'My friends from Australia', wrote Lord Carrington in January 1962, not long after his spell as High Commissioner in Canberra, 'still tell me that Bob is upset & bitter'.[5] Among the causes of his disenchantment, the ongoing transformation of the Commonwealth ranked high.

The Commonwealth in the early 1960s

The changes in the Commonwealth were a consequence of the working out of British colonial policy. The acceleration of the pace of colonial change meant allowing territories previously seen as far from ready for independence to join the decolonisation queue, from which they could be expected to proceed to membership of, or at least association with, the Commonwealth.

In so far as British leaders perceived the Commonwealth as a usable instrument for British purposes, they had a certain interest in augmenting it. One who remarked succinctly upon this was Shann in Australia House:

> I do not think we should over-estimate the extent of the acceptance in this country of the idea that we are all equal independent members of an association of Nations. Nor should we imagine that the United Kingdom is too worried about the possibility of many small unviable colonial territories gaining full membership. My own view is that the idea of sub-divide and rule is welcomed even in the highest quarters . . . [There is] a view often held here that Britain must dominate the Commonwealth in order to sustain her own position.[6]

Simultaneously, Britain was planning to consolidate its influence in the Atlantic and European spheres. This desire to have things all ways provided rich soil for confusion and contradiction, of the kind that President de Gaulle would shortly choose to exploit in making his case for vetoing

British accession to the European Economic Community. Moreover, as things turned out, Britain soon came sharply up against the limits of its power to shape developments in its former empire, much of which drifted into American spheres of influence in various parts of the world.[7] In fact, the perception of Commonwealth as somehow helping to serve Britain's major power status would barely survive into the middle 1960s. But at the beginning of the decade the perception was real enough.

The British were aware that the general movement in colonial and Commonwealth policy might be none too palatable to various existing members: South Africa, for obvious reasons, but also Australia, which was seen in London as anything but a proponent of rapid decolonisation, whether British or Australian, and as deeply attached to the old Common-wealth—'the old intimate association', as Menzies characteristically called it.[8] Obviously the Commonwealth countries had to be treated carefully and kept well informed, not least because they would eventually have to pass judgment on newly independent territories' applications for membership. This became an increasingly important concern for the Commonwealth Relations Office from the later 1950s. The Office had had a less than happy experience in 1956 when South Africa had created difficulties over the pro-posed admission of Ghana, and even Canada had complained that it had been given insufficient information to assess the anticipated application of Malaya. Thus by the end of the decade the Office had established the prac-tice of holding regular briefing sessions for Commonwealth diplomatic representatives in London on developments in colonial policy. One such briefing was on Sierra Leone, which, London decided in March 1960, would probably become independent before the end of 1961. As a Commonwealth Relations Office official noted, this prospect

> has filled certain of the Commonwealth representatives here [in London] with gloom. The Australian in particular was, I gather, somewhat nettled by the Colonial Office attitude about Independence . . . there is no doubt that this crash exercise on Sierra Leone may give rise to some further grumblings in various Commonwealth quarters.[9]

At the Commonwealth Prime Ministers Meeting of May 1960 Menzies indicated that he himself was resigned to the inevitability of decolonisation: 'Political independence is arriving or about to arrive in many States. It is a fact of life that they must be given their independence'.[10] He also recog-nised the implications for Australia's own colonial policy, as his subsequent Sydney airport statement—'if in doubt you should go sooner, not later'[11]—made clear. But this is not to say that he welcomed the acceleration in British policy. Indeed he was worried about its implications in at least two domains. The first area of concern was that of defence and security. In this respect his attitude was visibly in line of descent from the Australian attitude of the preceding decade; concern with the strategic importance of the colonial presence was giving way to a concern with the strategic problems posed by its absence. The irony of this is that Britain itself calculated that strategic interests would on the whole be better served by letting colonies go than by hanging on. In essence, it seemed to Whitehall that conferring independence would be the best way of securing the long-term alignment of African and Asian countries with the West. For Iain Macleod this, along with the need to avoid bloodshed, was the 'overriding consideration' in his decolonisation policy. It was an imperative so assiduously pursued that Sir Andrew Cohen, for one, began to worry that 'killing communism' seemed to have displaced the preparation of stable and viable regimes as the main objective.[12]

The notion of decolonisation as anti-communist prophylactic was well understood in Australia. In its editorial on Macmillan's wind of change speech, the Melbourne *Age* had put the case succinctly:

> Any survival of colonialism is anathema to these new and intensely national-istic countries. There have been examples in Asia of the folly of attempting to suppress these indigenous movements. If the West stands rigidly against them, the Communist world is ready and waiting to divert the tide of nationalism into its own channels, as it did in China and Northern Vietnam, [*sic*] Mr Macmillan does not wish this to happen in Africa.[13]

Menzies was no doubt alive to this line of argument. But he was not necessarily optimistic that decolonisation would have the desired preventative effect. In Canberra's geopolitical perspective, with 'Asian communism' so close to hand, the margin for policy error seemed narrow indeed. Thus Menzies was at least as attuned to the strategic risks attendant upon swift decolonisation as he was to its hoped for strategic benefits. At the Prime Ministers Meeting in London in 1960, his argument was that the economic poverty of new states 'provides soil for Communist exploitation and is, therefore, an element of very great danger ... From the point of view of world political balance, they must not be allowed by default to get into the Communist camp'.[14] And early in 1961 the Department of External Affairs, under Menzies as Minister, expanded on the implications of this for Australia. Britain was

> primarily concerned with the defence of the British Isles and is clearly looking for a way of reducing the cost of her colonial possessions. During the remaining period of tutelage for those possessions in South-East Asia and the South-West Pacific ... we may ... have to undertake a more direct burden in the development of these dependent territories in order to combat influences hostile to us. The future of all British territories in the area, including those assessed as unable to sustain independence, will be a matter of common concern.[15]

For Menzies and his senior officials, in short, the coming demise of British colonialism, especially in their own part of the world, was to be assessed quite largely in terms of Cold War threat scenarios. There seemed a real risk that decolonisation would create a situation which 'influences hostile to us' could seek to exploit. There was no certain way of preventing this militarily, and direct political control was no longer an option. In these circumstances, so External Affairs was arguing, aid programs took on an enhanced importance as a key to Australia's security. Menzies acquiesced in this view, and indeed had spoken in broadly similar terms in his earlier talks in London: in order to counter communism, 'it may be that these countries have to be assisted and therefore all of us, including the United Kingdom, may have to accept risks on the defence side in order to increase what we can give for the development of these new countries'.[16] Menzies' reference to defence spending was prompted partly by the fact that Macmillan had presented a paper to the meeting drawing a pointed contrast between Britain's high level of defence expenditure as a proportion of government outlay and the much lower levels attained by Australia, Canada and New Zealand. But in fact Britain did not need to be lectured on the need to move resources into the new states. The goal of maintaining British influence and political stability in the new Commonwealth had already led London to promise large increases in development capital from government funds, an undertaking which had doubled the value of British overseas aid between 1957 and 1960.[17]

Indeed, there seemed something of a consensus among the old-Commonwealth leaders on the issue of aid to the new states. This showed through most notably in their adoption of the multilateral Special Commonwealth African Assistance Plan in 1960. Australia's contribution to SCAAP, like the contributions of the other Commonwealth aid donor countries, was directed mainly towards technical and educational assistance. But as was shown in Chapter 4, the rationale for Australia's contribution, as outlined by Menzies to Cabinet in 1961, was conceived almost entirely in strategic terms. It reflected an aid policy whose political purpose was explicitly likened by Menzies to that of the Colombo Plan a decade earlier, with a concern to help in the consolidation of new states' independence being closely tied to broad geopolitical considerations and an avowed Australian self-interest. In short, it conformed closely with the instrumentalist model of development assistance in Cold War circumstances that Menzies and External Affairs were espousing at the time.

The second issue of concern was the impact of decolonisation on the nature of the Commonwealth itself. As of May 1960 the question of the precise form of association which the smaller ex-colonies would have with the Commonwealth was still, in principle, an open one. Ever since the late

1940s there had been intermittent discussion in Whitehall of how far it might be possible to devise arrangements which would accommodate small territories ('the tiddlers') but which would stop short of giving them full membership, thus preserving the club-like relationships among the older members that Menzies, among others, valued so highly.[18] A prime mover in the quest for a formula of this kind was the British official Sir Norman Brook, Cabinet Secretary and principal adviser to the Prime Minister. Brook was deeply attached to the old Commonwealth and had long taken a special interest in Commonwealth policy (to the point, indeed, where Commonwealth Relations Office officials were moved to complain to their Minister about his habit of trespassing on their turf[19]). In 1959, perhaps sniffing the coming wind, Brook secured Macmillan's agreement to the establishment of an official committee to re-examine the issue of two-tier membership.[20] Brook's personal position on the issue remained plain: as he wrote to Macmillan in April 1960, apropos the notion of a Commonwealth open to all comers, 'to me, this is a bleak prospect'.[21] It seemed increasingly apparent that not only were many of the potential aspirants for membership small and impoverished, but some, such as Cyprus and British Guiana, were also potentially awkward customers in a political sense.

But the more British officialdom wrestled with the problem, the more it was forced to the conclusion that a two-tier arrangement would be wholly unworkable. Cyprus let it be known in 1960 that it wanted full membership or nothing, and all indications were that other territories now hastening towards independence would take exactly the same line. By April 1960, with a Commonwealth Prime Ministers Meeting imminent, Brook had reluctantly accepted that a rapid expansion in full membership seemed inevitable. The only consolation lay in the hope that British influence would indeed expand with it.

Having accepted the new realities, Brook now became involved in a tactical effort to win over existing Commonwealth members, in particular the white dominions (as they were sometimes still called) to a similar acceptance. His idea, which was put to and endorsed by Macmillan, was that the Commonwealth meeting should be invited to establish a working party of its own, at official rather than political level, to consider the future of the smaller colonial territories.[22] Convening in May, the Prime Ministers agreed to do this. The resulting working party, with Brook in the chair, comprised officials drawn from Britain, Australia, Canada, New Zealand, India and Ghana. This was fairly much the membership list Brook had had in mind from the outset, and it was subtly devised; it represented the major regions of the Commonwealth and included both old and new members, but gave the heaviest representation to the group of old members thought to be in most need of persuading. The Australian representative was a man close to Menzies, Sir Allen Brown, formerly Secretary of the Prime Minister's Department and now Deputy High Commissioner in London.

The British aim in this exercise is apparent from the papers prepared in the Commonwealth Relations Office for consideration by Brook and British ministers—but not the Commonwealth representatives—before the working party met. The covert British aim was to 'get other Commonwealth countries used to the idea' that the current trends in colonial policy would necessarily create a different kind of Commonwealth:

> The old criterion of 'viability' is already out of date. How many Countries are 'viable' nowadays, anyway? They will get into the United Nations and it will be difficult to argue that the Commonwealth should adopt a more exclusive view in relation to countries 'within the family' . . . The conclusion is that, whatever paper plans we may lay now, we shall probably have, in ten or fifteen years, a Commonwealth of some twenty-five to thirty members, of which ten or so will not be of the 'standard' so far regarded as 'suitable'.[23]

Guided by Brook, the officials duly produced a report along these lines.[24] It was circulated to Commonwealth governments at the end of July 1960, and, rather against London's initial expectations, was received with hardly a murmur by Australia among the others. Possibly Brown had given Menzies advance notice of the report's message. But by this time, it may be supposed, the political impracticability of two-tier Commonwealth membership had become plain for all to see. Thus the report was quite probably regarded by its recipients as a statement of the obvious.

Once again, then, it can be said that Menzies recognised the inevitable. But once again it can be said that he did not welcome it. The first significant test case to arise after the Prime Ministers Meeting of May 1960 was that of Cyprus. Should a country which was not only very small and not obviously 'viable', but which had recently been locked in bitter military conflict with Britain, and which was closely aligned with a foreign power (Greece), be allowed in? Menzies and his senior advisers were in no doubt: 'We must agree to the Cyprus application for membership . . . It is evident that Cyprus is important to the United Kingdom, strategically at least, and that the United Kingdom wants it admitted. In that case Australia, though having no strong view of its own, would certainly not intervene to resist its membership'. And nor were they in doubt about the deluge that would follow: 'If Cyprus is admitted now, the issue of whether small independent territories are to be given full membership of the Commonwealth will, for all practical purposes, be decided. Once Cyprus is in, there is no basis for keeping others out'.[25]

This was simple political realism. But Menzies' heart was not in it. The actual admission of Cyprus at the Prime Ministers Meeting of March 1961 drew from him the heavily sarcastic comment (addressed privately to

McEwen in Canberra): 'You may like to know, His Beatitude, the Arch-
bishop of Cyprus, has arrived and been seated'.[26] From Menzies' point of
view the situation from that point onwards grew steadily worse. During the
year non-viable Sierra Leone and the much larger but deeply impoverished
Tanganyika were added to the ranks. By the end of 1961 Commonwealth
membership stood at thirteen, with the 'Crown Commonwealth' out-
numbered nine to four. 'When I ask myself', Menzies wrote to Macmillan
in January 1962, 'what benefit we of the Crown Commonwealth derive
from having a somewhat tenuous association with a cluster of Republics
some of which like Ghana are more spiritually akin to Moscow than to
London, I begin to despair'.[27]

Macmillan was well aware of the way Menzies saw things, and had for
some time been considering sending him a message, 'the main purpose of
which is to show that Australia is never out of our thoughts'.[28] Menzies'
letter stimulated him to make a major effort. The result was an eighteen-
page disquisition which ranged over world history since antiquity, extolled
the accomplishments of the British people, and came to the point on page
15 with a paragraph that made the case for the new Commonwealth essentially in terms of Cold War strategy:

> But if we are to stay in the United Nations it is all the more necessary to keep
> the New Commonwealth together with all its frustrations and difficulties. I am
> bound to confess that I now shrink from any Commonwealth meeting because
> I know how troublesome it will be, whatever the subjects immediately under
> discussion. I think it may be possible not to have a meeting until there is one
> specially related to the European Community question. But I think the real
> reason for keeping the Commonwealth together is that I believe we *can* influ-
> ence it, slowly and gradually, but effectively. Ghana is very dictatorial and
> almost crazy today; that makes Nigeria a little more moderate. And as the years
> pass I think it is possible with patience and putting up with a lot of trouble and
> insults from them that it will be worth doing. I think it is certainly worth doing
> while the Communist/Free World division really holds the front of the stage.
> Indeed in this situation we are forced to try.[29]

Macmillan's advisers saw this communication as extremely well geared
to its main purpose. Brook felt sure 'that this is the right medicine for his
[Menzies'] present malaise'.[30] And Lord Home commented: 'It may be just
possible to hold the modern Commonwealth together but our European
children are more sensitive than the mother country and they will deeply
resent any interference by the coloured brethren with their affairs. I think
Bob will like it'.[31] But Menzies was not, in the event, much mollified: 'I still
doubt the viability of the new Commonwealth . . . Any enthusiasm I had for
. . . [it] is waning fast. People like me are too deeply royalist at heart to live
comfortably in a nest of republics'.[32]

Stress points

The 1961 Prime Ministers Meeting in particular had left Menzies 'sad and depressed'.[33] It was the meeting of the Nehru incident, but, more substantively, it was the meeting that saw South Africa, under extreme pressure from the newer members with regard to its racial policies, quit the Commonwealth. Menzies fought to the end to keep South Africa in. He argued —and indeed believed, very strongly—that Commonwealth members did not and should not discuss each others' internal affairs, and that the moment they abandoned this well-established convention, the Commonwealth would cease to exist in any acceptable form. He supplemented his oratory on the general principle with an attempt to persuade the South African Prime Minister, Dr Verwoerd, to accept some compromise that might help to appease the critics; for example, the accreditation to South Africa of non-white diplomats. Macmillan too, by his own account at least, was fervent about trying to hang on to South Africa. In his epic letter to Menzies he described the 1961 conference as 'an absolute tragedy'. At the beginning of the conference, so he wrote,

> I thought we could have just got through it; and I suppose it may have been my fault in handling that led to failure. Looking back, I feel that if Dr Verwoerd had made even a small gesture on the lines you pressed upon him—the acceptance of African and Asian High Commissioners—we could have won through. Sometimes, again, I think that the whole thing was plotted against us from the start, and that some of our leading colleagues were not completely straightforward with me about it. However, it is over.[34]

It is of interest that Macmillan was so anxious to reassure Menzies that the two of them were on the same side on this issue. As late as 1971, with both of them long since retired, he could still hark back to the subject, referring in a letter to 'the terrible Commonwealth Conference . . . What an awful time it was'.[35] In fact, as Macmillan no doubt knew, Menzies felt that Macmillan did carry a share of the responsibility for the outcome of the conference, and was not inclined to forgive him for it. Menzies had gone into the conference believing that Macmillan and he were of a mind. To McEwen in Canberra he cabled his understanding of the position:

> Tomorrow, Monday, the South African question comes up. Macmillan and I have concerted our ideas as follows. Take the matter in two steps. First try to establish as a matter of routine for the future the proposition that where a member of the Commonwealth decides to become a Republic, this (as precedent shows) is its domestic affair and needs only to be notified to other members. Then say, on this procedural principle, South Africa should continue. Second, promote a full debate on African affairs, which will then be conducted

with South Africa as a participant and not with South Africa as a petitioner for continued membership. Verwoerd accepts this. He will not seek to avoid a full discussion. But Macmillan and I apprehend grave trouble, particularly if Nehru goes cunning.[36]

But the next day he had to report the collapse of this strategy:

> When Macmillan opened he did not take the matter in the two steps which I spoke about in last night's message . . . Instead, after a brief mention of the first point he moved to the second and threw it open to the meeting. Nehru got the first call and immediately said that he agreed there should be a common discussion on the two issues of continued membership and racial policies. I can only assume that this change in approach by Macmillan came from the meeting he had last night at Chequers with Nehru.[37]

Menzies further believed that Duncan Sandys had joined in pressuring Macmillan. In the outcome, Macmillan not only permitted discussion of the race issue—a discussion in which speakers such as Nehru, the Pakistani leader Ayub Khan and the Canadian John Diefenbaker made most of the running—but himself played a generally passive role in the debate. When at length he intervened, it was to submit a written statement, of his own drafting, which, while supporting South Africa's right to remain in the Commonwealth as a republic, noted that 'the other Prime Ministers' believed that the Union's policies were 'inconsistent with the basic ideals on which the unity and influence of the Commonwealth rest'.[38] Menzies considered this a loaded statement; in further debate, he registered his objections both to the phrase 'the other Prime Ministers'—he preferred 'various Prime Ministers'—and to Macmillan's placing of the 'other' Prime Ministers' views at the end of the statement, as if they constituted some sort of conclusion.[39] Macmillan then offered to add a further paragraph comprising Verwoerd's rejoinder to his critics. The whole package, Macmillan suggested to Menzies, should then add up to confirmation of South Africa's membership. But Menzies remained suspicious, cabling to McEwen his view that Macmillan's package would be insufficiently positive to be acceptable to Verwoerd.[40] To Menzies the basic meaning of the statement was very clear: 'South Africa is being given notice to quit'.[41]

Sir John Bunting, Menzies' Department Secretary, analysed Britain's motive thus:

> the United Kingdom, although it did not actively want this [South Africa's withdrawal] to happen, did make up its mind that it was not going to oppose the Afro-Asian group on the question . . . the truth is that the United Kingdom is defending, somewhat grimly, its standing and authority in the world. For this purpose, which is political rather than economic, it requires a certain amount of keeping in tune with India in particular.[42]

What further troubled both Menzies and Bunting was the precedent set by the Commonwealth's scrutiny of South Africa's domestic affairs: 'Moves against other individual countries must now be reckoned to be much more on the cards than ever before'.[43] Menzies feared that Australia's turn might soon come. As he wrote to Macmillan, the South African precedent meant that it would henceforth be 'quite legitimate' for the Commonwealth 'to discuss, for example, the Australian immigration policy which is aimed at avoiding internal racial problems by the expedient of keeping coloured immigrants out. I hope my fears are not justified'.[44]

During 1961 his unhappiness at the movements in British policy was compounded by two more reversals on specific issues. In April, for the first time, Britain decided to vote in the UN General Assembly in support of an Indian resolution condemning apartheid, thus contradicting its own, and Australia's, long-sustained argument that South Africa's race policies were a matter of domestic jurisdiction and so *ultra vires* the United Nations. The decision to change policy had been taken without prior consultation with Australia, on what the Australians saw as the very thin pretext that time had not permitted. Menzies at once transmitted his extreme displeasure to Macmillan at having his own position made 'intolerable', and insisted that Australia would stick to its guns and abstain on the vote. Shortly afterwards, however, Menzies bowed to duress and the urgings of some of his colleagues, and accepted that Australia was left with no choice but to follow the British lead.[45]

And then in November the British Government introduced its Commonwealth Immigrants Bill. A response to the backwash of empire, long planned but much delayed because of the acutely delicate problem of drafting, the Bill was clearly intended, as Alexander Downer, Minister for Immigration, told the Australian Cabinet in January 1962, 'to secure control over the influx of unskilled immigrants from the West Indies, Pakistan and India. To avoid any appearance of discrimination, however, the legislation is to apply to immigration from all Commonwealth countries'. As Downer understated it, the Bill brought home 'the extent to which Australia's traditional relationship to the United Kingdom is changing'.[46] For their part, British officials judged that although the Australians

> sympathise with and even welcome our wish to limit the number of coloured immigrants to Britain, they resent our unwillingness openly to admit this. They believe that in making the Bill non-discriminatory in terms we have shown ourselves ready once again to prejudice the interests of the older Commonwealth countries because we are unwilling openly to legislate against coloured Commonwealth immigrants. It is hoped that Australians will continue to be able to visit Britain in the same numbers as at present without

impediment and without vexatious formalities or delays. If it proves otherwise not only will an invaluable link between Britain and Australia be impaired, but the resentment caused will magnify the damage many times over.[47]

How to appease the Australians

Various of these grievances had been aired in Harrison's 'soot on the statues' meeting with Sandys in May 1961. Immediately after that meeting, Sandys had instructed his officials 'to think what gestures we could make to Australia in any field with a view to correcting this unhappy strain'. All Under-Secretaries at the Commonwealth Relations Office were charged with re-examining relationships with Australia in their own fields of responsibility. Other officials confirmed that Australian disgruntlement was not confined to Menzies personally: for example John Crawford, former Secretary of the Department of Trade, had told a British official 'that they were never surprised when the UK failed to consult them'.[48]

In June, just before Sandys was due to leave for Canberra to discuss the difficult and sensitive issue of Europe, his Permanent Secretary reported to him on the Office's efforts. There was a certain amount the Minister might say in Canberra by way of reassurance. First, on the Commonwealth issue,

> it seems that the Australians are in the frame of mind that, because we acquiesced in South Africa leaving the Commonwealth and followed it up by denouncing apartheid, we shall be ready to sell Australia down the river in an attempt to gain the favour of our African and Asian friends. We need to try to convince them . . . [that] there is no question about the 'respectability' of Australia's policies; no problems such as those affecting South Africa arise or can arise; nothing stands in the way of the closest association between Britain and Australia, which is what we want.

Second, in other matters of foreign affairs and defence, the Australians' main concerns were that they be consulted on all important issues (as they had not been on the apartheid vote), and that Britain should not get out of step with the United States on Southeast Asian policy 'as they are constantly afraid we may'. Thus 'it will be desirable to emphasise that we recognise the importance of SEATO and the need to keep up the morale of its members'. Third, there was intelligence cooperation, about which the Australians could have no grounds for complaint: 'Relations between the organisations in the two countries are good and for the most part very intimate'.

Finally there was the economic field: potentially the most difficult. Clearly, Anglo-Australian relations were going to be dominated by what happened about Europe: 'If we propose to join the European Economic

Community on terms which gave what Australians regarded as inadequate protection for their interests in the United Kingdom market, the effects could be very serious'. On top of that, Britain's trade agreement with Australia was due for renegotiation, and it was clear, to the British at least, that Britain would not be able to maintain in its current form the 'wheat clause', under which Britain 'endeavoured' to buy 750 000 tons of Australian wheat annually; to the Australians, this was the most important clause in the agreement. Britain's guaranteed price for Australian meat was also due for review. As the Office summarised the overall position, there were 'not at present any gestures of substance which we can make to please the Australians'.[49] The rhetoric of special friendship went visibly unmatched by offers of special deals.

Aftermath

What Canberra experienced as declining British interest in Australia was actually part of a larger phenomenon: declining British interest in the Commonwealth generally. The leadership's interest in the idea of using the augmented Commonwealth as an instrument of British influence was, as noted earlier, quite shortlived. Although many linkages remained between Britain and its former colonies, the series of financial and economic crises that afflicted Britain from the early 1960s, culminating in the devaluation of sterling in 1967, rather put paid to the idea that Britain would be able to go on shaping developments in the ex-empire to its own liking. Herein lay the 'metropolitan infirmity' which, various writers have suggested, quite quickly overtook the high hopes and ambitions of 1960.[50]

At bottom, Macmillan was in any case more interested in Britain's other two circles, the Atlantic one and the European one. As Commonwealth Prime Ministers Meetings became progressively more unruly, this differential probably increased. And his declining interest in the Commonwealth was plainly shared by most of his ministers, to whom, as the scale of Britain's economic difficulties became steadily more apparent, it began to seem axiomatic that the solution must lie in ever closer association with other highly industrialised powers.

At the same time, there were domestic political costs to be considered. Pro-Commonwealth (and anti-European) sentiments had by no means faded in the British electorate, perhaps least of all among Conservative voters. One senior British politician who became increasingly concerned at the disjunction between government policy and electoral sentiment was the former Foreign Secretary and Chancellor Selwyn Lloyd, whom

Macmillan had rather brutally dispatched to the back benches in his sweeping Cabinet reshuffle of July 1962. Lloyd took to touring the party branches, where he sensed much disillusion with the Government's policies. Fearing for the party's electoral prospects, he concluded that one way of reviving party support would be to revitalise the Commonwealth connection. In 1963 he made a number of speeches urging closer cooperation through such devices as a Commonwealth Economic Development Council, a Commonwealth Export Council, a Commonwealth Bank, and new commodity agreements. In mid-year he had a 'long talk' with Menzies, who showed interest in the Export Council idea 'but obviously had given up hope of anything happening under Mr Macmillan'.[51]

When in October Macmillan was succeeded as Prime Minister by Sir Alec Douglas-Home (the former Lord Home), Lloyd was brought back from the wilderness as Lord Privy Seal. Clearly he felt that Sir Alec, who had served five years as Commonwealth Secretary, would be more receptive than Macmillan had been to his views on the importance of Commonwealth. In a long private memo strongly critical of what he called 'the Macmillan regime', he told Douglas-Home of his recent activities and averred that following his speeches he had 'received quite extraordinary expressions of support, both from this country and overseas, particularly Australia'. He then set out, in vivid terms, the case for revitalisation of the Commonwealth:

> The facts that the Africans are opposed to us over Southern Rhodesia, that Mr Nehru has never really liked us, that Australia does not buy our aircraft, that Canada discriminates against us, that there are wide political differences over attitudes towards Communism, are no reason for giving up. In many large families there is the beatnik, the rebel, the irresponsible or the spendthrift, but one does not because of that abandon the attempt to keep the family together. So with the Commonwealth. The fact that there are differences is all the greater reason for economic co-operation, technical aid, educational activities, and the encouragement of bodies like the Commonwealth Press Council.

And then there was the politics of the matter:

> Quite apart from the merits of the case, your Government will not continue unless it commands wide-spread support. I believe that that support will be much increased if you make it clear that there is a change of emphasis with regard to Commonwealth co-operation on the part of your Administration.[52]

These arguments struck a chord with Douglas-Home. In January 1964 he presented Cabinet with a submission proposing new machinery for Commonwealth-wide technical and economic planning.[53] He followed this up in June with a letter to the veteran antipodean Prime Ministers Menzies and Holyoake and the new Canadian Prime Minister Lester Pearson, effectively putting the onus on the 'senior Members'—that is, the Crown Commonwealth—'to develop our association on a more genuinely co-operative basis'. Menzies showed interest in Douglas-Home's ideas.[54] But he was one of the few who did. Very little came of them. The Prime Ministers Meeting of July 1964 evinced a much greater interest in the Rhodesian situation than in proposals for technical cooperation. Most of the ideas for economic planning had already been killed off by opposition from Douglas-Home's own Cabinet colleagues, especially Edward Heath, most ardent of the pro-Europeans.[55]

It is noteworthy that even Richard Casey, since 1960 a member of the British House of Lords, became rather disenchanted with the British connection in this period, in part because the British political elite's interest in the Commonwealth was so rapidly and obviously fading. That he had difficulty in finding a British publisher for his 1963 book *The Future of the Commonwealth* must have seemed to him to be proof of a still wider lack of interest. By 1964, according to his biographer, 'he was angered and ready to abandon the British connection'. To a correspondent Casey wrote: 'I suppose I'll come over here [London] again, but I doubt if I'll do so with very much enthusiasm. Perhaps I'll go to America and Asia, where they seem to know what I'm talking about'.[56]

To Robert Menzies and many others of his generation the British connection still mattered a great deal in the early 1960s, on a variety of grounds embodying both sentiment—kinship, culture, history and the like—and material interest—trade, investment and to some degree defence. The problem was that in this era Britain was actively seeking to recast its future role, and was doing so in ways that Australian leaders judged harmful to Australia; and this at a time when Australia was not yet ready, or much inclined, to rethink its own role in more regional terms.

The Anglo-Australian relationship always lacked symmetry. It mattered a good deal more to parochial Australia than to metropolitan Britain. In the nature of such relationships, the metropolis set most of the terms. Because Australia had a greater investment in the old relationship it had more to lose, or thought it had, when the metropolis began to change the terms; more incentive to value the familiar, indeed familial. It was ironic, to say the least, that the old pattern of relationships should have unravelled so much during the long prime ministership of Robert Menzies, most devoted of Commonwealth men, and that the individual who did most to promote the major shifts in British policy should have been Harold Macmillan, with whom Menzies had believed his relationship to be especially close.

And yet Australia did begin to come to terms with the changes in the relationship. It was Menzies himself in 1965, his last year of office, who confirmed the changing order of things with two notable decisions. One was to appoint an Australian, none other than Casey, as Governor-General. The other was to commit Australian troops to the first war in which Australia had ever taken part without British involvement. Indeed, the Vietnam war would have a much greater long-term impact on the redefining of Australia's sense of itself and its international role than Menzies could ever have anticipated: a sense that entailed increasing identification with the fortunes of the Asia-Pacific region, less and less with the fortunes of distant Britain.

In 1966 Menzies assumed the Lord Wardenship of the Cinque Ports. It seemed a most apposite symbolisation of the things he had stood for. In a further irony, one that Menzies himself probably did not fail to remark, this post was the gift of a Labour Prime Minister.

6

Menzies, Macmillan and Europe

B RITAIN'S FIRST CAMPAIGN to join the European Economic Community was launched in 1961. Intensive negotiations at Brussels ensued, until President de Gaulle brought them to an abrupt end with his veto on British membership in January 1963. It is clearly the case that this episode was of central significance in the broader decline of the 'special links' between Australia and Britain. On the European issue the two countries' interests were in fairly direct opposition; and although this first attempt by Britain to enter Europe proved abortive, the long-term message for Australia was clear enough. If Britain remained determined to become European, then Australia would have to look for an alternative trading future.

It has been stressed already that it would be simplistic to see British policy in the early 1960s as comprising a turn 'away' from the Empire/ Commonwealth 'towards' Europe. For a time at least, Britain was hunting for ways of maximising its influence in both spheres. But from Australia's point of view these two tendencies did seem to be obverse and reverse of the same coin. And both of them meant a kind of betrayal of Australia.

Other works have described the ins and outs of the Anglo-Australian arguments over Europe in 1961–63, notably Harry Gelber's early study, meticulously detailed but necessarily based on materials in the public domain, and Stuart Ward's *Australia and the British Embrace*, the first full-length study of the issue to be based on the primary sources.[1] This chapter aims rather at a more tightly focused account that relates the European issue directly to the evolution of the Australian relationship with Britain, and for that purpose puts Robert Menzies at the centre of the story. What is especially intriguing is the British perception of Menzies as potentially a key player in their own game plan. This led to a British attempt to turn Menzies' Anglophilia to their own advantage. British politicians and senior officials evidently hoped that it might prove possible to persuade Menzies to accept their case for a British move towards Europe, on the merits of the argument and on high political grounds; and that his acceptance might then help to influence the Commonwealth more generally, and perhaps political and public opinion in Britain as well, to accept the case. At times he appeared to give them reason for such hopes. Nevertheless their attitude reflected a considerable misjudgment of Menzies. For all his British race patriotism, for all the support he had given Britain in (for example) the Suez crisis of recent memory, when it came to Europe he neither played the game Britain's way nor helped to deliver the results Britain wanted. To the extent that he was susceptible to pressure from others, he took rather more notice of John McEwen than of Harold Macmillan.

Early manoeuvres

The British Government began seriously to contemplate economic association with Europe in the mid-1950s. Spurred by the rapid movement of 'The Six'—France, Germany, Italy, Belgium, the Netherlands and Luxembourg—towards the establishment of a European Common Market, Macmillan, as Chancellor of the Exchequer, put to Cabinet in July 1956 a plan for a European Free Trade Association, designed to provide the British with a form of association with Europe on their own terms: that is, not within the EEC, and hence not under the domination of Germany.[2] Australian concern at this development was immediately and strongly felt. Early in 1957, with the Treaty of Rome imminent, Casey asked Lord Home, at that time Secretary of State for Commonwealth Relations, how fully the United Kingdom proposed to integrate itself with Europe. In a few words, Home's reply set the tone of the British position from that time forwards: the United Kingdom 'saw dangers in being left out of the economic structure of Western Europe . . . [he] thought that it would be wise for Australia to seek protection for her interests through GATT'.[3] Britain was at this stage maintaining that any lowering of British tariffs in Europe would not extend to agriculture, and that EFTA would make special arrangements for Commonwealth agricultural exports to Britain. Even so, it was being signalled already that Australia could not necessarily look to Britain, its major trading partner, for protection of its interests.

In the next few years 'Europe' became a significant source of strain between Australia and Britain. In 1960 the British High Commissioner in Canberra reported to London that 'The Australians are much concerned about common market and E.F.T.A. developments. They foresee that the

U.K. may be compelled to extend the free-trade system to agriculture'.[4] Later that year Menzies made his own major entry into the debate with a long letter to Macmillan on the closely related subject of the European Monetary Agreement. Somewhat belatedly the Australians had discovered that under the terms of the agreement European countries were provided by Britain with a dollar guarantee on the sterling balances held by their central banks. There had never been such a guarantee for the sterling held by Australia (or any other member of the sterling area). Menzies put it that the European countries had thus been granted a claim, of higher priority than Australia's, over the central gold reserves of the sterling area. His letter was a study in reproach. It included eloquent declarations of Australia's loyalty and the sacrifices Australia had made in defence of sterling, not least at the time of Suez:

> During the Suez crisis, when sterling was seriously threatened, you, as Chancellor of the Exchequer, asked us to sell the United Kingdom gold from our own reserves against sterling. We did so promptly and to the full amount of the $56 million for which you asked. This was at a time when, mistrustful of the future of sterling, a good many people, including residents of the United Kingdom, were selling it for other currencies.

And Menzies came to the point in this passage:

> Widely though the sterling system ramifies beyond the Commonwealth, its main strength has long rested on the steady support of the sterling area countries who are firm holders of sterling at all times and loyal collaborators with the United Kingdom in difficult times. I cannot but fear that the cohesion of this central group will progressively weaken if the United Kingdom continues to accord a preferred status to outside countries who owe no particular allegiance to the sterling system and who take no share in its responsibilities.[5]

The values of Anglo-Australian loyalty and Commonwealth cohesion which permeated the letter were fundamental to Menzies' world view, and Britain's failure to adhere to these values on this issue was one of the factors in the growth of his disenchantment with the British that became evident in the period immediately following. But it may be doubted that the British were much moved by Menzies' eloquence, given that they were well aware of Australia's own long-term moves to diversify its trade and exchange outside the sterling area. Both countries certainly knew where their material interests lay. And this points to what became the essence of the European problem: on no issue in Anglo-Australian relations up to that time had considerations of sentiment and material self-interest been so starkly at odds. In effect, the idea of loyalty would become a kind of normative underpinning to a largely materialistic debate, with each side seeking, in its own interest, to mobilise the putative loyalty of the other.

London proposes, Canberra opposes

The major catalyst of Australian anxiety came in 1961 when, following the failure of the EFTA scheme to make headway, Britain declared its intention to explore the possibility of joining the EEC. Shortly before the formal announcement was made, McEwen, as Minister for Trade, presented a submission to the Australian Cabinet on the economic implications for Australia. Cabinet duly formulated a policy position. Australia recognised the importance to be attached to 'promoting political unity in Europe', but 'this must be in ways which preserve Australia's major export interests'. Menzies, serving at the time as his own Minister for External Affairs, was concerned with the political no less than the economic aspects of the issue, and it was probably he who guided Cabinet to a further conclusion:

> On the political side, the Cabinet felt that if the United Kingdom were to join the E.E.C. its obligations as [a] member of that Community must have some effect, and perhaps a great deal of effect, on its freedom in Commonwealth political affairs. This could raise fundamental issues in Australia/United Kingdom political relations. The Cabinet therefore felt that this aspect, in addition to the trade aspect, should be given consideration within Australia and, in due course, raised with the United Kingdom.[6]

Accordingly the Department of External Affairs was charged with preparing an appreciation of the political implications for Australia. The essence of the Department's lengthy analysis was that Britain would feel obliged to prove itself a good European, and hence its entry into Europe

> would accelerate tendencies which are already established: towards the transformation of the United Kingdom into a European rather than a world power and towards a decline in its commitments beyond Suez; and towards the transformation of the Commonwealth into a looser group . . . This acceleration could reduce the prospects for Australia of getting effective action against the various forms of Communist expansion, and Chinese or Indonesian aggression, in Australia's North. It could require of us earlier adjustments than if the United Kingdom remained outside Europe.

The Department's 'prudent estimate' was that the European Community would not give Asian affairs a high priority, and that Australia would have a reduced capacity, once Britain was in Europe, to influence British policy towards Australia's region. Australia's interest would therefore lie in

> exploiting now all the arguments of sentiment and mutual interest available to us to obtain—for what it is worth—a public recognition from the United Kingdom that she will have continuing concern with the security of Australia and New Zealand. Our objective should be to try to avoid this objective being lost in a generalised acknowledgment by the United Kingdom of a sense of responsibility towards the welfare of the Commonwealth as a whole.

At the same time, the Department recognised that Britain for its part would doubtless 'use all the arguments it can employ to persuade us of the political necessity of its entry'; Australia would simply have to be prepared to deal with such arguments.[7]

The British were indeed preparing to muster their arguments. In the week that the External Affairs paper was being circulated to Australian ministers, Macmillan was instructing Commonwealth Relations Secretary Duncan Sandys on the line to take in his forthcoming visits to Canberra, Wellington and Ottawa. Sandys' brief was 'to bring Commonwealth Governments to understand . . . the broad political (and economic) case for our joining The Six'. He was instructed also to 'find out from Commonwealth Governments what are the essential interests which they wish us to try to safeguard', and to 'encourage the Commonwealth to make the arrangements necessary for the closest possible consultation in the period ahead', but at the same time to resist pressures for a Commonwealth Prime Ministers Conference until after Britain had begun negotiations with The Six and formed an idea of the terms of entry. Macmillan further advised Sandys that Australia, or at least Menzies, might see 'possible countervailing damage to the political cohesion of the Commonwealth', and be somewhat resistant on this account.[8] Macmillan was certainly right in this assessment, as subsequent exchanges would show, although he was perhaps underestimating the degree to which Australian opposition was already accumulating on other grounds, as expressed in Cabinet decisions and the External Affairs paper.

The Sandys mission has been amply described by Gelber, who has also provided a pithy summary: 'Mr Sandys apparently managed to irritate almost every Australian in sight'.[9] Sandys insisted that he was not seeking an Australian opinion on whether Britain should apply. But Australian ministers made it plain how strong their opinions were. Menzies, as anticipated by Macmillan, argued that British membership of the EEC would gravely weaken the Commonwealth. His deputy, McEwen, who was Leader of the Country Party as well as Minister for Trade, and who was thus especially concerned about the impact on Australian farmers of Britain's entry, led other ministers in seeking to extract from Sandys a guarantee of safeguards for Australian interests in the British market. This Sandys refused to provide, although he did say that Britain would do its best to protect Australian interests in the Brussels negotiations. McEwen and others then argued that Australia should be allowed to participate directly in the negotiations with The Six when items affecting Australian trade were under discussion. Again Sandys was unforthcoming. In the post-talks communiqué, the Australians tersely explained 'that the absence of objection should in the circumstances not be interpreted as implying approval'.

Menzies' view of this encounter was set out in a letter to Harrison, his High Commissioner in London:

> We had some fascinating exchanges with Duncan Sandys and produced a communiqué which he didn't like very much. Duncan always seems to me to have had so much of his own way that, when he comes up against some opposition and is finally compelled to bow to it, he is surprised and disappointed . . . The most interesting thing about the Sandys talks was that while constantly asserting that no decision had been taken, Duncan devoted a great deal of time to demonstrating the absolutely unanswerable nature of the arguments for going in.

Menzies was 'so much impressed by this' that he 'engaged in a good deal of cross-examination', as, evidently, did McEwen and others.[10] But the overall outcome was a sense of unresolved standoff.

In the next few months Australia grew still more worried about commercial matters, as it became clearer that the United States, for its own reasons, was anxious to see Britain move into Europe as quickly as possible. Washington evidently placed a rather higher priority on European unification, and thus the consolidation of the Western alliance, than on the protection of Commonwealth trade. In Canberra, a Cabinet committee noted in January 1962:

> The fact that the United States saw the Brussels negotiations as an opportunity to work towards the end of Commonwealth preferences is a development of considerable concern to Australia, particularly when coupled with indications that The Six wished the United Kingdom to dispense with preferences to Commonwealth countries, and the possibility that the United Kingdom is reconciled to their loss . . . ultimately Australia may be forced to rely solely on the assurances given by the British Government, and beyond this, on the attitude of British public opinion. Ministers agreed that the time had come for Australia to take up a public position on the preference issue.

It was decided to campaign hard on a commodity-by-commodity basis, even though, 'on a realistic assessment', not all commercial objectives might be realisable.[11]

Immediately before this Cabinet committee met to discuss trade questions, Menzies had written to Macmillan to voice his own worries about the impact on Anglo-Australian relations more generally:

> I have never denied the possibility of very great advantages, politically, in British membership. It could help to prevent the development of neutralism in Europe and serve to dispel the Communist idea that the issue is between the Soviet Union and the United States and that all the rest of us should be passive onlookers. But however great the weight of these considerations may be, I beg of you to realise that there is great uneasiness in my own country, which may

lead to some weakening of our historic and invaluable ties. If I may suggest it to you as an old friend, it would be valuable for you to take an opportunity of making a considered speech on what I will call the Commonwealth political aspects of the European Common Market.[12]

In short, by the beginning of 1962 the Australians had developed their objections to British policy on a mixed base of tangible and intangible considerations: regional security; Commonwealth trade preferences; and the 'historic and invaluable' ties of kinship. The first of these continued to be actively discussed with Britain. As events unfolded Australian concerns were somewhat assuaged, since Britain's creation of Malaysia, and then the need to defend this construct militarily against Sukarno's Confrontation, ensured that Britain maintained a security presence in the region for a while longer. But the second and third concerns were intensely felt, and through 1961 and 1962 the Australians mounted a major effort to persuade the British to meet them. With regard to these issues something of a division of labour emerged on the Australian side, with McEwen carrying most of the argument on trade and Menzies focusing on the high politics of Commonwealth unity. The British perceived this well enough, and also perceived some important differences between the two men. With Menzies, the proven friend of Britain, they felt they could probably arrive at an understanding. He alone among the Commonwealth Prime Ministers, as J. D. B. Miller has pointed out, 'was a figure of importance to British Conservatives. Holyoake, while approved of, was normally dismissed as provincial, and Diefenbaker, while extolled by the Beaverbrook press, was something of a figure of fun, when not an irritant. But Menzies typified for many Conservatives the sort of "loyalty" which they expected of Commonwealth countries'.[13]

McEwen seemed a very different proposition. He was seen as obstinate, uncompromising, bent only on securing Australian commercial advantage. There was an illustrative exchange in February 1962 when Harrison proposed to Edward Heath, Britain's chief Common Market negotiator, and Sir Frank Lee of the Treasury, that a Commonwealth Prime Ministers Conference might be held in May or June. This, he said, would be convenient for Mr Menzies, who 'would be a key figure in the consideration by the Prime Ministers of the major European issue', and who in any case 'increasingly disliked having to come to England during the winter'. When Heath and Lee pointed out that the Brussels negotiations would then be in midstream, Harrison responded that there could be a later meeting to work out details at which McEwen could represent Australia. 'The Lord Privy Seal [Heath] and I', Lee reported, 'made what I would like to describe as a discreet recoil from this last suggestion'. At this point Harrison, a former Cabinet colleague of both Menzies and McEwen, acknowledged that McEwen 'was essentially a "sectional leader" who would not be disposed, or indeed perhaps able, to make the same broad political judgment on the outcome of the negotiations as would Mr Menzies'.[14]

But a few weeks later McEwen came to London anyway, reiterating his demand that Australia be permitted to join in the negotiations with The Six in order to provide proper protection for Australian interests. Heath was deeply opposed to this idea. Although no other Commonwealth countries had made such a demand, he feared that if anything were conceded to the Australians along these lines other Commonwealth countries might want to join in, or, even worse, that France and the Commonwealth might gang up against Britain on cereals.[15] It was a forerunner of confrontations to come. Menzies for the time being reserved his position. 'McEwen returns to Australia on April 25th, after strenuous labours on your side of the world', he wrote to Macmillan, 'and will be able to report to us on the position as he sees it. I will then decide my own course of action'.[16] He shortly afterwards had useful intelligence from Harrison about the impact McEwen had made in London. R. A. Butler, the British Deputy Prime Minister, had told Harrison: 'This is some boy that you have out there, he kept four of our Ministers [Butler, Heath, Sandys and Soames] busy all the time and we tried to confuse him, but his clear thinking rather baffled us'. And Heath had added: 'I am greatly beholden to McEwen. I suppose we can say now that we understand Australia's case far better than we have up to the moment'. Harrison hoped that Menzies would be able to come to London himself, to 'put the coping stone on Jack's efforts'.[17]

Britain prepares the ground: stage 1

Meanwhile there was the question of the timing of the next Commonwealth Prime Ministers Conference, a delicate problem indeed for the British Government. Australia and Canada were pressing for an early meeting so that Commonwealth influence on the British negotiating position at Brussels might be maximised. Menzies had apparently formed the impression, British officials noted, 'that Mr Macmillan was resolved to "dodge" a conference if he could'.[18] This was certainly Harrison's suspicion, and one that he had conveyed to Menzies. He believed that the British were deliberately loading themselves with a series of mid-year meetings (SEATO, CENTO, NATO, a Sukarno visit) with the aim of forestalling the Commonwealth. Hence, he advised Menzies in January 1962, 'it might be as well to say something quickly about the Prime Ministers Conference'.[19] It was in order to 'say something quickly' that Harrison approached Heath and Lee in February with his proposal for a conference in May or June.

The British interest did indeed lie in putting off the conference for as long as possible. The main reason, as intimated in Macmillan's instructions to Sandys in mid-1961, was precisely to enable British negotiators to retain a relatively free hand at Brussels. British officials had an additional reason for wishing to keep the Australians in particular at bay: the Menzies Government's wafer-thin parliamentary majority after the 1961 election might well serve to 'prevent any Australian representative from taking up a forthcoming attitude'.[20] But in due course opinion in Whitehall began to crystallise in favour of a meeting in September, when the Brussels negotiations would be in recess.

Even more important than the question of timing was the problem of how best to control the proceedings. From late February the Commonwealth Relations Office was briefing Sandys on the need to 'take very careful steps to prepare the ground beforehand' in order to 'achieve the results we want'; to think out in advance 'suitable topics for discussion at the Meeting'.[21]

In March, Macmillan made an attempt to deflect any possible conflict with Menzies: 'You know . . . I hope, how deeply we feel the need to safeguard the Commonwealth in all this. If, therefore, our two Governments should have some differences on the tactics of the negotiations I know that you will not think this is because we are being intentionally unhelpful'.[22] It was however Sir Saville Garner, Permanent Under-Secretary at the Commonwealth Relations Office, who made the crucial suggestion as to how Menzies ought to be handled:

> It seems to me that Mr Menzies may be the key to everything. If he is prepared, for broad reasons of policy, to go along with us over Europe it would make the whole difference to the meeting—and also to the attitude of the Conservative Party. I think it is tactically very important that . . . the Prime Minister should send him a personal message (perhaps reviving the suggestion that Mr Menzies might come here in the early summer as well).[23]

Other officials agreed that Menzies was likely to be a key figure, not only at the meeting, 'but also in relation to public opinion in this country', and that the best idea would be to invite him over for preliminary conversations. Sandys concurred, adding the suggestion that Menzies might welcome the idea of 'combining business with pleasure at the Tests with Pakistan'. Macmillan needed little persuading; his invitation was sent at once, although with no mention of cricket.[24]

Menzies wrote back with a somewhat reluctant acceptance of a September date for the Prime Ministers meeting, which 'appears to suit most of our Commonwealth colleagues'. For his part, he feared that the meeting would be 'too late to be effective in relation to the Common Market negotiations' and that the debates would tend to be 'both generalised and retrospective'. He was also 'completely sceptical about a meeting of fourteen Prime Ministers, few of whom have trade problems in common, achieving concerted views upon such complex matters'. And he was disturbed by the movements in British policy: 'For example, Heath's recent statement on the political implications of acceding to the Treaty of Rome goes far beyond what Duncan Sandys was putting to us in Canberra. It envisages a political integration ... How this will affect the Commonwealth relationship is no doubt arguable'. For all these reasons, Menzies agreed that he should make an early visit to London. He looked forward, he said, to discussions with Macmillan 'in which, without benefit of Ghana or Ceylon, but with all the benefit of old and tried comradeship, we could speak together as men do, having "tired the sun with talking, and sent him down the sky"'. But if this clubmanlike sentiment seemed to be uttered in the voice of Menzies the true friend of Britain, he tempered it with the hard-edged insistence that the Australian Government was keen 'to pursue pragmatic lines of consultation, which involve much complicated detail'.[25]

He did not say as much to Macmillan, at least not in writing, but Menzies was well aware that Macmillan hoped to make use of him for domestic political purposes. In a mid-May despatch, Harrison briefed Menzies about the current divisions in the British Cabinet over Europe and stressed that

> Macmillan is also wanting some statement to be made by a prominent Commonwealth person that will ease the political situation as far as he is concerned ... The Conservatives are at the lowest political ebb, they want something to lift them out of it and any statement that might be made by you when you arrive giving the impression that Australia was satisfied with the negotiations would be seized upon by Macmillan as a Heaven-sent opportunity to allay the suspicions that are quite inarticulate but are being held by a great number of people in the electorates.[26]

Thus the Menzies–Macmillan meeting was set up, but with the two sides at cross purposes. For the British, as has been argued, the idea was to appeal to Menzies' 'higher' loyalty and to convince him of the political merits of the British case for entry, in the hope that he could then influence both his own colleagues and the Commonwealth meeting, and, incidentally, help rally the doubters in the Conservative Party and the British voting public behind the Government's policy. Or in terms that Macmillan would use later, it was hoped that Menzies would prove 'reasonable and statesmanlike'.[27] For Menzies, the goal was to appeal to loyalty somewhat differently conceived—namely, Britain's loyalty to the old Commonwealth —and to intervene in the British policy process on behalf of Australian and

Commonwealth interests before Britain had gone so far down the European road that these interests were effectively marginalised. His major intention, so he told Harrison, would not be to discuss in detail the economic and commodities problems with which McEwen had dealt, but rather to concentrate on political aspects, especially as they related to the future of the Commonwealth: 'In any event, Jack has his own methods and I have mine which are different, and between the two of us we may build up an all-round case which may have its value'.[28] The division of labour could not have been described more clearly.

No written record of the Menzies–Macmillan talks is available, but to judge by a subsequent note from Sandys to Macmillan, the British apparently felt that things went fairly much their way. Although Menzies had made some 'unfortunate public statements' in London, he now seemed 'very much happier about our attitude towards the Common Market'. Accordingly Sandys had invited him to return to London a few days before the Prime Ministers Conference so that he and British ministers could 'discuss together how the others should be handled. He said he thought there would be advantage in this'.[29]

The Washington gambit

Yet if London felt that it now had Menzies where it wanted him, London was mistaken. For Menzies' next move was to visit Washington for talks with President Kennedy and (among others) his senior advisers Robert McNamara, George Ball, Douglas Dillon and Averell Harriman. The US Government, as noted above, was keen to see Britain enter Europe. Significantly for Australia, it had also appeared to take the view that if the price of British entry was to phase out Commonwealth trade preferences, then this should be done. Menzies went to Washington with the political objective of persuading the Americans to moderate this view. But the Americans' objective was somewhat different. Kennedy had been advised that Menzies' attitude

> could be a major factor in preventing the UK from joining the EEC . . . It is important, therefore, for us now to be as forthcoming as is consistent with our basic position on preferences in order to meet the Australian problem and try to lead the Australians away from such a head-on collision. This will mean a direct appeal to Menzies' statesmanship.[30]

Menzies arrived in Washington on 17 June 1962. His talks with the American officials, mainly in one-on-one sessions, extended over some three days. The resulting communiqué was diplomatically bland;[31] but

Menzies later set out his own version of the talks in a distinctly guileful message to Macmillan, which merits quoting at length.

> My central theme [in talking to Kennedy] was this: 'If you exercise your influence with The Six to resist everything that resembles a Commonwealth preference or even a substitute for it, and, if as a consequence, The Six carry the principle of the disappearance of preferences by 1970 right down the board, you will impale the Government of the United Kingdom on the horns of a dilemma. It will then be said, and with great force, that Great Britain will be choosing between Europe and the Commonwealth. I believe that you are keen, for political reasons, on Great Britain going into the European Community. Harold Macmillan himself is much influenced by the overall political considerations. Surely this is not a time at which your common conception of an extended and powerful Europe should be put at risk by the presentation to Great Britain of a set of conditions which she might well find impossible of acceptance by her at the centre of the British Commonwealth.'
>
> The reactions to this were interesting and, I hope you will agree, valuable. The President took the opportunity of speaking very warmly about the importance of the Commonwealth and the necessity to build up its strength. You will see a reference to this in the communiqué which was issued and a copy of which, in case you have not seen it, I enclose.

The Americans went further. According to Menzies, George Ball, who was a convinced pro-European and 'whom I had expected to find as my chief opponent . . . said quite plainly that a phasing out of the existing Commonwealth trade arrangements by 1970 would be most unreasonable'. Kennedy added that 'our practical business seems to be to find a way between the horns [of the dilemma]'. The Americans agreed that they and the Australians should inaugurate their own discussions of the question of access to the European market on a commodity-by-commodity basis since, as Kennedy put it, 'we both have a lively interest in maintaining and developing our own trade entry into the extended Europe and in the avoidance of over-nationalistic economic policies in the Community itself. We therefore have a lot in common'. Menzies had willingly taken this cue: 'I at once arranged for this with John McEwen in Australia and the talks are now in hand'. His overall conclusion was that there was 'a reasonable flexibility in the American approach', and that the Americans realised that the price of British entry 'should not be too high'.[32] Menzies did not mention, however, that the meeting had also established (presumably because the Americans had wished this point to be registered) that Commonwealth preferences accounted for less than half of Australia's trade.[33]

Between its lines, Menzies' message was telling Macmillan that for Britain to accept the principle of exclusionist policies in an extended Europe might be to incur the risk of American displeasure. Having implied this,

Menzies sought to pressure Macmillan by proposing that all four old-Commonwealth leaders should meet immediately prior to the Prime Ministers Conference in order to work out a common line of approach.[34] But Macmillan saw the snare, and smoothly evaded it. 'I am quite sure that your visit will have been of great value, particularly in impressing on the President the importance of the Commonwealth interest in the Common Market problem', he wrote. 'But our task at the Conference would not be eased if the impression were created that the old Commonwealth were ganging up in advance'.[35] Britain's objective was still to maintain maximum freedom of manoeuvre in the negotiations, and thus it needed to avoid the potential entrapment of a discussion in which Australia, New Zealand and Canada would present a common front. Bilateral discussions between Britain and others could be more easily controlled, and hence in the lead-up to the full conference Britain insisted on bilateral discussions only.

The Washington ploy was no doubt worth trying; but it seems plain that Menzies could not realistically have expected to enlist American support to any significant degree. In August, presumably in response to a request from the Department of External Affairs, the Australian Embassy in Washington reported back in some detail on American attitudes towards the Commonwealth, and in essence confirmed that 'whatever positive value the United States may place on the Commonwealth is of relatively minor account by comparison with the U.S.A.'s vital interest in the formation of a strong, workable and co-operative European Community'.[36] And in September Kennedy specifically asked the British if there was anything he could say to Menzies at their next meeting that would help Britain achieve its European goal.[37] Arguably Australia's only real chance of leverage in Washington would have come from playing a very different card, namely the China one; for the State Department in 1962 was reportedly much disturbed by McEwen's push for the recognition of Communist China as part of a broader Australian trade drive into Asia to compensate for possible British entry into the EEC.[38] But since Menzies himself adamantly opposed McEwen on the China recognition issue, that card was never playable.

An incident at home, however, confirmed Menzies' backing for McEwen on the European issue, against, for example, the Treasury, which was now taking a somewhat less alarmist view of the consequences for Australia of British entry. On 25 July Leslie Bury, Minister Assisting the Treasurer, commented in a public speech on the exaggerated fears that were being expressed, and remarked pointedly that 'certain rural industries [that is, McEwen's bailiwick] may have to adjust any plans for future expansion, but in the aggregate their output is only a minor element in the total economic scene'. McEwen immediately protested to Menzies, who decided that these remarks ran counter to government policy and forced Bury's resignation. In a subsequent parliamentary speech he made it clear that the whole European issue was deeply troubling to him.[39]

Britain prepares the ground: stage 2

The British Cabinet met on 22 August to consider tactics for the Commonwealth conference, and in particular what to do about Australia and New Zealand. As Macmillan put it, 'at the forthcoming Commonwealth Meeting a great responsibility would rest with the Prime Minister of Australia'.[40] The problem was referred to the Ministerial Committee on the Common Market which was due to meet on 5 September, five days before the conference. Macmillan's minute to the Committee noted that

> The new Commonwealth countries are pretty well looked after [in the Brussels negotiations so far] and can have no economic grievances. If they choose to associate they can increase their potential markets. Moreover, to be frank, they carry little political weight in this country. Sentiment towards the Commonwealth is really centred upon the old Commonwealth countries, especially Australia and New Zealand. Their Governments, if they wished, could make it almost impossible for a Conservative, or indeed any Government, to carry Britain into the Common Market. That would be, in my view, a tragedy of the first order. It follows, therefore, that our tactics must be somehow or other to get them acquiescent if not wholly satisfied.[41]

In a separate minute, Sandys proposed a possible tactic. They should admit at once to Australia and New Zealand that the proposals regarding trade in temperate foodstuffs which had emerged from the negotiations up to that point were not good enough, and to promise that Britain would try to improve on them when negotiations were resumed in October; that is, after the Commonwealth conference.

Macmillan at first seemed inclined to accept this approach, noting in his minute to the Ministerial Committee that 'We could undertake to try and get these principles [on price policy] clothed with a little more flesh'. But at this point Sir Norman Brook, the formidably influential Cabinet Secretary, intervened with a minute of his own to Macmillan. Brook saw considerable danger in Sandys' proposal, from both a diplomatic and a party political point of view. If the Government led the old Commonwealth countries to believe that it could achieve something on these lines and then failed to pull it off, 'our last case will be worse than the first—especially if our failure becomes obvious in the opening stages of the resumed negotiations in Brussels early in October, just before the Party Conference'. Brook believed that the safer course would be to try to bring the old Commonwealth countries to 'face the realities' and to persuade them that they ought to concentrate on the future rather than seek cast-iron safeguards for their existing trade. This would mean stressing the fact that anything like a Commonwealth Common Market is impracticable; that it is their interest, as well as ours, that Britain should be prosperous and strong; that they will have a better chance of increasing their exports to Europe if Britain is a member of the Community than if she is not.[42]

Macmillan and the Ministerial Committee were, it seems, impressed by this advice. Macmillan had an immediate opportunity to put it into practice, for on the evening of 5 September, following the Ministerial Committee's meeting, he met Menzies for what turned out to be, in Macmillan's view, a 'very useful discussion'. Macmillan came away believing that Menzies was once again back in the fold: 'frank about his own difficulties', as Macmillan reported to Sandys, but indeed 'reasonable and statesmanlike'.[43] In other words, we may suppose, Macmillan now read Menzies as generally prepared to accept 'the realities', along the lines set out by Brook. But Menzies did ask one favour. Suppose that it did not prove possible at Brussels to make special arrangements for Australian temperate foodstuffs; suppose that Australia began in consequence to subsidise its exports; suppose that Australia was then attacked by 'other chaps' in GATT for dumping, and that GATT sought to take punitive measures against Australia; would Britain then support Australia in GATT? Macmillan was sympathetic, evidently seeing this as an acceptable quid pro quo. 'From my knowledge of GATT', he told Heath, 'I would hope that this would not be too difficult, for GATT is a slow-moving machine and it should be possible for us to circumvent it or to take this action almost indefinitely'.[44]

Thus it appeared that after all the toing and froing an understanding between the two Prime Ministers had been reached, just in time for the conference.

The Commonwealth confers

The minutes of the 1962 Commonwealth Prime Ministers Conference make remarkable reading. Macmillan opened with a magisterial review of the high politics of the issue. He was followed by Heath with a detailed account of the negotiations to date. Delegations then descended immediately to the low politics of economic self-interest, and stayed at that level for a full week of intense and often acrimonious discussion. In the event, Menzies did not give the Commonwealth the lead that the British had wanted from him. Rather, he made what Macmillan considered a '*very* damaging speech'.[45] In his address Menzies declared that he realised 'the sense of historic purpose inspiring Great Britain' and accordingly did not wish 'to record an objection in principle'. But he found the proposed safeguards for Commonwealth interests 'sketchy', and the conditions of Britain's entry 'vague and un-decided'. He did not think The Six had moved at all in the direction of the Commonwealth. He anticipated damage to Australian interests and insisted that 'there had to be compensating factors', of which there was as yet little sign. He lectured the meeting on the history of federalism, arguing that if federations were not to disintegrate their central authority was bound to grow, and that this was the outcome to be feared in Europe.[46] He then handed over to London's *bête noire*, McEwen, who made a great deal of the running for the rest of the week, circulating position papers on commodity agreements that were heavily loaded in Australia's favour and having many a sharp exchange with Heath on the temperate foodstuffs issue. Menzies intervened seldom, and when he did it was usually in support of McEwen. Other delegations were comparably tenacious in pressing their commercial interests and in demanding that the British negotiate concessions on their behalf. New Commonwealth leaders were just as vigorous in these demands as old; so much for Macmillan's belief that the new countries could have 'no economic grievances'.[47] All in all the British leaders, and Heath in par-ticular, had a difficult week. Macmillan noted in his diary that he felt shaken by the Commonwealth's attitude, while Heath, who was 'accus-tomed to Europeans who are courteous and well informed even if hard bar-gainers, was astounded at the ignorance, ill-manners and conceit of the Commonwealth'.[48]

That Macmillan and his colleagues were both disappointed and aggrieved is further evidenced by their reports back to Cabinet. Deputy Prime Minister Butler told the Cabinet that the other Commonwealth governments had been far more critical than had been expected, and had done their own cause little good by concentrating on their short-term econ-omic goals rather than accepting that their long-term interests would be better served by a stronger (that is, European) Britain. Ministers noted that Commonwealth leaders' public statements were fuelling the already exist-ing antipathy towards Europe among the British public; they 'would bear a heavy responsibility if, by their public statements at this stage, they made it impossible for the United Kingdom to join the Community'. It would, Butler bleakly remarked, be 'inexpedient' to have another Commonwealth conference so long as the Brussels negotiations were going on.[49] And Heath was especially critical of the Australians:

> they had demanded, not only access, but a guaranteed price remunerative to Australian producers. This was something which we could not have accepted even if our entry into the Community had not been in question, since it would have involved an undertaking to cover in advance and at our expense the effects of Australian inflation. New Zealand and Canada did not attach so much importance to the question of price because they were efficient producers. More should be done to explain these issues in public.[50]

Only on the final day of the conference, when a brief and neutral communiqué drafted by Macmillan and Brook was presented and adopted, did Menzies' attitude become, in British eyes, more cooperative. As Macmillan noted: 'Menzies (having, I suppose, made a sufficient demonstration for home politics) was reasonable. He reverted to his favourite sport of teasing Diefenbaker'.[51]

After the conference, Macmillan summarised the overall position for his Cabinet colleagues. The meeting had started badly. 'In spite of all the earlier consultation, Commonwealth Ministers had not clearly understood the under-lying considerations in favour of our entry'. It looked as if the Australians in particular would continue to try to drive hard bargains. But the meeting had ended as well as could have been expected. He hoped that the talks had at least helped to clear the Prime Ministers' minds and put the British position in a better perspective.[52]

This last was whistling in the dark. The meeting did nothing to help Britain in its major objective. Rather, to onlookers in Europe, and especially to President de Gaulle, the dissension and the air of indecision emanating from the Commonwealth Conference helped reinforce the impression that Britain was not yet wholeheartedly ready for Europe. De Gaulle's veto followed four months later. He cited Britain's continuing inability to make a clear choice between Commonwealth and Europe as a major factor in his decision.[53] Or as Robert Holland has put it, 'when de Gaulle finally vetoed British entry, he did so on grounds (that the UK was not a European power, but one with special responsibilities and duties in the wider world) which were exquisitely chosen to cause the greatest dismay in Whitehall'.[54] In effect, he was impaling Britain on the horns of that very dilemma that Menzies had described to Kennedy. Holland notes further the impact of this setback on Britain's policy towards the remnants of its formal empire. President de Gaulle's veto 'heightened the British belief that decolonisation had now to be pushed *à l'outrance*; hence the unseemly bustle with which the most ramshackle dependencies ... were pitched into independence during the mid-1960s'.[55]

Might the outcome of the 1962 conference have been different if the Commonwealth had collectively voiced its support for Britain's European ambitions? Probably not; there seems little doubt that de Gaulle had made up his mind to veto Britain's application anyway. But the more focused question to which this discussion gives rise is whether it was ever reasonable for the British to expect Menzies to help rally the support they required in the Commonwealth, to say nothing of the Conservative Party and the British electorate. In fact, each time they judged him their man, Menzies proceeded to go his own way—most spectacularly perhaps in his Washington initiative, but also in the conference chamber itself. To enlist Menzies to the British cause, they needed to detach his 'higher' loyalty to Crown and Commonwealth from his 'parochial' sense of Australian self-interest. But this strategy could not work because, on the European issue, Commonwealth loyalty and Australian interest were inseparable as far as Menzies was concerned—something he had made clear in his letter on the European Monetary Agreement, written well before the Common Market negotiations had even begun.

After the conference was over Menzies called on Macmillan, and, as Macmillan recounted to Butler, 'explained his conduct at the Conference by the weakness of his political position'. This was in part a reference to Menzies' parliamentary vulnerability at home. But there was also the McEwen factor. According to Menzies, 'Mr McEwen was at him all the time to take a much stronger line'. At least he had resisted, 'greatly to Mr McEwen's displeasure', joining in the demand for another Prime Ministers Conference. As Macmillan saw it, Menzies in this conversation 'was clearly trying to be as pleasant as possible and excuse himself for not having taken a more constructive position throughout the Conference'.[56] For all this, the gulf between the meanings the two leaders would have given to the idea of 'constructive position' remained very wide indeed.

Whether Menzies would have had much influence on the other Prime Ministers even if he had done as the British wished was another question entirely. Given the rapidly changing character of the Commonwealth at the time, and the manifestly poor relations between Menzies and such new-Commonwealth leaders as Nehru and Nkrumah, it must be doubted that he would have carried any great weight. Indeed, whatever influence he might have enjoyed with the new Commonwealth had probably been forfeited at the previous Prime Ministers Conference in March 1961, when he had made his last ditch attempt to keep South Africa as a member.

In short, British hopes were doubly misplaced. They hoped he would play their game; he did not. They hoped that in playing it, he would influence the outcome of the Commonwealth conference; almost certainly he would not, and could not, have done so.

How much does this case of post-imperial dissension tell us about the changing nature of the broader Anglo-Australian relationship? Stuart Ward has shown that it tells us a great deal. In his full-length study of the case, Ward argues convincingly that Britain's attempt to join the EEC in 1961–63 was central to the transformation of the relationship from something that was based, at least in part, on a sense of race patriotism to something that became increasingly instrumental and interest-based. Drawing on the theory of imagined communities, Ward argues that historically the idea of Anglo-Australian organic race unity was Australia's imagined community.

This did not mean that Australians failed to perceive their own interests, as distinct from Britain's. In fact disagreements between Australia and Britain were historically quite frequent (some examples bearing upon issues of formal empire were noted in Part 1). But disagreements were typically characterised as aberrations, with the 'web of culture' closing over each episode. Until, that is, the EEC episode, which posed a problem of a different order for Anglo-Australian relations since 'sentiment' and 'self-interest' were placed so fundamentally at odds.[57]

When Britain chose Europe (self-interest) over sentiment (the Commonwealth), Australia at first objected as much on cultural grounds as on grounds of interest, as if London had violated some imagined code of British conduct. Yet Australia's adaptation to Britain's shift came about more quickly than anyone in (say) early 1961 would probably have anticipated. Effectively, within the space of a year or so (1961–62), Australia's sense of betrayal was superseded by a resigned acceptance; and, more positively, by a remarkably swift adaptation among trade policy makers who set out to find new economic relationships that might compensate for European losses. At the heart of the shift, on the Australian side, was the fascinating political interplay between Menzies and McEwen. During 1961–62, Menzies led Australia to a relatively moderate oppositionist stance designed to balance Australia's economic concerns against the wider political need to retain great and powerful friendships in uncertain times. By contrast, for as long as the EEC battle lasted, McEwen strenuously fought for Australian economic self-interest with all the resources and tactics he could command; Britain had no more obdurate adversary. Yet McEwen was a politician who kept his options open, who searched for new trade partnerships wherever they might be found, and who did not cease to do so while the EEC battle was being fought; and this left him well placed to oversee Australia's policy response to the dwindling of the British market. The Australian adaptation can reasonably be seen as a product of the approaches these two leaders represented.

7

Confrontation in Southeast Asia

DIFFERENT ASPECTS OF THE ENDING of Britain's empire raised different kinds of issues for Australia. Britain's scheme for the conferring of independence on its remaining Southeast Asian colonial possessions in 1963 put Australia's regional diplomacy severely to the test. This was chiefly because Indonesia took strong exception to Britain's creation of the new Federation of Malaysia. Australia found itself trying to support Malaysia without alienating Indonesia, a truly demanding task. Then in August 1965 came the blow of Singapore's departure from the Federation; the repercussions of this dramatic event were such that 'the whole western policy of attempting to combine decolonisation with anti-communism seemed in danger of coming apart'.[1]

Australia's policies towards Malaysia and Indonesia in this difficult period have been described in a number of works, the more recent of them grounded solidly in the primary records.[2] Rather than retell in any detail what is by now an oft-told story, this chapter aims to use the story to illuminate the changing and sometimes problematic character of Anglo-Australian relations during this key episode in the winding up of imperial affairs. First, however, it is necessary to provide some context by sketching Australia's military relationships with both Britain and the United States in the period of Malaya's own decolonisation.

Background: regional defence

A decade and more after World War II the Anglo-Australian defence relationship in Southeast Asia was still, in important ways, extremely close. As of the mid-1950s the standardisation of equipment and military

139

procedures between Britain and Australia remained in effect. In Southeast Asia the ANZAM agreement provided a framework for coordination of British, Australian and New Zealand service planning. In 1955 Australian troops began operating jointly with British and New Zealand troops in the Commonwealth Strategic Reserve in Malaya. From Canberra's point of view these arrangements served both to help subdue subversion in a British dependent territory and to give substance to the Australian security doctrine of forward defence.

At the same time, in the wake of the collapse of French colonialism in Indochina and the subsequent creation of SEATO in 1954, Australia's American connection was growing in importance. The problem was that British and American strategic plans for Southeast Asia were diverging. Whereas the British were determined to commit resources only to the defence of their own colonial territories and showed little interest in SEATO planning, the American strategic vision encompassed the whole SEATO area. Menzies had initially hoped to reconcile the two approaches within the Malayan context at least; when he announced Australia's commitment of troops to the Commonwealth Brigade on 1 April 1955 he evidently believed that the United States would play a part in supporting the Commonwealth force. But in July he and his government were 'devastated'[3] to learn from Washington that the Pentagon would no longer tolerate a line of thinking that focused on committing ground forces to the internal defence of one country, Malaya. Rather the United States saw it as necessary to develop mobile striking power that could serve to defend Southeast Asia as a whole, and especially the arc of countries from Thailand to Vietnam which appeared most vulnerable to Chinese aggression. Canberra was warned that Australia would be unlikely to receive American military aid unless it tailored its Southeast Asian strategy to America's. Australia's military planners were in any case moving towards the view that adoption of the American approach would be more likely to enhance the 'defence in depth' of Australia, and more likely to generate American support should Australia come under direct threat.[4] Thus Canberra made its choice. By degrees between mid-1955 and early 1957, Australia turned towards the United States for its major strategic alliance in the region. The key Cabinet decision, taken in February 1957 and announced in April, was to create a flexible, mobile, Australia-based force that could in principle operate anywhere in the region in tandem with the Americans.[5]

Intertwined with these developments was the matter of Malaya's transition to independence. As noted in Chapter 1, a material factor for Australia in deciding to commit a battalion to the Commonwealth Strategic Reserve was the British assurance that constitutional change in Malaya would not be rapid. This was important for the Australian Government, since there was a degree of anxiety in Canberra that a self-governing Malaya might oppose the Reserve's broader strategic role in the region, effectively in support of American policy, as distinct from a role in combating subversion within Malaya. However, in July 1955, less than four months after Australia made its decision to commit the troops, elections were held in Malaya, and it quickly became apparent that the tempo of Britain's decolonisation was about to increase. This was disconcerting to the Australians, as indicated by Alan Watt's view, communicated to Richard Casey in June 1956, that if for any reason Australia had delayed its decision, the commitment of the battalion might never have taken place.[6] It remained to be seen, as Karl Hack notes, 'whether Britain could control decolonisation in such a way as to prevent Australia from deciding the Strategic Reserve was too circumscribed to be of value in supporting American policies in Southeast Asia'.[7]

Australian alarm at trends in British policy increased during 1956 and 1957. Canberra worried about Britain's now manifest plan to push for quick decolonisation and to conclude a new defence agreement with independent Malaya, since that might create a Malayan veto power over the use of the Reserve for regional purposes. In the same period Britain was moving towards a more nuclear-based defence strategy, giving rise to Australian concerns about possible cutbacks in British conventional forces East of Suez. These fears helped reinforce the movement in Australia's own policy towards strategic association with the United States.

For all that, even after Malaya's decolonisation Australia's commitment to the Commonwealth Strategic Reserve remained in place. As Hack puts it, 'Ultimately the political capital sunk in the Malayan commitment mitigated [*sic*] against withdrawal'.[8] Stretched between the two allies, Australian policy thus retained a certain ambiguity. But one thing that did proceed was an incremental standardisation of Australian military equipment with American. This process culminated in 1963 when Australia, in need of new fighter bombers to replace its veteran Canberras, had to decide between the British TSR2 and the American F-111A (neither of which was yet operational). In spite of Macmillan's shameless playing of the 'sentiment' card—'this seems to me rather more than a commerical [*sic*] transaction'[9]— Australia bought American. Attacked by the Labor Party in Parliament for his shabby treatment of the British, a situation not without irony, Menzies famously protested that he was British 'to the bootheels' but that his prime duty was to 'the safety of my own country'.[10] To his friend Sir Alec Douglas-Home, newly installed as British Prime Minister, he maintained that Australia's decision 'undoubtedly greatly satisfies the United States and sustains their interest in this corner of the world. This is a most important by-product of the decision and one which I hope may contain some merit from your point of view'.[11]

Malaysia proposed

Malaya had been independent for nearly four years when in May 1961 its Prime Minister, Tunku Abdul Rahman, proposed closer association between his country, the British colonies of Singapore, Sarawak and North Borneo, and the British trust territory of Brunei. The British were initially hesitant, but by October 1961 had given their support to the idea of a fully fledged federation. Motives varied. Tunku Abdul Rahman could see economic advantages in association with Singapore; in proposing the addition of the other three territories he was seeking primarily to ensure that ethnic Chinese would not form the majority of the grouping's population. For the British, the core concerns were Singapore's political instability and the radicalism that had been developing there since the mid-1950s, which aroused fears that an independent Singapore might associate itself with China. Singapore was the focal point of British military power in the region, and Britain was anxious that its base facilities not be placed in jeopardy. Yet demands for independence were strong and could not be fended off indefinitely. Thus Lee Kuan Yew, Prime Minister of Singapore from 1959, held the key to the situation. To the relief of the British, Lee was strongly anti-communist; and to their further relief he came out in favour of a merger with Malaya, both for economic reasons and because he saw the construction of a larger state —and hence a larger internal security apparatus—as the only way to contain his radical opponents and preserve his own leadership position in Singapore. This was the outcome that the British too desired.

The idea of grafting on the three Borneo dependencies was additionally attractive to the British, since it would enable them to cast off their remaining colonial responsibilities in the region. This motive was of a piece with broader British policy, for this was a period in which federation was much in favour in London as a device for managing awkward decolonisations, for example in the Caribbean and South Arabia. As London saw it, if there were no federal scheme in Southeast Asia the Borneo territories might well require British tutelage for years to come. Although the British governors of Sarawak and North Borneo were uneasy at the notion of a rush towards federation for their extremely undeveloped territories, London by the end of 1961 was no longer in any mood for prolonged tutelage. London did, however, promise to consult local opinion, and early in 1962 a British-Malayan commission of enquiry under Lord Cobbold was despatched to Borneo for that purpose.

In Canberra, the issue first came up for consideration by ministers in August 1961. Menzies, as Minister for External Affairs, presented a lengthy submission to an ad hoc Cabinet committee. He noted the economic case for merging Malaya and Singapore, but spent most of his time on the security arguments. Menzies stressed the goals of preserving Western interests and maintaining Australia's capacity to engage in forward defence in the region. He was aware of the risk that a new Malaysian government might impose restrictions on the mobility of the Commonwealth Strategic Reserve; on the other hand, the British bases in Singapore might have better prospects of remaining in place in a federation than in an independent Singapore. As for the Borneo territories, he was prepared to see them included in the federation, no matter how unready they might appear to be, given the possibility that if they were left out Indonesia might seek aggressively to incorporate them once British colonial authority had been withdrawn. In Menzies' words, 'If the price of maintaining Western interests in Singapore (and ultimately Malaya) were the early termination of United Kingdom sovereignty in the Territories, that price would be, from a political point of view, worth paying'. Overall, Menzies felt, the weight of the arguments tipped towards federation.[12] The Cabinet committee's response to this cautious advocacy was to record its support for the Malaysia proposal 'on balance'. It felt that Australia should not commit itself too strongly to the scheme lest it prove unfeasible, and should not become directly involved in consultations.[13]

Subsequently the Australian Government expressed its approval for the Britain-Malaya agreement of November 1961. When in the later part of 1962 the Cobbold survey in the Borneo territories came up with results that Britain felt able to interpret as supportive of federation, Britain and Malaya agreed in principle that Malaysia should be established by 31 August 1963, and once again Australia approved. It seemed that this exercise in tidying up unfinished imperial business was well on track.

Both Australia and New Zealand nevertheless remained constantly alert to the implications of British policy for their military security. A letter of Macmillan's to Menzies and Holyoake in October 1961 floated the less than welcome idea that whether or not Malaysia came into being, it was 'only realistic' to assume that over the next ten years the use of the Singapore bases was 'likely to be hampered by local susceptibilities'. Moreover, if Malaysia were indeed established, the transfer of responsibility for internal security to the Malaysian authorities would of itself lead to a reduction of British land forces.[14] Antipodean concern was evident in Holyoake's response that in that case, Australia and New Zealand might have to look even more to the United States for 'logistic support'.[15] Macmillan then offered an assurance that Britain proposed to maintain, 'if and when a Greater Malaysia is successfully set up, slightly greater naval and air forces than at present together with appropriate ground forces'.[16]

Large-scale British military withdrawal was not yet under discussion, but the Australians already had their suspicions about British long-term intentions. With regard to Malaysia, External Affairs in particular aimed to ensure that Britain would carry the responsibility for supporting the Federation under the Anglo-Malayan Defence Treaty of 1957, and would not simply 'federate and scuttle'.[17] Barwick, Minister for External Affairs from December 1961, stuck firmly to this objective, to the extent that some of his Cabinet colleagues appear to have been worried that his diplomacy might become 'unduly abrasive, especially towards Britain'.[18] Certainly Barwick wanted the British to stay in Southeast Asia in strength, but he was very much concerned to consolidate Australia's security relationship with the United States and to build good relations with Indonesia, and he did not want Australia to be diverted from these objectives by becoming drawn too far into what should by rights be a British commitment. According to David Marr, he had a further motive for remaining low key in his support for Malaysia: he wished to retain the option of Australia acting as mediator in the event of a serious dispute between Britain and Indonesia.[19]

By late 1962 some British officials had gained the impression that Australian policy makers not only doubted Malaysia's viability but were worried that the Indonesians, if not carefully cultivated, 'might make it their business to foment trouble' in the Borneo territories.[20] But even more than this, the British by this time sensed an atmosphere of External Affairs unwillingness to be too closely associated in Asian perceptions with British colonialism. As the High Commissioner in Canberra reported:

> We must in future expect Australian officials (and even some Ministers) in considering any particular question to pay less attention to the importance of the Commonwealth connexion as such and more to the possible effects of their policy on that question in the non-Commonwealth countries of Asia. The Australians are anxious nowadays, perhaps because they will soon be one of the few remaining colonial Powers, to dissociate themselves in Asian eyes from the colonial policies of others ... There is also a feeling in some Australian circles, particularly in the Department of External Affairs, that the British have dreamed up Malaysia as a rather transparent, intrinsically flimsy and probably impermanent device for solving their colonial problems in Singapore and the Borneo Territories. They suspect that in the long term we will withdraw from South-East Asia and leave them, with New Zealand, to hold the baby.[21]

Malaysia debated

The first indication that the Malaysia scheme might not proceed so smoothly after all came in December 1962 when the self-styled North Borneo National Army mounted a rebellion against the Sultan of Brunei. British forces sent from Singapore subdued the rebels, but the significance of the uprising was enhanced by Jakarta's manifest sympathy for it. From about this time President Sukarno voiced open hostility towards the Malaysia project. He branded it a neo-colonialist plot devised by Britain in collaboration with Malaya, with the intention of protecting British economic interests and destroying the Indonesian republic through subversion and encirclement. On 20 January 1963 his Foreign Minister, Subandrio, declared the policy of *Konfrontasi* (Confrontation), under which Indonesia would seek to thwart the creation of Malaysia by all means short of war. There ensued a period of intensive diplomatic activity among the Western allies principally involved: Britain, the United States, Australia and New Zealand. Since that time several studies have traced the ramifications of this diplomacy.[22] Here we focus on its Anglo-Australian dimension.

Matters were initiated by London. Alarmed at the possibility of further disorder in its Borneo dependencies, Britain in mid-January sought urgent talks with Australia and the United States with a view to formulating a common policy towards Indonesia (New Zealand was later added to the invitation list at Australia's suggestion). The British specifically asked if they could rely on Australian help in the military defence of Malaysia. In support of their initiative they also circulated a Foreign Office appreciation of Indonesia's motives. This paper characterised Sukarno as driven by grandiose political and territorial ambitions. Having recently acquired West New Guinea, he would aim now to take over the three Borneo territories, Portuguese Timor, East New Guinea, and perhaps even Malaya and the Philippines, so as to establish himself as leader of all the Malay people and of the 'newly emerging forces'. To this end he was building up Indonesian armaments with help from the Soviet Union. It was possible that he was planning outright war on Britain as the local colonial and neo-colonial power.[23]

Senior Australian officials promptly expressed scepticism at this analysis. Tange pointedly reminded London that its assessment of Indonesia had been very different when Australia had looked to Britain for support on West New Guinea.[24] Australia's Ambassador to Indonesia, Shann, judged the British document to be 'hardly deserving of serious consideration'; in his view Indonesia clearly wanted to acquire Portuguese Timor and block the creation of Malaysia, but that was as far as it went.[25] Officials in Canberra generally saw Indonesia as being opportunistic rather than driven by a grand design, and Sukarno as driven by domestic political factors as much as by international ones. They also saw Indonesia as understandably concerned about regional developments that might have implications for its own security, but about which it was not being consulted. The External Affairs view was that Western countries should recognise Indonesia's interests as not being irreconcilable with their own.[26]

In response to Britain's initial request, four-power (or 'quadripartite') talks were scheduled to be held in Washington on 11 and 12 February. On 31 January Barwick conferred with the senior External Affairs officials

Arthur Tange, Keith Waller and Gordon Jockel in order to work out an Australian position. It was agreed that Malaysia was primarily Britain's responsibility and that Australia at this stage need offer no more than moral support 'and the use of our ships'.[27] On 2 February Barwick wrote to Holyoake in New Zealand with an extended statement of his policy. He felt that Australian security interests required that Tunku Abdul Rahman's goodwill be maintained. This did not have to mean supporting Malaysia, a plan with 'many weaknesses'. Creating a state which faced the immediate hostility of its two major neighbours (for the Philippines had a territorial claim of its own to North Borneo) might not be good policy. On the other hand, Indonesian plans to subvert the Borneo territories would have to be firmly opposed. On balance Malaysia should be supported, but there should be no firm commitment to support Britain militarily and the legitimate interests of Indonesia and the Philippines must be recognised.[28] These were broadly the arguments that Barwick took to Cabinet three days later. There he had to contend with Menzies, whose officials regarded the External Affairs line as somewhat negative. In Cabinet Menzies counter-argued that in the face of the Indonesian threat British policy should have Australia's unqualified support. Barwick's line prevailed; Cabinet reiterated its approval of the Malaysia proposal and deplored Indonesia's tactics in Borneo, but endorsed Barwick's view that Britain had to carry primary responsibility for both the creation and the defence of Malaysia. Cabinet also gave explicit priority to the improvement of Australia's relationship with Indonesia.[29]

At the quadripartite talks, where Australia was represented by Tange and Howard Beale, the Ambassador in Washington, the three ANZUS countries all advised Britain to aim at securing Indonesian and Philippines acceptance of Malaysia by diplomatic persuasion. But according to Barwick's subsequent submission to Cabinet, it remained doubtful that Britain would 'seriously attempt to remove, by further consultation, any legitimate grounds there might be for Indonesian and Philippines opposition. The British delegate appeared unwilling or unable to accept that the two countries might have any other motives than cupidity or expansionism'. Australia, New Zealand and the United States also pressed Britain to ensure 'the maximum appearance' of popular consultation in the territories; on this Barwick observed, in similarly critical vein, that doubt remained 'as to whether the British are yet fully aware that there is substantially more for them to do to make Malaysia stand up to international scrutiny'. In fact, Britain put most of its effort at the talks into seeking firm assurances of support for Malaysia. Of greatest importance to Britain was the American attitude. The Americans made it clear that their main interest lay in maintaining their relationship with Indonesia, 'the vital nation in the region', which must on no account be lost to communism. At the same time they approved of Malaysia 'as basically anti-Communist, as a stabilizing force and a means of safeguarding Western interests, both political and military, in the area'. Nevertheless the development and protection of the new state against subversion must be a Commonwealth responsibility.[30] The Americans, as a British commentary on the talks later put it, 'were too deeply committed in Vietnam to wish to take on a second case of the same kind'.[31] The United States did at least indicate that 'in the last resort it would be unlikely to stand by and see a British, or a British-Australian defence of Malaysia fail'. But British attempts to elicit from the Americans a definition of the last resort were unsuccessful.[32]

In Canberra policy continued to evolve. In the week following the quadripartite talks conflicting messages came from Shann in Jakarta and his opposite number in Kuala Lumpur, Critchley (both of them, in Woodard's phrase, 'charismatic heads of mission'[33]). Shann wrote of Malaysia's 'shaky foundations' and suggested that Australia should perhaps pause for second thoughts rather than risk military confrontation with Indonesia. Critchley's view was that it was too late for second thoughts and that there was no option but to press on with Malaysia, if only because the British were determined to decolonise Singapore which it was in Australia's interest to see incorporated within the larger polity. More positively, Critchley felt fairly optimistic about Malaysia's prospects, and also believed that Britain had enough military capacity to deal with any armed threats. Faced with these assessments, External Affairs agreed with Shann that caution was necessary but agreed with Critchley that Malaysia had to proceed. Ultimately, Australia's security interest was a decisive factor. In the Department's judgment, Australia could not hope to divorce itself from Malaysia yet maintain its forward position in Southeast Asia.[34]

This last was certainly a key factor in Barwick's mind, as is apparent from the stress he gave it in his Cabinet submission of 26 February. By this time he had come to the view that in spite of the importance of the Indonesia relationship, Australia must support Malaysia more strongly 'and accept the very real risk that thereby we may cause tension in our relations with Indonesia and that we may be required for an indefinite future to prepare militarily to assist in the defence of the new Federation'. On 5 March Cabinet agreed, at the same time accepting a Defence Committee recommendation that Australia's defence capacity in the region be upgraded.[35] That Barwick had moved from his earlier reserved attitude to a more openly supportive one was interpreted by the British High Commissioner as 'yet another instance where Sir Robert Menzies has exerted his influence in a direction helpful to Britain'.[36] This, however, was to fail to take into account the continuing difference between Barwick and Menzies on the key practical issue of an Australian defence involvement. In a submission to the 5 March meeting prepared jointly with Athol Townley, the Minister of

Defence, Barwick had reiterated his argument against the Government making any formal commitment at this stage to the defence of Malaysia.[37] Menzies remained less than happy with this approach. He returned to the issue in a Cabinet meeting on 28 March, arguing that Australia's undertaking to defend Malaysia should be made firm and specific by way of a formal Australian accession to the Anglo-Malaysia Defence Agreement that would succeed the Anglo-Malaya Defence Agreement of 1957. Australia's current responsibilities in the Commonwealth Strategic Reserve covered defence against internal subversion and external communist aggression, but not Indonesian confrontation; acceding to the new agreement would significantly extend Australia's responsibilities. Against this, Barwick argued that such a step could lock Australia into a disproportionately large defence involvement and would be extremely provocative to Indonesia. Better that the commitment remain unspecified. In any case Australia should not make any firm commitment without some assurance of American backing. This time Cabinet's decision was to make no decision, for the time being at any rate.[38] The consequence was that Barwick remained free to continue formulating Australian policy on Malaysia.

During March Barwick had (against British advice) persuaded Indonesia to agree to a meeting with both the Philippines and Malaya. This initiative led to further meetings between the three and even to the short-lived idea of a loose 'Maphilindo' confederation. Barwick also worked hard in the next few months to garner support for Malaysia among the non-aligned nations. He was conscious of playing rather a lone hand, publicly remarking at one point that Menzies was European in his thinking and out of sympathy with Asia.[39] Not for the first time in Australian policy making, the middle months of 1963 saw bureaucratic tussling between External Affairs, which provided strong support for Barwick's emphasis on building Asian relationships, and the Prime Minister's Department, which under John Bunting usually took a pro-British line. In June, Menzies' sympathy for the British position was made clear once more during talks in London. To Sandys' remark that 'it would give great confidence in the area if Australia could sign a definite commitment to assist Malaysia', Menzies replied that 'this was his personal view but that he had not yet discussed the matter with his Cabinet'. But, he said, he had good news: on the basis of talks with Averell Harriman, the American Under-Secretary of State, he was confident that if Australian troops were engaged in Malaysia the ANZUS Treaty would apply and American support could be expected.[40] Others—including, in due course, President Kennedy—were a good deal less definite on this point.[41]

In London the wish to pin down Australia and New Zealand to specific undertakings to back Malaysia continued to run strong. Britain's motives were not just political and strategic; they were also financial. At a time when the Treasury was demanding economies in defence expenditure, the British Government's plans for a post-colonial settlement in Southeast Asia appeared to entail an actual increase in the defence budget. Pointing this out to Macmillan, the Cabinet Secretary, Sir Burke Trend, urged the importance of persuading the antipodean pair to 'bear a more significant proportion of the cost' of keeping Southeast Asia on an even keel.[42] The goal of inducing others to share the financial and military burdens that were concomitant with decolonisation had been an object of British thinking for some years, and it would remain one for some years to come. But on this occasion Lord Home, the Foreign Secretary, counselled restraint. Earlier Australian and New Zealand doubts about Malaysia 'could easily be revived if they got the impression that we wished to reduce our own military contribution and were asking them to take up commitments that we were going to lay down'. It might be advisable to wait until Malaysia was a *fait accompli* before pressing the matter.[43]

By August, however, with Malaysia's proclamation day looming—it was scheduled now for mid-September—Australian policy was in any case moving closer to the position that Britain was hoping for. The movement in policy followed from an attempt to resolve the tensions between the Prime Minister's Department and the Chiefs of Staff on the one hand and External Affairs on the other. Prime Minister's officials, particularly the senior foreign policy adviser Allan Griffith, took the view that External Affairs was still overly critical of the British and solicitous of Indonesia; their argument was that it was time for Australia to associate itself unambiguously with Malaysia, which was after all a pro-Western country of much strategic significance for Australia. But Tange and others in External Affairs continued to warn of the possibly adverse consequences for the Indonesia relationship. The outcome of interdepartmental discussion was a compromise recommendation, endorsed by the Foreign Affairs and Defence Committee of Cabinet on 12 August, that Australia should extend to all of Malaysia the defence commitments it currently provided through the Commonwealth Strategic Reserve in Malaya, while also stressing that the actual defence of Malaysia would still be primarily a British responsibility.[44]

Shorn of Brunei, which had opted for separate independence, and with North Borneo renamed Sabah, Malaysia came into being on 16 September. Around this time it appeared that a degree of ministerial discontent with Barwick's perceived soft line towards Indonesia was having an effect at Cabinet level, thus pushing policy further towards the Menzies line. Barwick showed the tougher side of his own position by engaging in some notably blunt talk with Sukarno during a stopover while on his way to Kuala Lumpur for the proclamation ceremony. This trend in policy was reinforced when, in reaction to the proclamation of Malaysia, rioters in Jakarta burned down the British (though not the Australian) Embassy. On 20 September Macmillan appealed directly to Menzies: 'I would be most grateful if you would consider allowing Australian forces to participate in operations against insurgents should the necessity arise ... their participation would be a further proof to Sukarno that Australia means to stand no nonsense: it would also I think have a valuable effect in further consolidating American support'.[45] In response to this approach, Cabinet decided that Australia should undertake to provide military assistance if asked, effectively on three conditions: that Australia would need to satisfy itself from its own sources that the military situation justified the request; that the formal request should be clearly supported by the Government of Malaysia; and that Australian assistance would supplement, not supplant, Britain's own military involvement. Menzies announced the Australian policy to Parliament on 25 September.[46] The Government appears to have felt able to make this decision because of its understanding that ANZUS would be operative, possibly on a reciprocal basis: that is, American help in Malaysia in exchange for Australian help in Vietnam.[47] It remained far from obvious what the Australian decision might mean in operational terms, but from late 1963 Barwick made it clear (to the British in the first instance) that Australia's overall approach would be one of 'carefully graduated response'.[48]

Malaysia defended

Through 1964 and into 1965 Sukarno stepped up his campaign. His 'crush Malaysia' policy was expressed both in his fierce rhetoric and in Indonesian border raids and military incursions into the Borneo states, supplemented from August 1964 by troop landings in peninsular Malaya itself. During this period dealings between London and Canberra regularly took the form of British requests for military assistance followed by Australian responses that reflected very considerable caution about taking the plunge. In Canberra's view, Barwick's assumption that Britain had to take the primary role still applied. Moreover, at least until August 1964 the Government's advisers doubted that the military circumstances actually warranted intervention. In any case the Government was still pursuing its policy of trying to improve the relationship with Indonesia. It was seeking also to remain in tune with American thinking which continued to emphasise the importance of not taking actions that might drive Indonesia closer to the communist powers. There was a further complexity, namely a nagging uncertainty among some policy makers as to how full-blooded the American commitment to support Australia under ANZUS actually was. Barwick was quite prepared to make public and private references to ANZUS as a means of putting pressure on

Indonesia, but there were indications that the Americans were put out by this, and Paul Hasluck, who succeeded Barwick as Minister for External Affairs in April 1964, was less outspoken. Hasluck felt—so he told the British—that the very applicability of ANZUS 'put Australia under a moral obligation not to take any action which might unnecessarily involve the United States in war with Indonesia'.[49]

In November 1963 the British had provided their first specific listing of the kinds of assistance they would like to receive. These ranged from anti-aircraft batteries for immediate use all the way up to strike aircraft and the use of an Australian battalion drawn from the Commonwealth Strategic Reserve in the event of full-scale fighting. Australia was slow to reply. In London there was concern that Australia might yet back away from its promise of support and, under American influence, revert to a soft line on Indonesia.[50] For this reason the new British Prime Minister, Douglas-Home, sent a personal note to Menzies on 17 December:

> We are quite confident that the Malaysians and ourselves with Australia and New Zealand can meet whatever threat the Indonesians mount. We intend to remain on top and to demonstrate beyond doubt to the Americans that we have the situation completely under control. I am sure that this more than anything else will bring them to adopt realistic policies . . . I wanted to let you know personally the importance we attach to assistance from Australia which would supplement the forces we and the Malaysians have committed. I hope you will agree to provide it.[51]

Cabinet's Foreign Affairs and Defence Committee, however, did not so agree. This was partly because of the Government's assessment that Britain did indeed have the military situation under control, and partly because of the palpable political importance of retaining influence in Jakarta. Australia, the High Commission in London argued in a despatch of 10 January 1964, 'must choose more subtle, more flexible and perhaps more complicated tactics than might suggest themselves to a retractable Briton sitting 8000 miles away'.[52] Yet there was also resentment that Britain seemed to be implying that Australia was not fully supportive of Malaysia. In the event the Foreign Affairs and Defence Committee decided to authorise nothing more than British military use of the Cocos Islands airfield. At the same time, in a nice illustration of the diplomatic tightrope Australia was walking, Barwick and Shann warned Indonesian leaders that Australia's promise of military support to Malaysia still held good.[53]

These exchanges set something of a pattern. The next few months brought several more formal requests from both Britain and Malaysia, often accompanied by a personal letter ('My dear Bob'). The Government considered these requests closely and showed itself willing to support its allies, up to a point. A policy more or less along the lines of 'carefully graduated response' began to take effect. By the middle of 1964 Australia had contributed transport assistance, a substantial quantity of matériel including two minesweepers and four helicopters, and personnel from all three armed services. What it had not contributed—and had on at least two occasions specifically refused to contribute—were combat troops, for which the Government's advisers continued to discern no military need. On the other side of the balancing act, the effort to stay on good terms with Jakarta continued. Australia's aid program for Indonesia remained in place; so too, notably, did the program of exchanges of military officers at staff colleges. And Shann, whom Sukarno liked personally, kept the diplomatic relationship in good order at the top level.

There were further factors underlying Australian reluctance to meet British and Malaysian requests in full. Very important was the growing conviction in some circles in Canberra that the major military threats to the region came not from Sukarno's harassment of Malaysia but from China and from the communist forces of North Vietnam. The United States was becoming ever more deeply involved in the defence of South Vietnam, and it seemed likely that Australia would be asked by its greatest military ally to join the struggle. But if Australia was to retain the capacity to respond to a worsening situation in Indochina, it would have to try to avoid having its forces tied down by Confrontation to the extent that the British apparently wanted. This was the view pushed by the Department of External Affairs, although there was a degree of resistance from the Prime Minister's Department where Griffith in particular continued to argue that it was more important to support the British with a view to keeping them in the region in strength.[54] Hasluck was strongly of the External Affairs view, and this was endorsed by Cabinet on 1 July. In addition to all this there was a local contingency to take into the reckoning: the possibility that Indonesian forces in Irian Jaya might infiltrate Australian New Guinea, there to mount covert operations. If this possibility became a reality, Australia would have to give priority to the New Guinea front over the engagement in Malaysia, where Britain still appeared to have matters generally under control.

But from August 1964 the situation grew more difficult. The notion that Confrontation was manageable was dented by the launching of Indonesian incursions not just into Sabah and Sarawak but into peninsular Malaya. Open warfare seemed in prospect. Early in September Tunku Abdul Rahman declared a state of emergency throughout the Federation and called on Britain, Australia and New Zealand for assurances of military support if the incursions continued. There ensued a flurry of Australian communications with London, Washington and Wellington, of which the main Australian outcome was a message to Kuala Lumpur conveying an assurance comparable to one Britain had already sent, that in the event of further Indonesian aggression against either peninsular Malaya or Singapore, it would be appropriate for Malaysia's allies to strike against Indonesian targets (meaning airfields). Not that Australia wanted to see this happen. External Affairs felt that any such action by Western forces would carry the risk of tipping Indonesia's internal political balance towards the Indonesian Communist Party (the PKI) and might also undermine the support for Malaysia among the non-aligned nations. Hence Australia urged Britain to share full details of its planning and to make no precipitate moves. At the same time Canberra pressed for further quadripartite talks in the hope of securing better coordination of British and American policies. But the idea of four-power talks remained unacceptable to Washington, with its Vietnamese preoccupations and its insistence that dealing with Confrontation was the Commonwealth's problem. Facing the possibility of armed conflicts in three separate theatres—Malaysia, Vietnam and New Guinea—the Australian Government decided in November that it had no option but to introduce conscription.

The tensions over Confrontation were increasing. Sukarno had proclaimed his 'year of living dangerously' on 17 August, the day of the first Indonesian landings on the Malayan peninsula, and at New Year he followed this with the announcement that Indonesia would withdraw from the United Nations. During January 1965 he spoke of collaborating with China to lead the 'newly emerging forces'. Within Indonesia the PKI was evidently gaining strength. In the same month the Indonesian military greatly augmented a build-up of forces in Borneo that had begun in December, with large numbers of these troops being moved close to the frontiers with Sabah and Sarawak.

On 15 January Douglas-Home's successor in Britain, the Labour Prime Minister Harold Wilson, cabled McEwen, Australia's Acting Prime Minister, about these developments. To meet the threat in Borneo, Wilson argued, there was a need for at least a battalion of troops in addition to the reinforcements that Britain was providing. He did not, in so many words, request Australian troops, and nor did McEwen promise any. But this was the turning point. After intensive discussion in Canberra and consultation with Kuala Lumpur, the Government decided on 27 January that the Australian battalion with the Commonwealth Strategic Reserve would serve in Borneo in rotation with Malaysian and British units. The decision was made public on 3 February, and the troop deployment took place later in the same month. Thus Menzies' pledge of September 1963 was at last fulfilled, but in circumstances far from the Government's liking; as Edwards puts it, 'Britain and America were each concentrating on one campaign, but Australia was being called upon for support in both'.[55] The commitment of an Australian battalion to Vietnam came less than three months later. For Australia too it had become a year of living dangerously. In the end Australia could not avoid making its dual commitment given the Government's powerful desire to keep both its major allies engaged in the region's defence.

Singapore's departure

Once Australia had taken the step of committing troops to the Borneo states the character of the exchanges between Canberra and London became somewhat different, since their main purpose now was to deal with the practicalities of military cooperation.[56] But the next political contretemps was not long in coming. It followed from Singapore's abrupt ejection from the Federation on 9 August 1965, an event which sprang from difficulties between Singapore and Kuala Lumpur and concerning which both Canberra and London were simply marginalised, being neither consulted nor given more than a few hours' warning of what was about to happen. Our interest here focuses on the repercussions of this dramatic event in Australia's dealings with Britain.

On 18 August Wilson cabled Menzies, Holyoake and President Lyndon Johnson proposing a quadripartite meeting to consider the implications of the Singapore-Malaysia rift for British policy in Southeast Asia. Some two weeks later a follow-up memorandum foreshadowed the line the British would take in the talks. Their scenario was very much a worst-case one. With regard to Indonesia, they expected that the PKI would remain powerful and that the policy of Confrontation would be maintained. The government in Kuala Lumpur, now that Singapore was gone and there was no longer a need to have outlying populations that would help to keep the ethnic Chinese in the minority, might come to see Sabah and Sarawak as liabilities and begin to think about letting them go. Increasing pressure on Britain to forsake its military bases in Singapore might also be expected. In these volatile conditions Britain's best option might be to seek a negotiated settlement with Indonesia, accepting that a major reduction in the British military presence would need to be part of the compromise; the implication was that long-term tenure of the Singapore bases could not be guaranteed.[57]

For the Australians the British memorandum was cause for unqualified alarm. Nothing of what it said was what they wanted to hear. Menzies replied to Wilson that the document envisaged simple capitulation, giving Sukarno the two things he wanted most: the dissolution of Malaysia and the departure of British forces.[58] Overall, it seemed to the Australians that the British policy towards the region had changed from firm to soft virtually overnight. The Wilson Government was well known to be under much greater domestic pressure than its Conservative predecessor had been to wind up Britain's post-imperial business in Southeast Asia. It was hard to avoid the conclusion that the Government was now seizing on Singapore's departure almost with gratitude as an excuse for getting Britain off its Southeast Asian hook.

Amid these tensions the four-power talks were convened at some speed, with the Americans this time only too willing to take part since Britain's new thinking had large implications for the United States position in Vietnam. In the talks the Australian, New Zealand and United States delegations made common cause and by all accounts pulled no punches, determined as they all were to hold Britain to its existing commitments. Under this pressure Britain backed away from the idea of early negotiations to end Confrontation. But this was only a tactical retreat. On 25 September Wilson wrote again to Menzies and the other leaders, with the message that Britain would not rule out reviving the idea of negotiations at a later date. On Singapore Wilson said nothing definite, but he did convey the view of his ministers that time was 'not on our side'.[59]

Just five days later there occurred in Jakarta the attempted military coup that led to a truly radical change in the configuration of Indonesian political forces. Over several months the events would unfold: the destruction—by massacre—of the PKI; the gradual easing of Sukarno from power and the consolidation of a primarily military government under Suharto; and, in August 1966, the formal ending of Confrontation. All of this would make it progressively easier for the British to proceed with the plans at which Wilson had hinted. But in mid-October 1965, Indonesia was in turmoil and there was no knowing where events might lead. In this historical moment of high tension and uncertainty, John Bunting prepared for Menzies a short briefing paper on British policy and the problems besetting the Anglo-Australian relationship. He noted that in the weeks since Wilson's message of 25 September, the British had been floating yet another new idea: the neutralisation of Southeast Asia, with neutrality to be maintained in the long term by a kind of natural balance among the political forces native to the region.[60] Bunting was strongly of the view that Menzies should resist such fatalistic thinking:

> Reduction of forces was put to us in the beginning in a financial and economic context. A new slant in British defence policy seems to be amending the context . . . It seems to me that if we disagree with the theory of natural balance in South-East Asia without a Western military presence—as I believe we do—now is the time to make this plain. Mr Wilson's latest message . . . mentions a continuing military posture. We need to cling to this and not let the 'neutralizers' take over.

What is most interesting here is that Bunting saw the differences over Southeast Asia as of a piece with the increasingly problematic character of the whole relationship: 'the sum of our attitudes to Britain in all spheres—defence, trade, external affairs, everything'. On this theme he wrote:

> I do not need to labour this. You know of it, and Hicks has referred to it in the field of aircraft purchases. We should take stock of our relationships and decisions. As things stand, there may be more debits than credits—which, if it continues, is bound to affect our defence interest adversely.[61]

These were remarkable views to be emanating from the Prime Minister's Department, which for so long had been known for the (generally) pro-London line it took in its dealings with other departments, notably the (often) rather less London-oriented Department of External Affairs. There could not have been a clearer indication of how things were changing.

The inauguration of Malaysia, Anthony Stockwell has argued, 'did more to aggravate Britain's problems than enhance Britain's influence in the region'.[62] Nevertheless, for London the formation of Malaysia served to resolve one of the more awkward difficulties of the decolonisation process. For Canberra it appeared more or less consonant with Australian security interests and so was a not unwelcome development. But as things turned out, the launching of the new federation precipitated a series of events that from Australia's point of view not only brought new problems in the already pressured bilateral relationship with Britain but also gave rise to unprecedented challenges in Australia's broader evolution as a foreign policy actor. Collaboration with Britain of course continued, extending in 1965 into joint military action in Borneo. Increasingly, however, there was dissonance and even an element of mistrust on the underlying issue of Britain's willingness, or lack of it, to sustain the military role in Southeast Asia that Australia had always seen as of high importance to regional stability and hence Australian security. As for Australia's development as a foreign policy actor, Confrontation was a steep learning experience. In fact Australia acquitted itself well in the testing task of maintaining good relations with both Indonesia and Malaysia during the period of their hostilities. In this respect it could be said that the problems arising from Britain's post-colonial dispensation in Southeast Asia were, for Australia, a blessing in disguise. Rather as Britain's turn towards Europe, seen at first as a thoroughly demoralising blow against Australian interests, had in fact pushed Australia into much greater, and generally fruitful, efforts to broaden its trade constituency, so in the Southeast Asian context Australia in the Confrontation period learned a good deal about coping with regional contingencies in regional terms. Though the imbroglio in Vietnam would do much to complicate the issues in the next several years, the lessons absorbed during Confrontation would give Australian policy makers a solid base for crafting regional relationships once the war, Australia's last on the Southeast Asian mainland, had run its course.

8

The troops go home

I~N~ F~EBRUARY~ 1965 Sir Robert Menzies outlined to the British Prime Minister, Harold Wilson, a tabulation of Australia's defence commitments in Southeast Asia. Perhaps the most interesting thing about it was the ordering: 'First, there was the almost instinctive obligation, unwritten but there nonetheless, to do all in their power to help Britain. Secondly, there were the contractual obligations under ANZUS. Thirdly, there was the Treaty obligation of SEATO . . . Fourthly, there was the commitment to Malaysia itself'.[1]

Not quite eighteen months later the Permanent Under-Secretary at the Commonwealth Relations Office, Sir Saville Garner, remarked to the Australian Deputy High Commissioner in London, J. L. Knott: 'I know you must appreciate that, if it wasn't for our concern for Australia's interests and protection, Britain would be out of the Far East, lock, stock and barrel and as quick as a flash'.[2]

The implication of both these statements is that the Anglo-Australian relationship remained unusually intimate, to the extent that each country felt a special solicitude towards the other. No doubt the statements were sincerely meant. They seemed, however, a little detached from certain operational realities of the time. By 1965 it was very plain that Australia's key strategic alliance was with the United States; indeed, Menzies was speaking to Wilson less than three months before despatching Australian troops to support the Americans in Vietnam, without benefit of British participation. And by mid-1966, when Garner spoke, it was equally plain that Australia was very far from being the major factor in Britain's calculations about the future of its military forces in Southeast Asia.

The question of what to do with these and other British forces East of Suez (in the Persian Gulf, in the Indian Ocean, in Hong Kong), left over as they all were from Britain's era of imperial authority, became in effect the last major item of 'end of empire' business for Britain. More specifically, for

157

the purposes of this study, in the middle to later 1960s the question of the durability of the British military presence in Malaysia and Singapore became the most salient matter of difficulty between Britain and Australia. In the Australian perspective, the prospect of British military withdrawal loomed as yet another in the series of blows that Britain had dealt Australia in the process of fashioning its post-imperial world role. In fact on this issue, as earlier on Europe, the two countries' interests (as they understood them) were thoroughly at odds, so that the scope for mutual solicitude was virtually non-existent. With hindsight their argument on the issue, which extended over three full years, can be seen as not just the last but also one of the most stressful of the Anglo-Australian interactions occasioned by the dissolution of Britain's empire.

What then was the significance of this episode in the evolution of the Australian relationship with, and attitude towards, Britain? Or, to recast the question in terms of the prospectus set out in the High Commission brief of 1962, which introduced Part II of this study: does the record of exchanges on the withdrawal problem suggest that, by the later 1960s, Australia had learned to look on Britain in an essentially demystified manner—no longer as the object of 'unrealistic sentimentalism', but as something like, at best, a 'business associate'; a 'close and friendly' associate perhaps, but one with whom deal-making was not necessarily going to be easy?

Early warnings

For all the importance Australia attached to the American connection, no one in Canberra wished to see the British quit Southeast Asia. In effect Australia sought to maintain the involvement of both its Western allies, the larger and the smaller. Australian policy makers hoped that the United States and Britain would routinely collaborate with each other and with Australia and New Zealand within a quadripartite framework, such that a shared security doctrine for the region might evolve. By mid-1965 the de facto division of labour that saw the United States and Britain at war in Vietnam and Malaysia respectively also saw Australian and New Zealand participation in both these conflicts. In these circumstances, the question of the durability of British involvement was a major one indeed for Australia.

Canberra was sensitive to the slightest warning signals that British resolve to stay in the region might eventually falter. Within the bureaucracy concerns were being felt as early as the mid-1950s, when doubts about Britain's long-term intentions had been a factor in Australia's progressive espousal of American strategic doctrine and acquisition of American equipment.[3] The Singapore base was described by an External Affairs analyst in March 1959 as 'an increasingly risky bet'.[4]

In May 1960 a British official paper, 'Study of Future Policy (1960–1970)' was discussed at a meeting in London of the Prime Ministers of Britain, Australia, New Zealand and Canada and their staffs. The Australians were quick to note a remark by Lord Mountbatten, Chief of the Defence Staff, that the security of tenure of the base at Singapore was uncertain. As External Affairs officials commented, 'This had not been so clearly stated before—on the contrary, the United Kingdom Government had been taking the line that it will maintain the Singapore base'.[5] Some months later Tange explored the implications in a letter to Bunting:

> Among other things, the [British] paper confirms the practical assumptions we had already made about the uncertain future of the Singapore base. It invites the question whether the United Kingdom will be able to afford to renew her present military apparatus in Asia . . . It is implicit in the paper that the United Kingdom expects Australia (and also New Zealand) to accept an increasing role and responsibility in South-East Asia. We must make this decision for ourselves, and, in making it, we must avoid the false assumption that the United Kingdom has substantial resources to deploy in the area between China and Australia, even in an emergency.[6]

Already, then, the feeling among senior officials in Canberra was that Britain would in due course be looking for a way out. But notwithstanding the hints in the British discussion paper (and Mountbatten's possibly unguarded remark), this was a feeling that the British did not yet wish actively to encourage. They stressed rather that no decisions had been taken. The danger, as British officials put it in a brief for Mountbatten, was that if the Australians came to believe 'that we were losing faith in the tenure of our bases', the consequences could include 'the breakup of ANZAM and further orientation towards America'—neither of which, evidently, the British wished to see.[7] Thus in June 1961 the Commonwealth Secretary, Duncan Sandys, was briefed to reassure the Australians that nothing in Britain's European ambitions stood in the way of existing British policies elsewhere, and that the alliance in Southeast Asia would be sustained.[8]

Not long after this, however, the tone of British communications began subtly to change. In a letter to Menzies and Holyoake in October 1961 Macmillan predicted that old-style military bases might become obsolete with the development of new (read nuclear) weapons and technologies. What Britain would then need would be 'forward operating facilities' rather than bases. He followed up these intimations with a letter in February 1962 which outlined scenarios for Australian and New Zealand defence based on the premise that British retention of bases in Southeast Asia had become impracticable, in which event 'our military contribution would, it seems to me, inevitably have to be mainly based on Australia'.[9]

For the antipodean prime ministers these were not welcome messages. Holyoake wrote of 'painful decisions with sentiment pulling one way and material considerations another'—that is, towards the United States. Menzies stressed that Australian policy remained premised on forward defence, and that 'we should guard against the development of a state of mind that in talking about the possible loss of the Malaysian bases we might come to accept their loss as inevitable'.[10] He showed no interest in Macmillan's hint about the use of Australian facilities, largely because to do so would have been to encourage the development of precisely the state of mind he was anxious to forestall.

Up to the mid-1960s Australia was still (in the words of the High Commission's 1962 brief) Britain's 'best friend in the world'. The evidence suggests that Britain was concerned not to undermine the friendship in any avoidable way, while for Menzies (if not for all of his colleagues) the 'almost instinctive obligation ... to help Britain' remained a powerful motivating factor. And yet there was a developing edginess, a mutual wariness. The matters of Europe, the Commonwealth and immigration were a source of much disaffection on the Australian side. As yet the issue of Britain's long-term plans for its forces in Southeast Asia was of lesser contentiousness. But the exchanges of 1960–62 on this issue show that both Britain and Australia were already formulating the positions that would become manifest in 1964–68, with British assurances having an increasingly conditional character and Australia refusing to concede that the British had any sort of case for departure.

Change in Britain

In October 1964 a Labour government came to power in Britain. Faced with the prospect of dealing with a Labour premier more than twenty years his junior, after the comforts of life with a series of Conservative elder statesmen in Downing Street, Menzies might well have wondered if 'the relationship' could ever be quite the same again. He resorted to wishful thinking, communicating to the vanquished Douglas-Home his belief that 'with the growing recognition in England of your qualities, you can have these boys out inside a year'.[11] It was not to be. Wilson was still there when Menzies retired in January 1966. While it would be simplistic to suggest that sentimentalist notions of race patriotism disappeared from Australia with Menzies' departure for the Cinque Ports—for many people continued to invoke them—his going did make a difference. At the Australian end the relationship was now in the hands of Harold Holt. There was thus a generational change of leadership in both countries. Coral Bell refers to Menzies' 'less anglophile' successors.[12] In fact, Holt unequivocally preferred the Washington connection.

The immediate practical significance of British Labour's arrival on the scene was that it brought a major review of defence expenditure. The new Government faced a financial crisis and was subjected to intense Treasury pressure to make budget economies. Yet at the same time its political constituency was demanding expanded social programs. Defence spending necessarily came under scrutiny. For all this, Wilson and his Defence Secretary, Denis Healey, insisted at the outset that Britain's major power status was not to be compromised. There would still be a British world role. Wilson later wrote that his belief in maintaining British forces abroad arose not from 'considerations of imperial splendour' but from 'thoughts of a contribution to international peacekeeping'.[13] In addition to this, it seems, the new Government at first accepted the rather traditional view that military bases were important for the protection of British trade, investment and supplies of raw materials. 'We cannot afford to relinquish our world role', Wilson told the Commons in December 1964.[14] There was also the not unimportant factor of pressure from Washington; as the Americans put it to British ministers, a British soldier in Hong Kong, Malaya or the Persian Gulf was more valuable to the alliance than one in Germany.[15] In essence, then, the goal of the defence expenditure review was to maintain major power status—but to do it less expensively.

Between late 1964 and early 1968, however, it became cruelly apparent that, far from being unable to afford to relinquish its world role, Britain could not afford to maintain it. A series of financial and economic crises (November 1964, July 1966, November 1967) alternated with defence white papers, defence reviews and Cabinet rethinks (February 1965, February 1966, February 1967, July 1967, January 1968). Wilson and Healey were forced by each fresh crisis to retreat from defence commitments which until then they had insisted were essential. Heavy domestic pressure from the pro-Europeans, the Labour left and the spending ministries intensified the strain on East of Suez policy. In Southeast Asia the ending of Confrontation in 1966 provided further incentive to scale down the military presence. What finally tipped the balance was the devaluation crisis of November 1967, which not only necessitated massive new expenditure cuts but also elevated the pro-Europeans to prominence in Cabinet under the leadership of the new Chancellor Roy Jenkins. In January 1968 the Southeast Asia timetable devised only six months earlier, which had provided for a 50 per cent reduction in the British forces in Singapore and Malaysia by 1971 and complete withdrawal by the mid-1970s, was scrapped; Britain would with-draw completely by 1971.

The story of this disorderly retreat has been much narrated already.[16] The concern here lies in observing the ways in which Australian and British policy makers interacted as it became increasingly apparent that their interests, as they respectively perceived them, were deeply at odds.

The Menzies–Wilson phase

As was shown earlier, Australian suspicions about the durability of Britain's will to remain in Southeast Asia predated by several years the Wilson Government's accession to power. With this culture of scepticism already permeating the Canberra corridors, the Australians must have feared the worst on learning that there would be a defence review—and must have been pleasantly surprised when Wilson and Healey seemed initially to be saying that commitments East of Suez would be protected from the defence cuts. A diplomatic report from London in December 1964 indicated that cuts were most likely to be made in Europe and in the nuclear program, and that the Far East was the area 'least lending itself to economies'.[17] Two months later Healey told Menzies that the British Government had 'more or less' taken a decision to give priority to East of Suez.[18] This was the period when Wilson was most openly determined to preserve the world role; hence these messages, which, if taken at face value, suggested that the interests of Britain and Australia might still be compatible.

But many in Canberra remained on their guard. A Defence Depart-ment commentary on the British Defence White Paper of February 1965 gave succinct expression to Australian doubts:

> The fundamental reason for the British defence review is the Government's determination to reduce the defence vote [by 400 million pounds] to 2000 million pounds. It seems that this objective will only be achieved if something is cut out. A situation could arise where the U.K. Government might wonder to what extent they are under an obligation to Australia to retain forces in the Indian Ocean area. It is a major Australian interest to retain British interest and military presence in the area East of Suez, and there may be a need for some deliberate action on Australia's part to bring this about.[19]

But what action? Nobody in Canberra seemed able to think of any. Pro-posals for 'some deliberate action' by Australia came rather from London. As the British put it in their White Paper, 'in meeting this worldwide role we have a claim upon our allies since we serve interests which are theirs as well as ours. If some of our burdens could be assumed or shared by our allies, we may not need the full range of military power we should require to carry them all alone'.[20] This kind of action was not on Australia's agenda. Many in Canberra believed that burden-sharing—or interdependence, as the British usually preferred to call it—would be used by the British as a device for easing their eventual departure. When the issue was debated in Cabinet in the later part of 1965, Harold Holt, as Treasurer, was one who argued that the idea of burden-sharing should be firmly resisted and that Australia should take a tougher line against London with American assistance.[21] There was also continuing ministerial and official resistance to suggestions from London that a British military base or bases might be established in Australia —a special case of burden-sharing. Again, as noted, this idea had been semi-formally on the agenda for some years. Canberra had several reasons for dis-liking it. Cost was one consideration. Another was the problem of explaining to the electorate why British forces should be stationed in Australia when Australian troops were fighting in Vietnam. But the point of most interest here is that to its opponents the idea carried the same risk as all other forms of burden-sharing, namely that it increased British options for getting out of Southeast Asia. As the Defence Department put it, the danger in even discussing the idea with London was that 'the alternative would develop into the policy'.[22] But with no counter-ideas to offer, Canberra found itself pushed by these British initiatives into a purely reactive stance.

Menzies himself, however, seems to have been, at least for a time, not so adamantly resistant to London's proposals. In July 1965 he met Wilson and Holyoake in London; he was accompanied by Bunting but not by any of his ministers. By this time Wilson's position on East of Suez appeared to have slipped a little, in that he expressed doubt about the long-term viability of the Singapore base. He then reiterated British views on the desirability of collaboration with Australia and New Zealand, 'sharing both the burdens and the facilities'. Menzies remarked that he was not surprised by what he had heard, and (as the British understood him) took the point about Singapore. He further mentioned that he did not think there would be any difficulties about British 'staging and bases' in Australia.[23] Later, Menzies argued in Cabinet that the early commitment of RAAF Mirages to the Butterworth air base in Malaysia might be the best means of persuading the British to stay on.[24] This was the antithesis of the line taken by Holt and others, that the British would use burden-sharing to get themselves off the hook. It might well be concluded that Menzies remained the most suscep-tible of all the Australian ministers to the siren song of race patriotism.

Be that as it may, Menzies reverted to a somewhat tougher line on East of Suez during his final months in office. An important stimulus was Wilson's message of September 1965, written in the wake of Singapore's departure from the Malaysian Federation. In addition to airing the ideas of a negotiated end to Confrontation and the neutralisation of Southeast Asia, Wilson made clearer than ever the view that 'time is not on our side' in Singapore. He mentioned the date 1970, suggested that it would be better to get out in good order than in humiliation, and repeated that future defence arrangements in Southeast Asia must be 'on a fully cooperative basis'.[25] Advising Menzies on a response, Bunting argued that the time had come for 'stiffening Britain' and tackling 'the 1970 complex' that seemed to be emerging:

> An earlier British paper spoke of retiring from Singapore 'in good order'. Mr. Wilson's message now speaks of being forced out of Singapore in humiliation. Translated, both of these things mean a policy of getting out while the getting out is good. Our policy, on the other hand, is that Britain stay there as long as she can, including, if necessary, in humiliation. This needs to be said.[26]

Menzies did say it, in a letter of 22 October. He argued that the British bases were not of merely regional significance but formed an integral part of total Western defence against China. Accordingly 'we should look towards means of staying, even in adversity'.[27] London was rather put out to find that Menzies was not so statesmanlike (that is, receptive to the British point of view) after all. Healey seized upon the phrase 'even in adversity' and minuted to Wilson: 'I believe that you should take him up on this and force him to think it through'.[28] Instructions to this effect were despatched to the High Commission in Canberra. Sir Francis Cumming-Bruce of the High Commission met Menzies who acknowledged that Britain should certainly leave Singapore if the Singapore Government demanded it. But he thought this most unlikely, since British departure would be flatly against the interests of both Singapore and Malaysia. To this Cumming-Bruce retorted: 'that would be correct if we were dealing with rational people'.[29]

Menzies' final word on the matter was contained in a letter to Wilson dated 19 January 1966, just one week before his retirement. The main purpose of this letter was to set out the basic features of a negotiating position that had clearly been settled in discussions with his successor (among others) in preparation for a forthcoming visit by Denis Healey (which his successor would have to handle). Having described it as 'fundamental' that the British should not contemplate total withdrawal from the Far East, he first withdrew his earlier cautious support for the idea of bases and facilities in Australia: they would provide 'no adequate substitute'. They would in any case be extremely expensive for Australia. (By implication, this would be too large a share of Britain's burden for Australia to contemplate.) He next sought a formal statement of Britain's overall strategic concept for Southeast Asia, as a prerequisite for substantive discussions. (The British would have well understood the import of this: a declared strategic concept could prove a useful tool for the Australians in all subsequent exchanges.) Finally, he maintained that the problems of Southeast Asian security could not be resolved through bilateral talks; rather there should be quadripartite talks involving New Zealand and the United States. (The implication of this too would not have been lost on the British, since they knew that New Zealand and the United States were no less keen than was Australia on the continuation of a British presence. Quadripartite talks would pit three against one.)[30]

The Holt–Wilson phase

This was very much the policy platform of the new Prime Minister, Harold Holt, and of such Cabinet colleagues as William McMahon (Treasury), Paul Hasluck (External Affairs) and John Gorton (Works). Holt's mettle was soon tested; within a week of his elevation, Healey arrived in Canberra with a party of officials and military brass for the first full-scale discussion between the two governments on the East of Suez issue. The Australian record of the meeting shows that Holt held to his predetermined position almost (but not quite) throughout the two days of talks. Repeatedly he stated that the real need was for a round of quadripartite talks and the development of a joint strategic concept. Only then could consideration of practicalities be undertaken. As for the British desideratum of burden-sharing, Holt and McMahon set out in their opening addresses to pre-empt any close consideration by presenting facts and figures which purported to show that Australia was in no position to contribute more to the defence effort than it was already doing. They argued that Australia's forces were already at full stretch (not only in Malaysia but in Vietnam and New Guinea), and that Australian resources should be directed not into expanding the defence budget but into national development, since in the long term this would constitute Australia's best contribution to regional security.[31]

Healey found the Australians, with the exception of Hasluck, 'not over-impressive'; and even Hasluck was 'rigid and unimaginative'. He noted that Gorton, Fairhall (Defence) and Hulme (Postmaster General) did not speak at all during the talks, and later recalled the meeting as a seminar conducted by himself. For that matter he was not much impressed by Canberra: 'a sort of Milton Keynes with wallabies'. But most of all he was unimpressed by the Australians' inflexibility. On the second day things became a good deal more heated. According to the New Zealand minister who was present, Healey became increasingly impatient and resorted to startlingly colourful language.[32] Having stressed several times that although the British were determined to maintain their world role it was necessary to consider all contingencies, Healey was eventually moved to utter a none too veiled threat: if his Cabinet colleagues 'were not satisfied with the kind of response which he had received in Canberra, the British would remain free to act unilaterally'.[33] Shortly afterwards Holt backed down on the Australian bases issue, at least to the extent of agreeing that officials could, without commitment, proceed to examine questions of feasibility. This was written into the communiqué. For his part, Healey agreed to let it be said in the communiqué that Britain intended to maintain a military presence in the Far East, that four-power talks would be held and that a strategic concept would be developed. In the judgment of the British High Commissioner Sir Charles Johnston, who had attended the talks, the very specific concession by Holt was more significant than Healey's imprecise assurances, leaving the British holding 'an unqualified advantage'.[34]

In the event nothing came of the bases plan. Healey later remarked that 'we held out our hand [with the bases proposal], and the Australians, if they had had any sense, could have nailed it. But they didn't'.[35] Yet it was at least possible that the British themselves were never entirely serious about the plan. T. B. Millar suggests that it was essentially a Healey gambit 'to give the Australians something else to think about while the British forces beat their final retreat'.[36] An opinion supportive of this view comes, interestingly, from Richard Crossman, the left-wing British minister (and Australian *bête noire*) who was one of the strongest advocates of speedy withdrawal. It was Crossman's impression that the Cabinet Defence Committee 'very much hope the Australians will turn us down when we ask for a British presence there . . . it is only on this assumption that we can possibly keep our defence budget within the limit the Cabinet has set'.[37]

From the time of the Holt–Healey talks until the denouement two years later, the British offered but a single sop to the Australians. In a speech in Canberra in June 1966 the Foreign Secretary, Michael Stewart, declared that in the event of an attack on Australia, Britain, mindful of the antipodean efforts on Britain's behalf in two world wars, would unhesitatingly come to Australia's defence. He invoked sentiment: this was not a matter of treaties or legal obligations, it would simply be 'unthinkable' for Britain to do otherwise. This was intended to be a statement of some significance; its wording had been fine tuned, it had been cleared at Cabinet level, and British officials thereafter went out of their way to draw the Australians' attention to it. But it failed to mollify Holt and his colleagues. The guarantee they wanted was not a British expeditionary force, but a British regional presence.[38]

The difficulties besetting Holt through 1966 and 1967 might be summarised thus. First, he wanted the British to stay but was reluctant to pay their price; his fear was that burden-sharing would have the counter-productive effect of making it easier for them to leave. Second, he wanted to tie them into quadripartite planning for the region on the basis of a shared strategic doctrine, but they were not going to fall for that one. Third, he commanded no significant bargaining chips, or other means of putting pressure on Britain. He could not try to turn Australia's role in Confrontation to political advantage, for by mid-1966 Confrontation was effectively over, and it would have been out of the question to threaten to withdraw Australia's forces from the Commonwealth Strategic Reserve. Fourth, the Australian factor was in any case declining rapidly in relative importance from London's point of view. The main forces pushing the Wilson Government towards its East of Suez decisions arose from economic crises and political conflicts at home; against these, and *pace* Sir Saville Garner, Canberra's concerns were relegated to a minor place. Ergo, fifth, all Holt could do was to try to regain London's attention from time to time by sheer force of argument.

Holt, thought by British officials to be 'in a considerable stew',[39] took a good deal of advice, especially from Hasluck and Bunting, on the best way of framing Australia's case. The task was not easy. His advisers stressed that he should leave the British in no doubt as to the strength of Australian feelings. But to argue from naked self-interest would make it too easy for Britain to do likewise. In addition Bunting insisted that he should say nothing that might imply 'something less than full confidence' in Wilson—difficult advice to accept, since Holt's confidence was indeed less than full. Generally, Hasluck felt, he should try to exploit Wilson's sense of Britain's historic world role. Certainly he should invoke 'ties of family sentiment and dangers undergone together'. He should also stress the psychological importance of Britain's stabilising influence in Southeast Asia—a coded way of rebutting the British argument that 'white faces' had ceased to be acceptable on the Asian mainland.[40]

Further counsel came from the Australian High Commissioner in London, Sir Alexander Downer. By far the most Anglophile of the senior Australians, and one much given to invoking the 'unbreakable ties of affection, family, institutions and history'[41] between the two countries, Downer was nevertheless deeply disturbed by the policies and attitudes of the British politicians currently in power. Sensing perfidy, he argued for much greater forthrightness from Holt; his fear was that if the Australians were too polite, 'our British friends, with intellectual dishonesty, will twist our phrases publicly into signifying acquiescence . . . Many prominent people here are now in a mood to use every weapon to justify their desertion of the Old Commonwealth'.[42]

As High Commissioner, Downer was Australia's front line representative. But he was apparently unable to make much of an impression on the

Wilson Government. In May 1966, following a mini-revolt in the British Labour Party against the East of Suez policy (on the grounds that the Government was delaying withdrawal too long), Holt instructed Downer to call on Wilson to seek assurance that he would hold firm against his back bench. Wilson was angered by what he saw as Holt's panic reaction: 'I don't like this at all . . . it is none of his business', he minuted to his officials. Downer went ahead with his visit and evidently believed that it was successful ('I always find him a very easy man to talk with . . . I formed the impression that Wilson was perfectly genuine in what he said' about holding the line).[43] Downing Street's perception was rather different. Wilson was 'at pains' to convey his irritation to Downer—but Downer appears not to have spotted this. 'They have been *very* stupid', noted Wilson's private secretary.[44] Several months later Healey remarked with calculated candour to Alf Parsons, the Australian High Commissioner in Singapore, that 'poor old Alex . . . really doesn't understand us and we find there is not much point in talking to him . . . how much longer does he have to serve?' Parsons, as he confesses in his memoirs, could not bring himself to report Healey's pointed remark to Canberra, 'consoling myself that any such report would only add to the tension between the two governments'.[45]

Meanwhile Downer was expending effort in London in a search for British allies. He was depressed to find that their number was small and dwindling. 'What does worry me is the growing body of vociferous opinion, not only in the Labour Party, but amongst our Conservative friends, which seems to favour Britain withdrawing', he reported in June 1966.[46] Thirteen months later he found 'quite shocking' the fact that *The Times* had come out for withdrawal. Only the *Daily Telegraph* and the *Daily Express* and a few Conservative peers, it seemed, were still willing to take Australia's, and more generally the Commonwealth's, part.[47]

But by this time even the *Sydney Morning Herald* at home was editorialising on the inevitability of Britain's departure and the need for Australia to adjust. Allan Griffith in the Prime Minister's Department attributed the *Herald*'s line to the paper's editor J. D. Pringle, 'who is an Englishman with no deep commitment to Australia . . . I would suspect that Pringle is a friend of Richard Crossman'. The matter should be taken up with the *Herald*, Griffith felt, 'at Warwick Fairfax's level'.[48] This suggests something of a siege mentality in the highest policy-making circles. The greater the pressure on the Australian Government to modify its stance, the more inflexible it seemed to become.

Through all this, Holt was doing his best to reconcile the strands of advice he had received and to present a coherent case. He sent Wilson a steady stream of hortatory letters, and twice, in June 1966 and June 1967, flew to London to press the case in person.[49] Wilson, grappling with his crises at home, remained unmoved, and in fact Holt's efforts were fore-doomed as long as Australia refused either to concede any part of Britain's case or to make offers of material support for Britain to consider. The record of the June 1967 meeting—the last between Wilson and Holt—reveals that Holt did budge a fraction, with a suggestion that old-Commonwealth coun-tries, including Australia, might be able to contribute to the cost of a resi-dual British presence in Singapore. But this was too little too late, evidently; the British showed no interest.[50] More typical of Holt's tactics was his pre-sentation of a document which quoted back at the British the various pledges they had made over the years: 'He wished to assure the Prime Minister that this had not been done in any carping or critical spirit; but . . . it was important that there should be no misunderstanding about the extent to which Australians believed that Britain was committed to a certain posi-tion in the area'.[51] This too cut no ice.

The Australians had one card left to play: the American one. The British might have stopped listening to Canberra, but must surely take Washington seriously. Cabinet approved in May 1967 the text of a letter for Holt to send to President Johnson:

> The course which Britain appears to have set must cause you great concern—not necessarily so much in the matter of the loss of defence potential, but in matters such as the stability and confidence of Asia, your own presence in Asia and, in fact, British/American co-operation on the wider world sphere. I would have thought that we, for our part, but also you particularly, must seek to persuade the British back into a full role in world affairs.[52]

Some degree of collaboration on the issue did develop between Canberra and Washington. Holt visited Johnson in Washington in June 1967, while Hasluck and Dean Rusk regularly compared notes and on various occasions, in company with the New Zealand foreign minister, confronted the British Foreign Secretary George Brown in a quadripartite context.[53] But in fact the Americans did not need any urging from Canberra. They were mired in Vietnam and only too anxious not to be left as the sole Western power in Southeast Asia. Johnson's messages to Wilson and Rusk's to Stewart and Brown were a good deal more robust, even peremptory, than any messages that emanated from Canberra. 'This is not the time to be rocking the boat', Rusk snapped in July 1967.[54] In the end none of these representations made any difference. Tom Critchley reported from the External Affairs Office in Australia House just before the last great debate in the British Cabinet that 'external factors such as United States influence or pressure from Australia New Zealand Malaysia and Singapore are unlikely to have much effect'.[55] This was in January 1968, by which time the Australian Government, without Holt who had recently died by drowning, knew very well that the game was up.

The end came after what was by all accounts a bitter struggle in the British Cabinet, with Roy Jenkins' pro-Europeans making common cause with Richard Crossman's left-wingers to defeat a last ditch attempt by George Brown's Bevinites to hold off the final withdrawal until the mid-1970s. The news that the date had been advanced to 1971 was brought to the Australian Cabinet in person by a somewhat hapless British emissary, the Commonwealth Relations Secretary George Thomson, to whom the Australians listened 'with dismay and anxiety'.[56] Yet once their 'profound' disagreement had been registered for the record,[57] the Australians under their new Prime Minister, John Gorton, did adjust, and quickly. A Malaysian proposal for a five-power defence arrangement involving Britain, Australia, New Zealand, Malaysia and Singapore had been in circulation for some six months. So far the Australians had declined to take part in discussions of this plan, in conformity with their strategy of not creating an alternative which might then become policy. But now they became willingly involved. It is relevant to note that Gorton himself had earlier argued in Cabinet—contra both Menzies and Holt—that there was no point in seeking to dissuade the British from a course they were certain to take, and that Australia must look to the future.[58] With the British decision made, his opportunity had come to take part in the construction of alternative arrangements.

To the end some people in both countries continued to talk about the traditional bonds. Immediately before the final round of debates in the British Cabinet, the British Defence Planning Staff was asked to prepare a paper outlining the purposes of a post-East of Suez defence policy. In an echo of Michael Stewart's pledge, it suggested as one of these purposes: 'to meet our moral obligations to contribute to the defence of Australia and New Zealand if they were attacked'. The phrase 'moral obligations' is of interest, suggesting as it does a British perception, even among defence planners, that the relationship was still something more than instrumentalist. The paper went on, however: 'we further assume that our special moral obligation towards Australia and New Zealand would be regarded, at the least, as open to review'.[59] Here, then, was another of those documents from which, had they known about it, Canberra and Wellington could not have drawn much comfort. But at this particular historical moment they would perhaps not have been much surprised either.

From time to time officials on both sides expressed concern at the possible impact of the East of Suez dispute on the wider relationship between Australia and Britain. Late in 1965, as will be recalled, Bunting had written to Menzies about the defence and other problems clouding the Anglo-Australian relationship: 'We should take stock of our relationships and decisions. As things stand, there may be more debits than credits'. At about the same time Sir Charles Johnston sent a warning message to London: 'This is an issue on which Australians of all shades of opinion feel deeply. Unless it is very carefully handled it could have a deplorable effect on our relations with this country'.[60]

Yet in the course of the East of Suez dispute each government focused on the pursuit of its perceived interest with little apparent regard for the wider task of nurturing the relationship. To the pragmatic Wilson, the Australian factor probably became something of a nuisance, and was certainly of diminishing importance, as the argument wore on. To Holt and Gorton, Anglophilia meant a good deal less than it had done for Menzies; both always looked more to the United States.[61] Even so, the notion that the Anglo-Australian connection was evolving towards a relationship between 'business associates', dealing with each other in a straightforward, no-nonsense fashion, does not seem to capture the full reality. What is revealing is that matters became so fraught. The protracted exchanges on East of Suez tended, as James Richardson has put it,

> To bring out the worst in both governments: on the British side, the tendency to reiterate firmer pledges than the situation allowed, leading inevitably to a sense of betrayal; on the Australian side a failure of anticipation, an apparent blindness to the pressures building up in Britain, a chiding tone and a lack of generosity and gratitude towards a power which had been carrying a disproportionate share of the burden of the security of Australia's own region.[62]

Here, in brief, was a dispute very similar in kind to the earlier argument over the Common Market. On each occasion the metropolitan country re-evaluated key interests and changed policy direction in the process of fashioning a post-imperial role for itself. And on each occasion the peripheral country felt abandoned and cried foul. These were not easy passages between Britain and Australia. Suspicion and exasperation pervaded their exchanges. With reference to Australia, Richardson's phrase 'sense of betrayal' is not too strong. The point is that the very strength of these feelings suggests how intimate the relationship had been until only a short time before. Hurt feelings were a legacy of the way things had been. All of which suggests that in 1964–68, it would have been premature to use the notion of business associates as if it provided a sufficient characterisation of the relationship.

But this is not to say that the traditional ties still functioned in the relationship as some kind of significant determining variable. It is true that for some individuals traditional sentiments were still sincerely felt. It is also true that in the Holt–Wilson period each side could still seek to apply moral pressure on the other by invoking the traditional ties. But such use of sentimentalist argument was plainly self-interested. Moreover, each side remained largely unmoved by the other's appeals to sentimental considerations. Looking at this matter from the Australian point of view, it becomes tempting to introduce metaphor: if the Common Market dispute left race patriotism seriously wounded, the East of Suez dispute administered the *coup de grâce*. Tempting, and no doubt facile. The demise of a sentiment cannot be so neatly dated. After all, monarchism lives on in Australia to this day. But what can certainly be argued is that the two great disputes of the 1960s, along with the removal of the personal influence of Robert Menzies midway through the decade, effectively concluded the role of race patriotism as a motivating force in Australian external policy.

By way of final illustration, we might note a pair of decisions taken by the Holt Government on some quite different matters. One was the decision in 1967 to remove the words 'British' and 'British subject' from Australian passports—a move never contemplated in Menzies' time. The other, mooted first in 1966 and approved in the following year, was the decision to limit appeals from the High Court to the Privy Council in matters of federal jurisdiction. The politics of this second matter is of particular interest, since Cabinet considered the issue with East of Suez very much in mind. In 1966 Cabinet balked at finalising the decision precisely because 'regard needed to be had to the importance of maintaining links with Britain in the context of encouraging the maintenance of a British presence East of Suez'. When a year later the Attorney-General, Nigel Bowen, again recommended the abolition of appeals, he pointed out to Cabinet that 'now that the British have announced withdrawal of land forces East of Suez', this consideration had lost its weight. Cabinet accepted Bowen's recommendation apparently without demur. Holt thereupon wrote disingenuously to Wilson: 'My purpose in writing is to assure you that there is no special significance to be attached to this decision nor the timing of it'. And the British played along. Anticipating press queries, the Commonwealth Office in London assured the High Commissioner in Canberra that 'we shall firmly discount any suggestion that Australian decision stems from some sort of disillusionment with Britain (e.g. over E.E.C. or East of Suez policy) or that it represents any weakening of the close relations between the two countries'.[63]

This at least was the diplomacy of the matter. But to revisit once more the language of the High Commission's 1962 brief: even if it remained true (as it quite possibly did; this is a relative judgment) that Australia was Britain's best friend in the world, it was also true that the drift towards different futures had become reality.

Conclusion

THIS BOOK HAS SOUGHT to make a contribution to the understanding of Australia's evolution as a foreign policy actor by taking two themes that have generally been construed as separate narratives and bringing them into a single framework. The first theme is that of the terminal phase of Britain's formal empire: the management of empire in the 1950s, the dissolution of empire in the 1960s, and the aftermaths of that dissolution. The second theme is the development of Anglo-Australian relations in the same period. Systematic consideration of the connections between these themes has not been attempted before. Yet without such consideration the understanding of Australia's changing relationship with Britain and the broader development of Australian external policy in the 1950s and 1960s must be seen as less than complete. The book has attempted to demonstrate this by reconsidering various well-studied themes in the history of Australian foreign policy in that period (such as policies towards 'Europe', and 'security'), with particular reference to their imperial and post-imperial aspects; by bringing to light some other relevant themes which have barely been studied at all (such as Australian mini-imperialism); and by combining these concerns in a single integrated narrative. In these ways the book has aimed not to supplant, but certainly to supplement, the already existing wisdoms.

Commonly the development of Australian external policy in the post-war decades has been interpreted largely in terms of a Cold War explanatory framework. In this respect studies of Australian policy can be seen as quite representative of writings on the history of post-war international relations in general. The work of John Darwin has been quoted more than once in this work, but here it is worth quoting again: 'much of the literature on post-war world politics has been highly Amerocentric in its interests and outlook, preoccupied with Superpower rivalry and intra-West relations. It has been easy to regard most of the world as a series of regional sideshows to the great drama of East-West conflict.'[1] And because decolonisation occurred during the Cold War period, it has perhaps been just as easy to interpret its significance largely in terms of the Cold War preoccupations, such as the East-West balance. Of course an understanding of the Cold War is relevant to the interpretation of decolonisation; that is one of the themes pursued in this book. But the converse also holds true. For 'imperialism' and 'colonialism' need to be seen as important explanatory categories in their own right, just as they had been since long before the Cold War—and indeed, the twentieth century—began. By positing a distinctive explanatory role for imperial/colonial concerns, and by using them as a kind of prism through which to view familiar material differently, this study has tried to bring out the interplay between imperial/colonial concerns and strategic/geopolitical ones, and so to modify the kind of thinking that, in dealing with Australia's international policies of the post-war period, has tended to rely excessively on the explanatory power of the Cold War.

To get down to some specifics: in the 1950s the relevance of the British colonial empire to Australia's concerns was a good deal stronger than has generally been perceived. This was the case in a number of realms. First, in the psycho-cultural realm the existence of formal empire was perceived by the Australian political leaders quite largely in terms of their sense of their own Britishness, contributing thereby to their generally pro-imperialist understanding of the world order. Put differently: empire helped to express and to underwrite Britain's larger world role, something that Australia still valued highly even as it increasingly looked to the United States for global leadership. Second (and relatedly), there was the matter of Australia's physical security, something that in Australian thinking had always been strongly associated with the proximity of colonial empires. In the 1950s Australia's perceived security interests were still quite extensively bound up with the fortunes of the British Empire, especially in the Southeast Asian region but also, to varying lesser extents, in such regions as the Indian Ocean, the South Pacific, and even Africa. Third, there was an established pattern of Australian economic interests in British dependent territories. Fourth, there was the realm of Australia's own policies as a colonial power, especially in Papua and New Guinea, for which many saw British imperial experience as a template. And fifth, there was the broader realm of Australia's policies as an international actor, for example in the multilateral contexts provided by the United Nations, where imperial and colonial issues were constantly under scrutiny, and the Commonwealth, where the same kinds of issues became ever more salient as the years passed.

From the Australian point of view, in short, the fact of colonial empire not only played its part in the modalities of the Anglo-Australian relationship but also bore directly upon material Australian interests. The Government knew very well that devolution of power in the remaining areas of formal empire was going to come eventually. But it was in no hurry to contemplate the necessary policy adjustments, and until quite late in the 1950s simply did not anticipate any need to do so in the short to medium term.

But then, from 1960 onwards, came the second great wave of decolonisation. The speedy dissolution of Britain's formal empire had important implications both for the Anglo-Australian relationship and for the larger evolution of Australian external policy. For a start, the fact that so many of the post-colonial new states were at best non-aligned in world politics, and at worst anti-Western, posed a number of problems. The need to foster the goodwill of new states, and in the process to counteract the proselytising efforts of the Soviets and the Chinese, became a significant Cold War concern; so too did the wish to protect Australia's supply and communications routes to and from the northern world. There was also a concern to minimise the disruptive potential of post-colonial Afro-Asian alliances in international bodies, not only for reasons to do with the Cold War but also with a view to preserving Australia's domestic policies on race and immigration from international attack; South Africa's forced departure from the Commonwealth in 1961 seemed all too ominous a precedent. And meanwhile the wind of change, now so swiftly sweeping away all the major European empires, could perhaps be seen as carrying a message for Australia's own colonial policy. By June 1960 Menzies was prepared to concede that 'if in doubt you should go sooner, not later'. In the case of Papua and New Guinea, however, it seemed that 'sooner' was still, in the eyes of the Government, open to latitudinarian interpretation.

In addition to these matters, there were difficulties arising from Britain's effort to reconstruct its world role in the aftermath of empire. There would now be a much greater emphasis in British external policy on nuclear defence and on relations with the industrialised north (Europe, the United States) at the partial expense of relations with the agrarian south (the old Empire, including its Commonwealth components). From the early 1960s Australian policy makers struggled to come to terms with several unwished for problems arising from these changes in British policy. The impact of decolonisation on the Commonwealth itself provided a leading example, made the more problematic for Australia's leaders in that Britain's desire to use the Commonwealth as a vehicle for continuing influence beyond NATO entailed the cultivation of leaders such as Nehru of India, who stood for most of the values that Menzies (in particular) found most alien. The backwash of empire led also to the revision of British immigration policy such that Australians—bearers of 'British passports' though they were—no longer enjoyed the right of automatic entry to Britain. On the security front, de-colonisation was associated with shifts in British defence doctrine towards a more nuclear-based strategy; the clear and unwelcome implication of this was that British conventional forces in Australia's region would be cut back. And then there was Britain's approach to the European Economic Community, an episode that was quite central to the loosening not just of the commercial ties but of the sentimental ones as well.

As the 1960s unfolded, Britain's retreat from empire brought still further problems for Australia. To facilitate the decolonisation of Southeast Asia Britain put together the Federation of Malaysia. It thereby aroused the wrath of Indonesia. Australia found itself in the awkward position of trying to stay on good terms with both sides. Once Confrontation had developed to the point of armed hostilities, Australia felt bound to become involved militarily on the Malaysian-British side. It was then saved from what might have become a serious military confrontation of its own with Indonesia only by the providentially timed fall of Sukarno. Thus was Australia inducted into the hard world of post-colonial international politics in its immediate neighbourhood.

Finally came the British military withdrawal from Southeast Asia. Though this development had long been regarded by officialdom in Canberra as inevitable, the Australian Government fought to the end to fore-stall, or at least delay, the outcome. It bears repeating that empire never did provide a security guarantee. Its role in the Cold War era was little more than supplementary to the American role in Australian strategic thinking. Nevertheless, for the Australian Government a special kind of value attached itself to the British military presence in the region. For historical reasons, Britain was, along with New Zealand, Australia's most natural ally. In one way or another the three countries had operated together in the region since the 1940s, and they had fought together against a regional adversary as recently as the mid-1960s. In the event, none of this counted for much in the estimation of a post-imperial Britain. Southeast Asian bases were an imperial relic that had become both militarily irrelevant and economically unsustainable. And so Australia learned another in its series of post-imperial lessons. The essence has been well captured by John Subritzky: 'withdrawal from East of Suez did not merely change Britain's national identity from that of global to European power. It also fundamentally transformed Australia and New Zealand from outposts of the Empire/Commonwealth to nations whose identity and future now rested entirely in the Asia-Pacific region'.[2]

Almost all the events described in this book took place during Robert Menzies' lengthy second term as Prime Minister. Menzies came to accept the inevitability of the passing of formal empire. But as one whose world 'had been ordered largely by colonial empires',[3] he was saddened by the process and did not find it easy to cope with some of its major consequences. Decolonisation brought, for example, the 'nest of republics', a development that hastened the demise of the older ideal of organic empire by which Menzies had once set great store. In this context the quality of the Anglo-Australian relationship itself seemed to suffer. Beyond that, as has been stressed in the book, the repercussions of decolonisation extended into areas as diverse as Cold War strategy, regional security, European integration and the politics of the United Nations. In all these areas Menzies saw changes, or potential changes, for the worse.

Yet although Menzies regretted Britain's turning away from the imperial circle to fashion its future elsewhere, Australia during his prime ministership acted not very differently from Britain in that it greatly expanded the pursuit of its interests in international contexts other than the imperial one. Sentimental considerations aside, the instrumental importance of empire to Australia came to be considerably outweighed by the importance of relationships with the major Pacific powers. This was already the case by the end of Menzies' prime ministership. Nothing showed this more clearly than the fact that at the very end of his tenure Australia found itself embarking upon an Asian war in collaboration with the United States—an experience that would prove to be a major watershed in the history of Australia's efforts to find its 'place' in its own region.

The historical irony, in short, was that the imperial factor lost its importance in Australia's external policies during the prime ministership of Robert Menzies, a leader who had always drawn a significant strand of his personal and political identity from a sense of imperial belonging. It was symbolically appropriate that his retirement from politics occurred in the mid-1960s, just when empire was ceasing to be.

Notes

Abbreviations

CO	Colonial Office
CPD, HR	*Commonwealth Parliamentary Debates*, House of Representatives
CRO	Commonwealth Relations Office
DEA	Department of External Affairs
DFAT	Department of Foreign Affairs and Trade
FAD	Foreign Affairs and Defence Committee
FO	Foreign Office
NAA	National Archives of Australia
NLA	National Library of Australia
PRO	Public Record Office, London

Introduction

[1] Quoted in Ward, *Australia and the British Embrace*, p. 3.

[2] Mandle, *Going it Alone*; John Arnold, Spearritt and Walker (eds), *Out of Empire. The Demise of the Imperial Ideal* is the subtitle of Ward's *Australia and the British Embrace*.

[3] Bolton, 'The United Kingdom', p. 220.

[4] See for example Alomes, *A Nation at Last?*; Meaney, 'Britishness and Australian identity'.

[5] See for example Bridge (ed.), *Munich to Vietnam*; Lee, *Search for Security*.

[6] See for example Crawford (ed.), *Australian Trade Policy*; Dyster and Meredith, *Australia in the International Economy*.

[7] Many of the contributions in John Arnold, Spearritt and Walker (eds), *Out of Empire*, discuss cultural issues.

[8] Ward, 'Sentiment and self-interest', p. 107.

[9] Connors, 'Identity and history', p. 136.

[10] Macintyre, 'Australia and the Empire'.

[11] Connors, 'Identity and history', p. 133.

[12] Rickard, 'Imagining the unimaginable?', p. 128.

[13] Davidson, 'The de-dominionisation of Australia', pp. 149–51.

[14] This phrase derives from Carrère d'Encausse and Schram, *Marxism and Asia*, p. 5. For these authors dis-Europeanisation began with the Japanese defeat of Russia in 1904–5 and culminated in the American failure in Vietnam.

[15] Darwin, 'Decolonisation and world politics', p. 7. Emphasis in original.

[16] Ward, *Australia and the British Embrace*.

[17] Eric Harrison, Australian High Commissioner in London, in conversation with Duncan Sandys, Commonwealth Relations Secretary, as reported in F. Mills to Sir Alexander Clutterbuck, Under-Secretary, CRO, 24 May 1961, DO161/161, PRO.

[18] Holland, *The Pursuit of Greatness*, p. 330.

Part I Living with Britain's empire

[1] Hughes, 'Introduction', p. xiii.

1 Empire: the view from Canberra

[1] Quoted in Parkinson, 'America dismissed Australia's war hopes'.

[2] Dunn, *Australia and the Empire*, p. 156.

[3] Day, 'The US alliance? Same as it ever was'.

[4] Meaney, 'Britishness and Australian identity', p. 81.

[5] Ibid., p. 87.

[6] Bridge, 'Globalisation?'

[7] Ibid.

[8] Spender, *Exercises in Diplomacy*, p. 39.

[9] Barclay, *Friends in High Places*, p. 42.

[10] Menzies to Fadden, 3 August 1950, in Holdich, Johnson and Andre (eds), *The ANZUS Treaty*, p. 19.

[11] Sir Keith Officer, 'Notes on talk concerning a Pacific Pact', 13 October 1950, in Holdich et al. (eds), *The ANZUS Treaty*, p. 26.

[12] Millar (ed.), *Australian Foreign Minister*, pp. 24, 84 (Casey's diary entries for 14 July 1951 and 3 August 1952).

[13] Gifford, 'The Cold War across Asia', p. 183.

[14] Pitty, 'The postwar expansion of trade', pp. 241–2, 451–2 note 37; Fraser's remark quoted from Peter Golding, *Black Jack McEwen: Political Gladiator*, Melbourne University Press, Carlton, 1996, p. 192.

[15] Spender to Eric Harrison, Australian Minister Resident in London, 21 February 1951, in Holdich et al. (eds), *The ANZUS Treaty*, pp. 94–9.

[16] Lee, *Search for Security*, pp. 127–34.

[17] Ibid., ch. 5.

[18] Note by Eden, Foreign Secretary, 'Indo-China', 15 June 1954, CAB129/68, C(54)199, PRO.

[19] Quoted in Hudson, *Blind Loyalty*, p. 131.

[20] Home to Menzies, 15 January 1957, Menzies Papers, MS4936, Series 1, Box 10, Folder 82, NLA. 'Selwyn' was Foreign Secretary Selwyn Lloyd.

[21] Quoted in Hudson, *Blind Loyalty*, p. 130.

[22] On which see Lorna Arnold, *A Very Special Relationship*.

[23] Reynolds, *Australia's Bid for the Atomic Bomb*. Reynolds also argues (pp. 168–70) that Menzies' nuclear ambitions were a factor in his Suez policy.

[24] Menzies to Macmillan, 29 June 1961; Macmillan to Home, 24 July 1961; numerous intra-Whitehall minutes; Macmillan to Menzies, 14 August 1961; all in PREM11/3202, PRO.

[25] Woodard, 'Best practice in Australia's foreign policy', p. 86.

[26] Quoted in Philip Bell and Bell, *Implicated*, p. 138.

[27] Ibid.

[28] Hasluck to Menzies, 8 November 1956, A1838/283, 338/1/1, part 4, NAA.

[29] For a discussion see Ward, *Australia and the British Embrace*, ch. 1.

[30] Menzies to Eden, 1 November 1956, DO35/6336, PRO.

[31] Lowe, 'Making sense of decolonisation', p. 444.

[32] Quoted in Cabinet memo by Lord Swinton, Commonwealth Relations Secretary, 'Commonwealth membership', 16 February 1955, CAB129/73, C(55)43, PRO.

[33] Quoted in Tsokhas, *Making a Nation State*, p. 145.

[34] Pemberton, 'An imperial imagination', p. 164.

[35] The Australian Labor Party's colonial policy is a theme of interest in its own right, but it is not pursued further here since this work is a study of government-to-government relations in a period when the ALP was not in government. For a discussion see Waters, 'War, decolonisation and postwar security', pp. 110–11, 121–3. Further insights into the ALP's approach to colonial problems while in office during the 1940s can be gleaned by following up the index references to 'Australian Labor Party' and 'Evatt' in Hudson, *Australia and the Colonial Question at the United Nations*.

[36] Quoted in Lowe, 'Making sense of decolonisation', p. 438.

[37] Gurry, *India: Australia's Neglected Neighbour?*, p. 5; Gurry, 'A tale of missed opportunities', pp. 14–15.

[38] *CPD*, HR, 24 September 1947, vol. 193, p. 79.

[39] Report, 'Joint United Kingdom-Australian mission concerning development of food and raw material production in Papua and New Guinea, 1948–9', DO35/3734, PRO.

[40] Ben Cockram to Lord Salisbury, Commonwealth Relations Secretary, 18 July 1952, DO35/7036, PRO.

[41] CO, 'Note of a meeting with Mr Hasluck, Minister of Territories, Australia, in Sir Hilton Poynton's room at 10 a.m. on Tuesday, 10th May, 1960', DO35/10699/86, PRO.

[42] For a detailed study of these matters see Edwards with Pemberton, *Crises and Commitments*; and for a summary account, Millar, 'Anglo-Australian partnership in defence of the Malaysian area'.

[43] British High Commission in Canberra to Office of Commissioner-General in Southeast Asia, 21 June 1955, CO1030/99/1, PRO.

[44] Quoted in Hack, *Defence and Decolonisation*, p. 141.

[45] British High Commission in Canberra to London, 19 April 1956, DO35/6294/1, PRO.

[46] DEA, 'Directive for Australian Commissioner, Singapore', 28 October 1960, pp. 1, 4, 5, A1838/280, 3024/10/6/1, NAA.

[47] Note of meeting in the CRO, 14 May 1959, DO35/9390/4, PRO.

[48] Darwin, *Britain and Decolonisation*, pp. 235–44.

[49] Gifford, 'The Cold War across Asia', p. 446 note 22.

[50] DEA, 'Directive for Australian Commissioner, Singapore', 28 October 1960, p. 2 and Annex B, A1838/280, 3024/10/6/1, NAA.

[51] Quoted in Thompson, 'Winds of change in the South Pacific', p. 163.

[52] J. L. F. Buist, CO, to W. Peters, CRO, 2 June 1960, DO35/10177/7, PRO.

2 Australia and Britain as colonial powers

[1] Note on file by G. J. Emery, 19 May 1950; Gordon Walker to Williams, 5 December 1950; both in DO35/3154, PRO.

[2] Williams to Gordon Walker, 3 January 1951, DO35/3154, PRO.

[3] Note for Gordon Walker, 'Suggested appointment of an Australian to a colonial governor-ship in the Pacific area', n.d. (June 1950), DO35/3154, PRO. The 'late Australian Minister for Immigration' was Arthur Calwell.

[4] Minute on file by Gordon Walker, 18 September 1950, DO35/3154, PRO.

[5] Department of Immigration to Australian Commissioner in Singapore, 30 July 1951, MP464/3, 99/1/498, part 1, NAA.

[6] Carrington to Lord Home, Commonwealth Relations Secretary, 6 June 1958, DO35/7889, PRO.

[7] Nelson, 'Papua and New Guinea', quoting Hasluck and Rowley on pp. 161 and 163 respectively.

[8] Kirk-Greene, *On Crown Service*, p. 29.

[9] Cabinet decision 17, 28 May 1951, A4909 CA3, NAA.

[10] CO, 'Note of a meeting with Mr Hasluck, Minister of Territories, Australia, in Sir Hilton Poynton's room at 10 a.m. on Tuesday, 10th May, 1960', DO35/10699/86, PRO.

[11] Mathieson to Sir John Martin, 27 January 1955, CO1036/115, PRO.

[12] H. P. Hall, CO, to J. Chadwick, CRO, 15 September 1959, CO1036/331/18, PRO.

[13] Minute on file by Formoy, 20 June 1956, CO1036/115, PRO.

[14] Quoted in Kirk-Greene, *On Crown Service*, pp. 118–19. Crocker went on to a distinguished Australian career, serving as Professor of International Relations at the Australian National University, as a diplomat (his posts including two separate tenures of the office of High Commissioner to India), and as Lieutenant-Governor of South Australia.

[15] Watt, *Australian Diplomat*, pp. 229–30.

[16] Gifford, 'The Cold War across Asia', p. 194.

[17] Record of conversation between Menzies, Harold Wilson and Sir Keith Holyoake, London, 1 February 1965, PREM 13/889, PRO.

[18] See Thompson, *Australian Imperialism in the Pacific*.

[19] CO, 'Draft brief for Mr Amery for discussions with Australian and New Zealand ministers in Wellington, 16–17 September 1960', n.d. (mid-1960), para. 14(iii), DO35/10699/123, PRO.

[20] Australian Mission at the UN to Canberra, 8 June 1959, A1838/1, 311/8/1, NAA.

[21] CO, 'Draft brief for Mr Amery for discussions with Australian and New Zealand ministers in Wellington, 16–17 September 1960', n.d. (mid-1960), paras 6 and 19, DO35/10699/123, PRO.

[22] Note by L. E. Storar of meeting in CO, 3 June 1959, DO35/10699, PRO.

[23] 'Nauru. Record of meeting with Australian Ministers on 27th May', 31 May 1960, DO35/10699/78, PRO; Department of Territories, 'Resettlement of the Nauruans', 26 August 1960, copy in DO35/10699/115, PRO; CO, 'Draft brief for Mr Amery for discussions with Australian and New Zealand ministers in Wellington, 16–17 September 1960', n.d. (mid-1960), para. 8, DO35/10699/123, PRO.

[24] CO, 'Draft brief for Mr Amery for discussions with Australian and New Zealand ministers in Wellington, 16–17 September 1960', n.d. (mid-1960), para. 13, DO35/10699/123, PRO; Amery to Macleod, 20 September 1960, DO35/10699/141, PRO.

[25] Australian Mission at the UN to Canberra, 8 June 1959, A1838/1, 311/8/1, NAA.

[26] W. G. Wilson, CO, to A. H. Reed, CRO, 19 September 1952, DO35/7036/6, PRO.

[27] Minute on file by A. H. Reed, 22 September 1952, DO35/7036, PRO.

[28] Brief by R. H. Belcher for Sir A. Clutterbuck, 13 January 1960, DO35/10631, PRO.

[29] Williams to D. M. Cleary, CRO, 25 November 1954, DO35/10618/1, PRO.

[30] M. E. Allen to Cleary, 31 December 1954, DO35/10618/4, PRO. Geofroy Tory signalled from the British High Commission in Canberra: 'You may take it that his former colleagues here are well aware of Spender's characteristics. Most of them (and certainly the Prime Minister) would prefer him at a distance in the United States rather than as a colleague here'. Tory to W. A. W. Clark, CRO, 8 February 1955, DO35/10618/5, PRO.

[31] Sir Pierson Dixon, British Mission at the UN, to Sir Gilbert Laithwaite, CRO, 21 June 1956, DO35/10618/14, PRO.

[32] Brief by P. E. Ramsbotham for Dixon, 6 February 1956, DO35/10618/9, PRO.

[33] J. R. Rowland, DEA Representative, Australia House, to R. Scrivener, FO, 13 August 1957, DO35/10618/21, PRO.

[34] Lord Lothian, British Mission at the UN, to Home, 6 January 1957, DO35/10705/15, PRO.

[35] Note by Storar, 12 January 1960, DO35/10618/26, PRO.

[36] Cohen to H. T. Bourdillon, CO, 15 May 1959, DO35/10699/4, PRO.

[37] Cohen to C. G. Eastwood, CO, *c.* 1 December 1959, DO35/10631/6, PRO.

[38] The revealing phrase, 'it may take all our influence over her to keep her in line', appears in a minute from Storar to Clark, 17 June 1959, DO35/10699, PRO. When this minute went up to Lord Home as a brief, the perhaps too candid words 'over her' had been deleted (Clark to Home, 24 June 1959, same file).

[39] Cohen to C. G. Eastwood, *c.* 1 December 1959, DO35/10631/6, PRO. For further discussion of Australia's approach to colonial issues at the UN see Hudson, *Australia and the Colonial Question*, and Lowe, 'Australia at the United Nations in the 1950s'.

40 Brief by Belcher for Clutterbuck, 13 January 1960, DO35/10631, PRO.
41 Belcher, CRO, to N. Pritchard, British High Commission in Canberra, 22 January 1960, DO35/10631/48, PRO.
42 Report by Cohen, 'Visit to Australia and New Guinea, Feb. 7th to 22nd, 1960', 2 March 1960, para. 24(i), DO35/10631/61, PRO.
43 Tange to Menzies, 12 April 1960; Canberra to Australian High Commission in London, 3 May 1960, A1838/1, 894/11/1, part 2, NAA.
44 Harry to Menzies, 6 April 1960; Canberra to Australian High Commission in London, 3 May 1960, A1838/1, 894/11/1, part 2, NAA.
45 *Age*, 5 February 1960.
46 Pritchard to Belcher, 21 March 1960, DO35/10631/64, PRO.
47 Report by Cohen, 'Visit to Australia and New Guinea', Feb. 7th to 22nd, 1960', 2 March 1960, para. 24(iii), DO35/10631, PRO. For the Australian record of the Cohen talks, see DEA, 'Report of discussions between Sir Andrew Cohen and representatives of the Departments of External Affairs and Territories, Canberra, ACT; 8–10 February 1960', 26 pp, A1838/1, 894/11/1, part 2, NAA.
48 Cabinet submission by Hasluck, 'Legislative Council for Papua and New Guinea', 6 April 1960, A5818/2, vol. 15, NAA.
49 DEA, 'Brief account of discussion between the four Prime Ministers', 13 May 1960, A1209/79, 1961/544, NAA.
50 CO, 'Note of a meeting with Mr Hasluck, Minister of Territories, Australia, in Sir Hilton Poynton's room at 10 a.m. on Tuesday, 10th May, 1960', DO35/10699/86, PRO.
51 Transcript of press conference, 20 June 1960, A1838/283, 201/11/1, part 3, NAA.
52 The British High Commission in Canberra, for example, promptly reported them to London. See Commonwealth Study Group (UK) 60 (1), 'The dependent territories of other member governments: and United Kingdom dependencies in the Pacific. Note for United Kingdom delegation', 6 July 1960, DO35/7876/57, PRO.
53 DEA, 'Discussion with Sir Hugh Foot: colonial problems', 30 March 1962, para. 16, A1838/2, 909/8/1/5, NAA.
54 Foot to A. F. Dingle, 12 May 1963, A1838/2, 909/8/1/5, NAA.
55 Ibid.
56 Thompson, 'Winds of change in the South Pacific', p. 169.
57 Bolton, *The Middle Way, 1942–1988*, p. 153.
58 Lee, 'The origins of the Menzies Government's policy', p. 74.
59 Quoted in Thompson, 'Winds of change in the South Pacific', p. 164.
60 This discussion of West New Guinea draws in part on a passage co-written by the author in Gifford, 'The Cold War across Asia', pp. 213–15.
61 Chauvel, 'Up the creek without a paddle'.
62 Tange to Shaw, 28 October 1960, Tange Papers, DFAT.
63 Marginal comment by Tange on letter from Peter Hastings to Tange, 18 July 1990, Tange Papers, DFAT.
64 Submission, Tange to Menzies, 20 February 1961, p. 1, Tange Papers, DFAT.
65 Doran, 'Toeing the line', pp. 13–14.
66 Marr, *Barwick*, p. 170.
67 Doran, 'Toeing the line', pp. 13–14.
68 Statement by Barwick, 'Netherlands New Guinea', *Current Notes on International Affairs*, vol. 32, no. 12, 1961, p. 16.
69 Statement by Barwick, 'Netherlands New Guinea', *Current Notes on International Affairs*, vol. 33, no. 1, 1962, p. 41.
70 Marr, *Barwick*, p. 170.
71 Barwick to Howard Beale, Australian Ambassador in Washington, 15 January 1962, Tange Papers, DFAT.
72 Thompson, 'Winds of change in the South Pacific', p. 164.
73 Marr, *Barwick*, p. 171.

[74] Barwick to Tange, 19 January 1993, Tange Papers, DFAT.
[75] Barwick, 'Australia's foreign relations', p. 6.

3 British islands, Australian ambitions

[1] Hamilton to Plimsoll, 15 January 1954, A1838/283, 338/1/1, part 3, NAA.
[2] E. J. Williams to Patrick Gordon Walker, Commonwealth Relations Secretary, 3 January 1951, DO35/3154, PRO.
[3] CRO to Australian High Commission in London, 6 March 1951, MP464/3, 99/1/498/1, NAA.
[4] Correspondence in DO35/3828–9 (1947), PRO; minute on file by L. E. Storar, 1 December 1958, DO35/10699, PRO.
[5] Reynolds, *Australia's Bid for the Atomic Bomb*, p. 87.
[6] P. Coleman, Department of Defence, to Director-General of Civil Aviation, 18 October 1949; Williams to Chifley, 21 June 1949; both in MP464/3, 99/1/498/1, NAA.
[7] Spender to Menzies, 8 June 1950; minute by Casey, 14 June 1950; McBride to Menzies, 6 July 1950; Menzies to Attlee, 24 August 1950; all in MP464/3, 99/1/498/1, NAA.
[8] Reynolds, *Australia's Bid for the Atomic Bomb*, p. 87.
[9] Williams to Menzies, 14 February 1951, MP464/3, 99/1/498/1, NAA; Cabinet memo by Lord Swinton, Commonwealth Relations Secretary, and Oliver Lyttelton, Colonial Secretary, 'Transfer of the Cocos Islands to Australia', 10 June 1954, CAB129/68, C(54)193, PRO.
[10] Heyes to Watt, 25 June 1951, MP464/3, 99/1/498/1, NAA.
[11] Australian High Commissioner in London to Canberra, 10 August 1951, MP464/3, 99/1/498/1, NAA; Watt to other Department Secretaries, 14 September 1951, MP464/3, 99/1/498/2, NAA.
[12] DEA, 'Summary record of inter-departmental conference regarding the transfer to Australia of administrative responsibility for the Cocos Islands', 21 August 1951, MP464/3, 99/1/498/1, NAA.
[13] Cabinet submission 143 by Casey, 'Transfer of Cocos (Keeling) Islands to Australia', for meeting of 15 October 1951, MP464/3, 99/1/498/2, NAA.
[14] Cabinet decision 205, 15 October 1951, A4909 CA3, NAA.
[15] Canberra to Australian Commissioner in Singapore, 14 July 1952, MP464/3, 99/1/498/2, NAA.
[16] Cabinet submission 143 by Casey, 'Transfer of Cocos (Keeling) Islands to Australia', for meeting of 15 October 1951, MP464/3, 99/1/498/2, NAA; G. E. Crombie to Sir R. Hone, 10 November 1954, DO35/6093, PRO.
[17] Casey to Swinton, 6 December 1954, A1838/2, 67/2/2, part 1, NAA.
[18] United Kingdom, House of Commons, *Debates*, vol. 536, 7 February 1955, cols. 1553–87.
[19] A. D. Dodds-Parker to Swinton, 8 and 16 February 1955, DO35/6094, PRO.
[20] Australian High Commission in London to Canberra, 22 February 1955, A5954/1, 1444/1, NAA.
[21] Australian High Commission in London to Canberra, 23 February 1955, A5954/1, 1444/1, NAA.
[22] Cabinet decision 325, 2 March 1955, A4910 CA3, NAA.
[23] British High Commissioner in Canberra to London, 6 April 1955, DO35/6094/310, PRO.
[24] Acting British High Commissioner in Canberra to London, 23 April 1955, DO35/6094/322, PRO.
[25] Clark to Sir Saville Garner, Deputy Under-Secretary, CRO, 29 April 1955, DO35/6094, PRO.
[26] London to Acting British High Commissioner in Canberra, 2 May 1955, DO35/6094/324, PRO.
[27] Acting British High Commissioner in Canberra to London, 5 May 1955, DO35/6094/326, PRO.
[28] Acting British High Commissioner in Canberra to London, 6 May 1955, DO35/6094/328, PRO.

[29] Cabinet decision 406, 10 May 1955, A4910 CA3, NAA.

[30] Correspondence in DO35/6095, PRO.

[31] Lambert to Shedden, 12 October 1954, A816/52, 2/301/466, NAA.

[32] Defence Committee minute, 21 October 1954, A816/52, 2/301/466, NAA.

[33] Cabinet decision 219, 24 November 1954, A4910 CA3, NAA.

[34] Australian High Commission in London to Canberra, 10 October 1955, A816/52, 2/301/466, NAA.

[35] Casey to Menzies, 26 February 1956, A816/52, 2/301/466, NAA.

[36] Menzies to Eden, 21 March 1956, printed as Annex 1 in Cabinet memo by Alan Lennox-Boyd, Colonial Secretary, 'Christmas Island', 1 August 1956, CAB129/82, CP(56)196, PRO.

[37] Cabinet conclusion, 'Christmas Island', 3 October 1956, CAB128/30, part 2, CM68(56)7, PRO.

[38] Canberra to Australian High Commission in Wellington, 26 October 1956, A816/52, 2/301/466, NAA.

[39] Minute by Deputy Secretary (Military), Department of Defence, 13 June 1956, A816/52, 2/301/466, NAA.

[40] Defence Committee minute 262/1956, 'Strategic value of Christmas Island', 20 December 1956, A816/52, 2/301/466, NAA.

[41] Tange to Shedden, 29 November 1956, A816/52, 2/301/466, NAA. The date of this letter precedes that of the minute cited in the previous note. The Defence Committee's reappraisal took the form of an endorsement of Joint Planning Committee report 61/1956 of 20 November 1956; Tange's letter was written in response to the Planning Committee's report.

[42] Cabinet decision 622, 5 February 1957, A4910 CA3, NAA.

[43] Sir Edwin McCarthy, leader, Australian delegation in London, to Canberra, 25 February 1957, A816/52, 21/301/466, NAA.

[44] Cabinet memo by Lord Home, Commonwealth Relations Secretary, and Lennox-Boyd, 'Christmas Island', 1 March 1957, CAB129/86, C(57)51, PRO; Cabinet conclusion, 'Christmas Island', 4 March 1957, CAB128/31, part 1, CC15(57)4, PRO.

[45] Australian High Commission in London to Canberra, 12 March 1957, A816/52, 21/301/466, NAA.

[46] Cabinet memo by James Griffiths, Colonial Secretary, Gordon Walker, and Kenneth Younger, Minister of State, 'New Hebrides', 26 June 1950, CAB129/40, CP(50)136, PRO.

[47] Reported in ibid.

[48] Annex to ibid., Spender to Philip Noel-Baker, Commonwealth Relations Secretary, 14 January 1950; Cabinet conclusion, 'New Hebrides', 29 June 1950, CAB128/17, CM40(50)8, PRO.

[49] Report of meeting between Casey and Hasluck on 15 May 1952, A1838/283, 338/1/1, part 3, NAA.

[50] Defence Committee minute 223/1951, 'New Hebrides', 17 July 1951, A5954, 2346/2, NAA.

[51] Report of meeting between Casey and Hasluck on 15 May 1952, A1838/283, 338/1/1, part 3, NAA.

[52] McIntyre to Officer, 12 October 1951, A1838/283, 338/1/1, part 2, NAA.

[53] Australian High Commission in London to Canberra, 2 January 1952, 3 January 1952 and 9 April 1952; Canberra to Australian High Commission in London, 3 January 1952; all in A1838/283, 338/1/1, part 3, NAA.

[54] Report of meeting between Casey and Hasluck on 15 May 1952, A1838/283, 338/1/1, part 3, NAA.

[55] Casey to Lyttelton, 19 June 1952, A1838/283, 338/1/1, part 3, NAA.

[56] Memo by F. Mills, 11 July 1952, DO35/5255, PRO.

[57] British High Commission in Canberra to Prime Minister's Department, 7 September 1953, A1838/283, 338/1/1, part 3, NAA.

[58] Brown to Watt, 1 October 1953, A1838/283, 338/1/1, part 3, NAA.

[59] Cabinet agendum, 'Condominium of the New Hebrides: proposed transfer of United Kingdom responsibilities to Australia', 8 February 1954, pp. 3–4, A1838/283, 338/1/1, part 3, NAA.

[60] Brown to Official Secretary, British High Commissioner in Canberra, 12 March 1954, A1838/283, 338/1/1, part 3, NAA.

[61] J. M. McMillan, DEA, to Plimsoll, 4 March 1955, reporting meeting between McIntyre and H. P. Hall, CO, A1838/283, 338/1/1, part 3, NAA.

[62] Sir John Gutch, Solomon Islands, to Philip Rogers, CO, 19 November 1956, CO1036/115/37, PRO.

[63] Hasluck to Menzies, 8 November 1956, A1838/283, 338/1/1, part 4, NAA.

[64] Minute by W. H. Formoy, 20 June 1956, CO1036/115, PRO.

[65] Lambert to Watt, 11 February 1954, A1838/283, 338/1/1, part 3, NAA; Cumpston to Plimsoll, 23 June 1955, A1838/283, 338/1/1, part 4, NAA.

[66] Lambert to Watt, 11 February 1954, A1838/283, 338/1/1, part 3, NAA.

[67] Hasluck to Casey, 11 February 1954, A1838/283, 338/1/1 part 3, NAA. The trusteeship agreement would have been involved because the 'Australian Solomons' were administered as a UN trust.

[68] Hasluck to Casey, 23 January 1956, A5954, 2346/2, NAA.

[69] Gutch to Sir John Martin, CO, 26 March 1956, CO1036/115/24, PRO.

[70] Minute by Formoy, 20 June 1956, CO1036/115, PRO.

[71] Defence Committee minute 58/1956, 'Strategic importance of the British Solomons and New Hebrides', 8 March 1956, A5954, 2346/2, NAA.

[72] Cabinet agendum 36, 'British Solomon Islands Protectorate and New Hebrides Condominium', 14 February 1956, A1838/283, 338/1/1, part 4, NAA.

[73] Brief for Casey by A. H. Loomes, 'Solomons and New Hebrides', 7 May 1956, and handwritten note by Casey, 18 May 1956, A1838/283, 338/1/1, part 4, NAA; Cabinet decision 194, 18 May 1956, A4910 CA3, NAA.

[74] Hyam, 'Introduction', in Hyam and Louis (eds), *The Conservative Government*, vol. 1, p. lxxxi.

[75] Macmillan to Lennox-Boyd, 16 June 1959, DO35/8095, PRO.

[76] Minute on file by Home, n.d. (*c.* 30 June 1959), DO35/8095, PRO.

[77] For the relevant CO and CRO papers see Hyam and Louis (eds), *The Conservative Government*, vol. 2, docs 554–9.

[78] Commonwealth Study Group (UK) (60)1, 'United Kingdom dependencies in the West and South Pacific', 6 July 1960, DO35/5256/179, PRO.

[79] CO, 'The British colonies in the South Pacific', August 1963, DO169/185/171, PRO.

[80] 'Report by the Joint Planning Committee at a meeting on 8th October, 1959', A1209/23, 57/5709, NAA.

[81] Ibid.

[82] Quoted in Thompson, 'Winds of change in the South Pacific', p. 164.

[83] Cabinet submission 590 by Barwick, 'Guidelines for Australian policy in the Pacific islands area', 8 March 1963, A5819/2, vol. 15, NAA.

[84] CO, 'The British colonies in the South Pacific', August 1963, paras 3 and 4, DO169/185/171, PRO.

[85] 'Evolution of the Commonwealth. Report by a working party of [British] officials', 24 April 1962, para. 34, copy in A1209/79, 1961/544, NAA.

4 Australia discovers Africa

[1] Casey to White, 26 February 1954, A1838/274, 145/10/6, NAA.

[2] Casey to McGuire, 26 February 1954, A1838/274, 145/10/6, NAA.

[3] Report of McGuire's conversation with Liesching, 6 April 1954, DO35/4574, PRO.

[4] T. W. Eckersley to Canberra, n.d., late May 1954, A1838/274, 145/10/6, NAA.

[5] A. F. Morley to Garner, 8 April 1954, DO35/8012, PRO.

[6] Report of McGuire's conversation with Liesching, 6 April 1954, DO35/4574, PRO.

[7] T. G. Gisborne to I. M. R. Maclennan, 9 November 1954, DO35/8012, PRO.

[8] Minute by British official (illegible signature), 25 September 1954, DO35/8012, PRO.

[9] McGuire to Casey, 14 June 1954, A1838/274, 145/10/6, NAA.

[10] 'K.W.' [Keith Waller?] to Plimsoll, 24 June 1954; minute on file by B. C. Hill, 7 July 1954, A1838/274, 145/10/6, NAA.

[11] Tange to Central Branch, 5 July 1954, A1838/274, 145/10/6, NAA.

[12] Oldham, 'British African territories—Australian representation', 14 July 1954, A1838/274, 145/10/6, NAA.

[13] Draft brief, 'British territories in Africa', n.d. (November 1954), A1838/274, 145/10/6, NAA.

[14] British High Commission in Canberra to London, 21 September 1954, and R. C. Ormerod to A. F. Morley, 23 September 1954, both in DO35/4574, PRO; Lord Halifax to Swinton, 9 November 1954, DO35/10618/4A, PRO.

[15] Tothill, Australian diplomatic reporting from South Africa, p. 22.

[16] Gilchrist to Tange, 5 April 1957, A1838/238, 201/10/1, part 2, NAA.

[17] Gilchrist to Tange, 'Australia and Africa', 3 March 1959, A1838/2, 155/7/4, part 1, NAA.

[18] Information about this secret NATO initiative had been leaked to the Australian Embassy in Paris; F. J. Blakeney, 'Western policies in Africa', draft, n.d. (June–July 1959), A1838/2, 155/7/4, part 1, NAA.

[19] Jamieson despatches 13, 14 and 37 of 1959 to Canberra; Dexter, 'Western policy in Africa', 22 June 1959; all in A1838/2, 155/7/4, part 1, NAA.

[20] Heydon to Jamieson, 20 March 1959, A1838/2, 155/7/4, part 1, NAA.

[21] Note of meeting in CRO, 14 May 1959, DO35/9390/4, PRO.

[22] Blakeney, 'Western policies in Africa', draft, n.d. (June–July 1959), A1838/2, 155/7/4, part 1, NAA.

[23] Dexter, 'Draft brief for Prime Minister. Africa', 4 June 1959; Dexter, 'Western policy in Africa', 22 June 1959; Jamieson to Tange, 7 July 1959; all in A1838/2, 155/7/4, part 1, NAA.

[24] DEA, 'The world in 1960', draft brief, 14 April 1960, p. 8, A1838/269, TS899/6/6, part 2, NAA.

[25] B. C. Hill (for Tange) to Secretary, Department of Defence, 25 June 1959; JIC, note 4/30/4, 'Defence significance to Australia of Africa South of the Sahara', September 1959; Dexter to JIC, 'Significance of Africa South of the Sahara', 4 March 1960; Rowland to L. H. Border (Head, Intelligence Coordination Branch), 20 February 1961; all in A1838/2, 155/7/4, part 1, NAA.

[26] DEA, 'The world in 1960', draft brief, 14 April 1960, pp. 8–9, A1838/269, TS899/6/6, part 2, NAA; also Jamieson to DEA, 'Radio Moscow—African broadcasts', 9 November 1959, and DEA Office, Australian High Commission in London, to Canberra, 'Communist China—penetration of Africa', 23 March 1960, both in A1838/2, 563/2/9, NAA.

[27] DEA, 'ANZUS Meeting. Agenda item 1. East West relations. Assessment of current Soviet policy in Africa', paper for Australian delegation, n.d. (April 1962), A1838/2, 155/7/4, part 2, NAA.

[28] DEA to Australian missions in Cairo, Pretoria, Lagos, Accra, 3 August 1961, A1838/2, 155/7/4, part 3, NAA.

[29] Dexter to JIC, 'Significance of Africa South of the Sahara', 4 March 1960, A1838/2, 155/7/4, part 1, NAA.

[30] DEA, 'African nationalism: Africa South of the Sahara', brief for Prime Ministers Conference, 11 April 1960, A1838/2, 155/7/4, part 2, NAA.

[31] Plimsoll to Canberra, 18 February 1960, A1838/2, 155/7/4, part 1, NAA.

[32] DEA, 'Notes for Heads of Mission Meeting at Geneva, 1961. The Commonwealth in Africa and its future', n.d. (February 1961), A1838/2, 155/7/4, part 2, NAA.

[33] Quinn and Dexter to Tange, n.d. (c. 22 February 1960), A1838/2, 155/7/4, part 1, NAA; Quinn to Tange, 11 April 1960, A1838/2, 155/7/4, part 2, NAA.

[34] Tange to Menzies, 'Policy towards Africa', 21 June 1961, A1838/2, 155/7/4, part 3, NAA.

[35] Heydon to Menzies, 4 August 1961, A1838/1, 155/7/4/3, NAA.

[36] Woodard, 'Best practice in Australia's foreign policy', p. 94.

[37] Shann to Tange, 6 April 1962, covering report, A1838/1, 155/7/4/3, NAA.

[38] Hyam, 'Introduction', in Hyam and Louis (eds), *The Conservative Government*, vol. 1, pp. lxv–lxvi, and Hyam and Louis (eds), *The Conservative Government*, vol. 2, docs 336–8.

39 Hyam, 'Introduction', in Hyam and Louis (eds), *The Conservative Government*, vol. 1, pp. lxv–lxvi.
40 Transcript of Menzies press conference in London, 18 May 1960, A1838/283, 201/11/1, part 3, NAA.
41 Cabinet submission 986 by Menzies, 'Aid to Africa', 3 February 1961, A5818/2, vol. 23, NAA.
42 DEA, 'Review of need for aid: Africa', 21 December 1964, A1838/264, 155/7/4/2, NAA.
43 DEA, 'Notes for Heads of Mission Meeting at Geneva, 1961. The Commonwealth in Africa and its future', n.d. (February 1961), A1838/2, 155/7/4, part 2, NAA.
44 J. C. G. Kevin to Tange, 13 September 1963, A1838/2, 155/7/4/1, part 1, NAA.
45 Plimsoll, 'Visit to Nigeria', 14 July 1959, A1838/2, 155/7/4, part 1, NAA.
46 Tange to Menzies, 'Policy towards Africa', 21 June 1961, A1838/2, 155/7/4, part 3, NAA.
47 These episodes are discussed in Chapter 5.
48 Tothill, Australian diplomatic reporting from South Africa, pp. 26–7.
49 Kevin to Tange, 13 September 1963, A1838/2, 155/7/4/1, part 1, NAA.
50 Cabinet submission 883 by Barwick, 'Apartheid', 5 September 1963; Cabinet decision 1012, 10 September 1963; both in A5819/2, vol. 22, NAA.
51 Garner to British High Commissions, 31 May 1962; Garner to Sir Arthur Snelling, 12 June 1962; Costar to Garner, 7 June 1962; all in DO161/95, PRO.
52 Garner to J. Chadwick, 13 September 1962, and MS annotation on this document, DO161/95, PRO.
53 FO, 'Secretary of State's visit to Canberra 25 June – 1 July 1966: Australian attitudes towards sanctions against Rhodesia', n.d. (June 1966), FO371/785912, PRO.
54 D. P. R. Mackilligan to M. Palliser, 8 July 1966; MS annotation by Palliser, 19 July 1966; both in PREM13/729, PRO.
55 For an account of the changes in Australian policy towards Africa in the 1970s, see Higgott, 'Australia and Africa 1970–80'.

Part II Coping with the end of empire

1 Darwin, 'The Pacific and decolonization', p. 409.
2 For an introduction to the historiography of Britain's decolonisation, see Darwin, 'Decolonization and the end of empire'. Hack, *Defence and Decolonisation*, pp. 1–12, offers an overview of theoretical approaches.
3 Martel, 'British decolonisation after Suez'.
4 Percox, 'Internal security and decolonization', p. 92.
5 Martel, 'British decolonisation after Suez', p. 405.
6 Jones, 'Creating Malaysia', p. 86.
7 Holland, 'The imperial factor in British strategies', p. 181.
8 Darwin, *Britain and Decolonisation*, pp. 243–4.
9 Hyam and Louis (eds), *The Conservative Government*, vol. 1, docs 1–3.
10 Macmillan to Lord Salisbury, chair of Cabinet Colonial Policy Committee, 28 January 1957, CAB 134/1555, CPC(57)6, PRO.
11 Quoted in Hyam and Louis (eds), *The Conservative Government*, vol. 2, doc. 554.
12 Quoted in Horne, *Macmillan*, p. 358.
13 Holland, 'The imperial factor in British strategies', pp. 179–80.
14 Louis, 'The European colonial empires', p. 100.
15 Menzies to Crocker, quoted in Martin, *Robert Menzies*, p. 439.
16 Stockwell, 'Malaysia', p. 138.
17 Peter Ramsbotham, quoted in Hyam, 'Introduction', in Hyam and Louis (eds), *The Conservative Government*, vol. 1, p. xxxvi. Ramsbotham contributed substantially to two major policy papers in which Britain's plans for the future were spelt out: 'The position of the United Kingdom in world affairs' (1958) and 'Future policy study, 1960–1970' (1960). See Hyam and Louis (eds), *The Conservative Government*, vol. 1, docs. 4–18.

[18] British High Commission in Canberra, 'Visit of the High Commissioner to London, 1962: steering brief: Anglo-Australian relations', March 1962, pp. 1, 2, 3, DO169/2, PRO.

[19] Ibid., p. 5.

[20] Ibid., p. 7.

[21] Ibid., p. 5.

[22] Ibid., pp. 5–6.

5 Things falling apart: Menzies, Britain and the new Commonwealth

[1] F. Mills to Sir Alexander Clutterbuck, 24 May 1961, DO161/161, PRO.

[2] J. Chadwick to Clutterbuck, 24 May 1961, DO161/161, PRO.

[3] Beale, *This Inch of Time*, pp. 139–41.

[4] Mills to L. J. D. Wakely, 7 September 1961, DO161/161, PRO.

[5] Carrington to Timothy Bligh, Macmillan's private secretary, 9 February 1962, PREM11/3665, PRO.

[6] Shann to Canberra, 21 March 1960, A1209/23, 1957/4588, part A, NAA.

[7] Louis and Robinson, 'The imperialism of decolonization'.

[8] Quoted in Cabinet memo by Swinton, 'Commonwealth membership', 16 February 1955, CAB129/73, C(55)43, PRO.

[9] Chadwick to British High Commissioners, 24 March 1960, DO35/7869, PRO.

[10] DEA, 'Brief account of discussion between the four Prime Ministers', 13 May 1960, A1209/79, 1961/544, NAA.

[11] Transcript of press conference, 20 June 1960, A1838/283, 201/11/1, part 3, NAA.

[12] Hyam, 'The primacy of geopolitics', p. 45.

[13] *Age*, 5 February 1960.

[14] DEA, 'Brief account of discussion between the four Prime Ministers', 13 May 1960, A1209/79, 1961/544, NAA.

[15] DEA, 'United Kingdom "Study of future policy (1960–1970)"; observations by the Department of External Affairs', 12 January 1961, A1209/79, 1961/544, NAA.

[16] DEA, 'Brief account of discussion between the four Prime Ministers', 13 May 1960, A1209/79, 1961/544, NAA.

[17] Darwin, *Britain and Decolonisation*, p. 239.

[18] See McIntyre, 'The admission of small states to the Commonwealth'.

[19] Garner to Sandys, 1 May 1962, DO161/95, PRO.

[20] Brook to Macmillan, 17 February 1959, PREM11/2910, PRO.

[21] Brook, 'The future development of the Commonwealth', covering note dated 28 April 1960, p. 4, PREM11/3220, PRO.

[22] Ibid.

[23] Report, 'Smaller colonial territories', with covering note from Sir Henry Lintott to Clutterbuck, 25 May 1960, paras 2 and 5, DO35/7876/39, PRO.

[24] Report, 'The constitutional development of the Commonwealth: report by a group of Commonwealth officials', 23 July 1960, CAB129/102, part 1, PRO.

[25] Bunting, 'Note arising from a meeting with the Prime Minister', 2 September 1960, A1838/2, 201/11/1, part 4, NAA.

[26] Menzies to McEwen, 15 March 1961, A1838/283, 201/11/1/1, part 2, NAA.

[27] Menzies to Macmillan, 15 January 1962, Menzies Papers, MS4936, Series 1, Box 22, Folder 187, NLA.

[28] Philip de Zulueta, Macmillan's private secretary, to A. C. Samuel, FO, 25 July 1961, PREM11/3204, PRO.

[29] Macmillan to Menzies, 8 February 1962, Menzies Papers, MS4936, Series 1, Box 22, Folder 187, NLA. Emphasis in original.

[30] Brook to Macmillan, 12 February 1962, PREM11/3665, PRO.

31 Home to Macmillan, 19 February 1962, PREM11/3665, PRO.
32 Menzies to Macmillan, 18 April 1962, Menzies Papers, MS4936, Series 1, Box 22, Folder 187, NLA.
33 Ibid.
34 Macmillan to Menzies, 8 February 1962, Menzies Papers, MS4936, Series 1, Box 22, Folder 187, NLA.
35 Macmillan to Menzies, 18 January 1971, Menzies Papers, MS4936, Series 1, Box 22, Folder 187, NLA.
36 Menzies to McEwen, 12 March 1961, A1838/283, 201/11/1/1, part 2, NAA.
37 Menzies to McEwen, 14 March 1961, A1838/283, 201/11/1/1, part 2, NAA.
38 Ibid.
39 Menzies to McEwen, 15 March 1961 (telegram 1188), A1838/283, 201/11/1/1, part 2, NAA.
40 Menzies to McEwen, 15 March 1961 (telegram 1194), A1838/283, 201/11/1/1, part 2, NAA.
41 Menzies to McEwen, 14 March 1961, A1838/283, 201/11/1/1, part 2, NAA.
42 Bunting, 'Prime Ministers' Meeting: South African membership', 23 March 1961, p. 7, A1838/283, 201/11/1/1, part 3, NAA. The leading scholarly study of the subject concludes, however, that Macmillan was genuinely shattered by the conference outcome: Hyam, 'The parting of the ways', pp. 171–2.
43 Bunting, 'Prime Ministers' Meeting: South African membership', 23 March 1961, p. 11, A1838/283, 201/11/1/1, part 3, NAA.
44 Menzies to Macmillan, 15 January 1962, Menzies Papers, MS4936, Series 1, Box 22, Folder 187, NLA.
45 Menzies to Macmillan, 5 April 1961, A1838/269, TS852/10/2/3, NAA; Cabinet decision 1277, 7 April 1961, A4943, NAA.
46 Cabinet submission 21 by Downer, 'The United Kingdom Government's Commonwealth Immigrants Bill', 12 January 1962, A5819/2, vol. 2, NAA.
47 British High Commission in Canberra, 'Visit of the High Commissioner to London, 1962: steering brief: Anglo-Australian relations', March 1962, p. 2, DO169/2, PRO.
48 Chadwick to Clutterbuck, 24 May 1961; G. D. Anderson to Chadwick, 5 June 1961; both in DO161/161, PRO.
49 Report, 'British relations with Australia', with covering note from Clutterbuck to Sandys, 21 June 1961, DO161/161, PRO.
50 As is noted for example by Stockwell, 'Malaysia', p. 138.
51 Lloyd to Douglas-Home, 7 November 1963, PREM11/4640, PRO.
52 Ibid.
53 Cabinet memo by Douglas-Home, 'Commonwealth policy', 3 January 1964, CAB129/116, part 1, CP(64)6, PRO.
54 Douglas-Home to Menzies, Holyoake and Pearson, 3 June 1964, and Menzies to Douglas-Home, 12 June 1964, both in PREM11/4623, PRO.
55 Cabinet memo by Heath, 'Commonwealth policy', 8 January 1964, CAB129/116, part 1, CP(64)6, PRO; Cabinet debate, 17 January 1964, CAB128/38, part 2, CM(64)5, PRO.
56 Hudson, *Casey*, pp. 292–3.

6 Menzies, Macmillan and Europe

1 Gelber, *Australia, Britain and the EEC*; Ward, *Australia and the British Embrace*.
2 Cabinet note by Macmillan and Peter Thorneycroft, President of the Board of Trade, 'United Kingdom commercial policy', 27 July 1956, CAB129/82, CP(56)191, PRO.
3 Record of Casey's conversation with Home, London, 14 March 1957, A1838/269, TS501/1, part 1, NAA.
4 Sir William Oliver to Clutterbuck, 22 March 1960, PREM11/2908, PRO.
5 Menzies to Macmillan, 15 September 1960, Menzies Papers, MS4936, Series 1, Box 22, Folder 186, NLA.

6 Cabinet submission 1108 by McEwen, 'Possible association of the United Kingdom with the European Economic Community', 5 May 1961; Cabinet decision 1356, 9 May 1961; both in A5818/2, vol. 26, NAA.

7 DEA, 'The political implications for Australia of United Kingdom entry into the European Economic Community', 26 June 1961, passages quoted from pp. 16, 18, 2, A5818/2, vol. 28, NAA.

8 Cabinet note by Macmillan, 'The Commonwealth and Europe', 28 June 1961, CAB129/105, C(61)87, PRO.

9 Gelber, *Australia, Britain and the EEC*, pp. 78–82, quoted from p. 81.

10 Menzies to Harrison, 21 August 1961, Menzies Papers, MS4936, Series 1, Box 14, Folder 122, NLA.

11 Ad Hoc Committee decision 19, 16 January 1962, A5819/2, vol. 2, NAA.

12 Menzies to Macmillan, 15 January 1962, Menzies Papers, MS4936, Series 1, Box 22, Folder 187, NLA.

13 Miller, *Survey of Commonwealth Affairs*, p. 331.

14 Note by Lee, 'Discussion with the Australian High Commissioner', 12 February 1962, DO161/194/70, NAA.

15 Heath's memos to Macmillan, PREM11/4620, PRO.

16 Menzies to Macmillan, 18 April 1962, Menzies Papers, MS4936, Series 1, Box 22, Folder 187, NLA.

17 Harrison to Menzies, 30 April 1962, Menzies Papers, MS4936, Series 1, Box 14, Folder 122, NLA.

18 British High Commission in Ottawa to London, 16 March 1962, PREM11/4620, PRO.

19 Harrison to Menzies, 30 January 1962, Menzies Papers, MS4936, Series 1, Box 14, Folder 122, NLA.

20 CRO brief for Sandys, 'Prime Ministers Meeting 1962', n.d. (probably late February 1962), DO161/194/73, PRO.

21 Ibid.

22 Macmillan to Menzies, 17 March 1962, PREM11/3657, PRO.

23 Garner to Sandys, 28 March 1962, DO161/194, PRO.

24 F. Mills to T. Bligh, 30 March 1962, DO161/194/103, PRO; Macmillan to Menzies, 31 March 1962, DO161/194/105, PRO.

25 Menzies to Macmillan, 18 April 1962, Menzies Papers, MS4936, Series 1, Box 22, Folder 187, NLA.

26 Harrison to Menzies, 15 May 1962, Menzies Papers, MS4936, Series 1, Box 14, Folder 122, NLA. Harrison added a PS: 'Bob, please, I hope I have not given you the impression that I want you to help the Conservatives. That is not the object of this letter'.

27 Macmillan to Sandys, 5 September 1962, PREM11/3663, PRO.

28 Menzies to Harrison, 14 May 1962, Menzies Papers, MS4936, Series 1, Box 14, Folder 122, NLA.

29 Sandys to Macmillan, 14 June 1962, PREM11/3660, PRO.

30 Briefing paper quoted in Martin, *Robert Menzies*, p. 448.

31 It can be found in *Current Notes on International Affairs*, vol. 33, no. 6, 1962, pp. 36–7.

32 Menzies to Macmillan, 11 July 1962, Menzies Papers, MS4936, Series 1, Box 22, Folder 187, NLA.

33 Martin, *Robert Menzies*, p. 448.

34 Menzies to Macmillan, 11 July 1962, Menzies Papers, MS4936, Series 1, Box 22, Folder 187, NLA.

35 Macmillan to Menzies, 20 July 1962, Menzies Papers, MS4936, Series 1, Box 22, Folder 187, NLA.

36 Australian Embassy in Washington to Canberra, 'United States attitude towards the Commonwealth', 27 August 1962, A1838/2, 899/8/1, NAA.

37 Martin, *Robert Menzies*, p. 452.

38 Costar, 'The politics of coalition', p. 101.

[39] Ibid., pp. 102, 109.
[40] Cabinet debate, 22 August 1962, CAB128/36, part 2, CC 55(62)1, PRO.
[41] Macmillan to Ministerial Committee, 4 September 1962, PREM11/3660, PRO.
[42] Brook to Macmillan, 5 September 1962, PREM11/3660, PRO.
[43] Macmillan to Sandys, 5 September 1962, PREM11/3663, PRO.
[44] Macmillan to Heath, 5 September 1962, PREM11/3663, PRO.
[45] Diary entry quoted in Horne, *Macmillan*, p. 355. Emphasis in original.
[46] Minutes of Commonwealth Prime Ministers Conference, 5th meeting, 11 September 1962, DO161/196, PRO.
[47] Minutes of Commonwealth Prime Ministers Conference, especially 11th meeting (13 September 1962), 13th and 14th meetings (both 14 September 1962), 17th meeting (15 September 1962), and 18th meeting (17 September 1962), DO161/196, PRO.
[48] Diary entry quoted in Horne, *Macmillan*, p. 356.
[49] Cabinet debate, 13 September 1962, CAB128/36, part 2, CC 56(62)3, PRO.
[50] Cabinet debate, 20 September 1962, CAB128/36, part 2, CC 57(62)2, PRO.
[51] Diary entry quoted in Horne, *Macmillan*, p. 356.
[52] Cabinet debate, 20 September 1962, CAB128/36, part 2, CC 57(62)2, PRO.
[53] For an account of de Gaulle's press conference of 14 January 1963 see Gelber, *Australia, Britain and the EEC*, pp. 223–5.
[54] Holland, 'The imperial factor in British strategies', p. 182.
[55] Ibid.
[56] Macmillan to Butler, 20 September 1962, PREM11/3663, PRO.
[57] Ward, *Australia and the British Embrace*, especially ch. 1.

7 Confrontation in Southeast Asia

[1] Edwards, 'Singapore and Malaysia', p. 188.
[2] The pioneering works include Greenwood, 'Australian foreign policy in action', esp. pp. 94–112, and Mackie, *Konfrontasi*. More recent studies include Edwards with Pemberton, *Crises and Commitments*, chs 14, 15, 17; Dennis and Grey, *Emergency and Confrontation*, chs 10–18; Subritzky, *Confronting Sukarno*; Marr, *Barwick*, ch. 16; Dee, In Australia's Own Interests; Lee and Dee, 'Southeast Asian conflicts', pp. 264–79; Edwards, 'Singapore and Malaysia'; Lee, 'The origins of the Menzies Government's policy'; Woodard, 'Best practice in Australia's foreign policy'; Jones, 'Creating Malaysia'.
[3] Lee, *Search for Security*, p. 132.
[4] Hack, *Defence and Decolonisation*, p. 245.
[5] Lee, *Search for Security*, pp. 131–4.
[6] Hack, *Defence and Decolonisation*, p. 184. Watt was then Australian Commissioner in Southeast Asia.
[7] Ibid., p. 184.
[8] Ibid., p. 246.
[9] Macmillan to Menzies, 3 October 1963, DO164/27/41, PRO.
[10] *CPD*, HR, vol. 40, 29 October 1963, p. 2373.
[11] Menzies to Douglas-Home, 24 October 1963, DO164/27/74, PRO.
[12] Cabinet submission 1304 by Menzies, 'Political and economic association of Singapore, the Federation of Malaya and the Borneo territories', 11 August 1961, A4940/1, C3389, NAA.
[13] Cabinet decision 1534 (HOC), 16 August 1961, A4940/1, C3389, NAA.
[14] Macmillan to Menzies and Holyoake, 20 October 1961, PREM11/4189, PRO.
[15] Holyoake to Macmillan, 13 December 1961, PREM11/4189, PRO.
[16] Macmillan to Menzies and Holyoake, 5 February 1962, PREM11/3644, PRO.
[17] Woodard, 'Best practice in Australia's foreign policy', p. 86.
[18] Edwards with Pemberton, *Crises and Commitments*, p. 254.
[19] Marr, *Barwick*, p. 194.
[20] Minute by A. S. Fair, CRO, November 1962, DO169/2, PRO.

21 British High Commissioner in Canberra to Sandys, 'Australian attitude towards Malaysia', 8 April 1963, DO164/39, PRO.

22 See for example Dee, In Australia's Own Interests, chs 3–5; Edwards with Pemberton, *Crises and Commitments*, pp. 257–69; Lee, 'The origins of the Menzies Government's policy', pp. 77–86; Subritzky, *Confronting Sukarno*, ch. 2.

23 British High Commission in Canberra to Bunting, 15 January 1963, A4940/1, C3739, NAA.

24 Tange to A. Eastman, Australian High Commission in London, 16 January 1963, A4940/1, C3736, NAA.

25 Shann to Canberra, 2 February 1963, A1838/280, 3034/7/1/1, part 1, NAA.

26 Lee, 'The origins of the Menzies Government's policy', pp. 78–9.

27 Woodard, 'Best practice in Australia's foreign policy', p. 90.

28 Barwick to Holyoake, 2 February 1963, A4940/1, C3739, NAA.

29 Cabinet decision 632, 5 February 1963, A4940/1, C3739, NAA.

30 Cabinet submission 576 by Barwick, 'Quadripartite talks on Indonesia', 26 February 1963, quoted from pp. 5, 9 and 2, A5819/2, vol. 15, NAA.

31 Home to Macmillan, 'The future defence of Malaysia', 16 April 1963, PREM11/4189, PRO.

32 Cabinet submission 576 by Barwick, 'Quadripartite talks on Indonesia', 26 February 1963, quoted from p. 11, A5819/2, vol. 15, NAA.

33 Woodard, 'Best practice in Australia's foreign policy', p. 85.

34 Lee, 'The origins of the Menzies Government's policy', pp. 80–1.

35 Cabinet submission 576 by Barwick, 'Quadripartite talks on Indonesia', 26 February 1963, quoted from p. 10, A5819/2, vol. 15, NAA; Cabinet decision 675, 5 March 1963, A5819/2, vol. 15, NAA.

36 British High Commissioner in Canberra to Sandys, 'Australian attitude towards Malaysia', 8 April 1963, DO164/39, PRO.

37 Subritzky, *Confronting Sukarno*, p. 65.

38 Lee, 'The origins of the Menzies Government's policy', p. 85.

39 Edwards with Pemberton, *Crises and Commitments*, p. 262.

40 'Record of a conversation at Admiralty House at 11 a.m. on Monday, June 24, 1963', Prem11/4096, PRO.

41 Edwards with Pemberton, *Crises and Commitments*, pp. 265–6; Woodard, 'Best practice in Australia's foreign policy', p. 92.

42 Trend to Macmillan, 'South East Asia', 2 April 1963, PREM11/4189, PRO.

43 Home to Macmillan, 'The future defence of Malaysia', 16 April 1963, PREM11/4189, PRO.

44 Edwards with Pemberton, *Crises and Commitments*, pp. 266–7. Emphasis in original.

45 Macmillan to Menzies, 20 September 1963, PREM11/4101, PRO.

46 CPD, HR, vol. 40, 25 September 1963, pp. 1338–9.

47 Edwards, 'Malaysia and Singapore', p. 188.

48 Barwick to Harrison, Australian High Commissioner in London, 16 December 1963, A4940/1, C1473, part 1, NAA.

49 Record of conversation between Hasluck and R. A. Butler, British Foreign Secretary, 6 July 1964, FO371/175054, PRO.

50 Subritzky, *Confronting Sukarno*, p. 89.

51 Douglas-Home to Menzies, 17 December 1963, PREM11/4101, PRO.

52 Quoted in Subritzky, *Confronting Sukarno*, p. 90.

53 Edwards with Pemberton, *Crises and Commitments*, pp. 285–7. The narrative in the remainder of this section draws mainly on the detailed accounts provided in this text, pp. 285–92, 315–23, 340–44; Subritzky, *Confronting Sukarno*, pp. 108–11, 119–21, 133–40; and Dee, In Australia's Own Interests, chs 6 and 7.

54 See especially Subritzky, *Confronting Sukarno*, p. 111.

55 Edwards with Pemberton, *Crises and Commitments*, p. 342.

56 For a discussion of Australia's military operations after the Borneo deployment, see Dennis and Grey, *Emergency and Confrontation*, chs 14–17.

[57] Wilson to Menzies, 18 August 1965, in British High Commission in Canberra to Menzies, 19 August 1965, A4940/1, C4266, NAA; Australian High Commission in London to Canberra, 2 September 1965, A4940/1, C4266, NAA.

[58] Canberra to Australian High Commission in London, 3 September 1965, A4940/1, C4266, NAA.

[59] Edwards, 'Singapore and Malaysia', pp. 192–3.

[60] Bunting did not say so, but this idea had echoes of a plan that President de Gaulle had been pushing for some time; see Waters, 'The Menzies Government and de Gaulle's proposal'.

[61] Bunting to Menzies, 'British presence in South-East Asia', 19 October 1965, A1209/80, 1966/7203, NAA. 'Hicks' was Sir Edwin Hicks of the Prime Minister's Department.

[62] Stockwell, 'Malaysia', p. 139.

8 The troops go home

[1] Record of conversation between Menzies, Wilson and Holyoake, London, 1 February 1965, PREM13/889, PRO.

[2] Conversation reported in Knott to Bunting, 12 July 1966, A1209/80, 1966/7335, part 1, NAA.

[3] Lee, *Search for Security*, p. 134.

[4] Gilchrist to Tange, 3 March 1959, A1838/2, 155/7/4, part 1, NAA.

[5] DEA, 'Summary of U.K. paper', *c.* May 1960, and 'Brief account of the discussion between the four Prime Ministers', 13 May 1960, both in A1209/79, 1961/544, NAA.

[6] Tange to Bunting, 13 January 1961, A1209/79, 1961/544/21, NAA.

[7] CRO, 'Draft brief for Lord Mountbatten's tour. The background of Australian defence policy', 26 January 1961, DO164/39/2, PRO.

[8] CRO, 'Note for the Secretary of State's visit to Australia and New Zealand', n.d. (*c.* June 1961), DO164/39/7, PRO.

[9] Macmillan to Menzies and Holyoake, 20 October 1961 and 5 February 1962, PREM11/4189, PRO.

[10] Holyoake to Macmillan, 13 December 1961, and Menzies to Macmillan, 31 August 1962, PREM11/4189, PRO.

[11] Menzies to Douglas-Home, 23 October 1964, Menzies Papers, MS 4936, Series 1, Box 10, Folder 82, NLA.

[12] Coral Bell, *Dependent Ally*, p. 85.

[13] Wilson, *The Labour Government 1964–70*, p. 212.

[14] Quoted in Dockrill, *British Defence since 1945*, p. 86.

[15] Crossman, *The Diaries of a Cabinet Minister*, vol. 1, p. 95 (diary entry for 11 December 1964).

[16] Britain-centred accounts include Darby, *British Defence Policy East of Suez 1947–1968*, ch. 9; Dockrill, *British Defence since 1945*, ch. 6; Darwin, *Britain and Decolonisation*, pp. 289–98; Healey, *The Time of my Life*, ch. 14; Darwin, 'Britain's withdrawal from East of Suez'; Ovendale, *British Defence Policy since 1945*, ch. 4; and Pickering, *Britain's Withdrawal from East of Suez*, chs 6–8. Australia-centred accounts include Richardson, 'Australian strategic and defence policies', pp. 242–9; Coral Bell, *Dependent Ally*, ch. 5; and McDougall, 'Australia and the British military withdrawal from East of Suez'. All but Healey's are secondary-sourced accounts.

[17] Australian High Commission in London to Canberra, 2 December 1964, A1209/80, 1965/6124, NAA.

[18] Australian High Commission in London to Canberra, 11 February 1965, A1209/80, 1965/6124, NAA.

[19] Department of Defence, 'United Kingdom defence review', June 1965, p. 6, A1209/80, 1965/6124, NAA.

[20] Quoted in Department of Defence, 'United Kingdom defence review', June 1965, p. 2, A1209/80, 1965/6124, NAA.

21 Aitkin (ed.), *The Howson Diaries*, p. 181, quoted in McDougall, 'Australia and the British military withdrawal from East of Suez', p. 188.

22 Department of Defence, 'United Kingdom defence review', June 1965, p. 5, A1209/80, 1965/6124, NAA.

23 Record of meeting between Menzies, Wilson and Holyoake, London, 1 July 1965, PREM13/889, PRO.

24 Aitkin (ed.), *The Howson Diaries*, p. 181, quoted in McDougall, 'Australia and the British military withdrawal from East of Suez', p. 188.

25 Wilson to Menzies and Holyoake, 24 September 1965, PREM13/889, PRO.

26 Bunting to Menzies, 19 October 1965, A1209/80, 1966/7203, NAA.

27 Menzies to Wilson, 22 October 1965, PREM13/889, PRO.

28 Healey to Wilson, 1 November 1965, PREM13/889, PRO.

29 Cumming-Bruce to London, 24 November 1965, PREM13/889, PRO.

30 Menzies to Wilson, 19 January 1966, PREM13/889, PRO.

31 'Defence consultations. Summary record of discussions held in the Cabinet Room, Parliament House, Canberra', 1–2 February 1966, attachment to FAD decision 22, 'Defence consultations', 2 February 1966, A5839, vol. 1, NAA.

32 Subritzky, *Confronting Sukarno*, pp. 182–3.

33 Healey to Wilson, 3 February 1966, PREM13/889, PRO; Healey, *The Time of My Life*, p. 291; 'Defence consultations. Summary record of discussions held in the Cabinet Room, Parliament House, Canberra', 1–2 February 1966, p. 21, attachment to FAD decision 22, 'Defence consultations', A5839, vol. 1, NAA.

34 Johnston to London, 2 February 1966, PREM13/889, PRO.

35 Quoted in Coral Bell, *Dependent Ally*, p. 84.

36 Millar, 'Anglo-Australian partnership in defence of the Malaysian area', p. 86.

37 Crossman, *The Diaries of a Cabinet Minister*, vol. 1, p. 456 (diary entry for 14 February 1966).

38 Johnston to London, 26 June 1966, and Palliser to British High Commission in Canberra, 29 June 1966, both in PREM13/1454, PRO; Knott to Bunting, 12 July 1966, A1209/80, 1966/7335, part 1, NAA.

39 Johnston to London, 1 June 1966, PREM13/726, PRO.

40 These points have been compiled from Hasluck to Plimsoll, 27 May 1966, and Bunting to Holt, 31 May 1966, both in A1209/80, 1966/7335, part 1; and Hasluck to Holt, 19 April and 20 April 1967, and Bunting to Holt, 24 April 1967, all in A1209/80, 1966/7335, part 2.

41 Speech by Downer, delivered to the English Speaking Union, Liverpool, 23 October 1967, in A1209/80, 1966/7203, NAA.

42 Downer to Holt, 20 July 1967, A1209/80, 1966/7335, part 6, NAA.

43 Holt to Downer, 27 May 1966, and Downer to Holt, 1 June 1966, both in A1209/80, 1966/7335, part 1, NAA.

44 Minute by Wilson (n.d.) on copy of Holt's message of 27 May 1966 to Downer; London to British High Commission in Canberra, 1 June 1966; Palliser to Wilson, 2 June 1966, emphasis in original; all in PREM13/726, PRO.

45 Parsons, *South East Asian Days*, p. 81.

46 Downer to Holt, 13 June 1966, A1209/80, 1966/7335, part 1, NAA.

47 Downer to Holt, 18 July 1967, A1209/80, 1966/7335, part 6, NAA.

48 Griffith to Bunting, 28 July 1967, A1209/80, 1966/7335, part 6, NAA.

49 For examples of Holt's letters: Holt to Wilson, 12 May 1966, PREM13/728, PRO; Holt to Wilson, 21 April 1967, A1209/80, 1966/7335, part 2, NAA.

50 'Record of conversation between the Prime Minister and the Prime Minister of Australia', 13 June 1967, PREM13/1323, PRO.

51 'British statements about the retention of forces in South East Asia', with covering note dated 16 June 1967; record of conversation between Holt and Wilson, 15 June 1967; both in PREM13/1323, PRO.

52 Holt to Johnson, n.d. on file copy but approved in Cabinet on 2 May 1967, A1209/80, 1966/7335, part 2A, NAA.

53 See, for example, Hasluck to Holt, 20 April 1967, A1209/80, 1966/7335, part 2, NAA.

54 Rusk to Brown, 8 July 1967, copy in A1838/346, TS691/1/1, part 2, NAA.

55 Critchley to Canberra, 1 January 1968, A1838/346, TS691/1/1, part 3, NAA.

56 DEA, 'Text of the Australian note' [to Britain], 12 January 1968, A1838/346, TS691/1/1, part 3, NAA.

57 Ibid.

58 Aitkin (ed.), *The Howson Diaries*, p. 181, quoted in McDougall, 'Australia and the British military withdrawal from East of Suez', p. 188.

59 Defence Planning Staff Papers 1967, no. 98: 'Implications for each of the Services of decision to terminate our commitments in the Far East and the Persian Gulf by March 1972', 28 December 1967, DEFE6/104, PRO.

60 Bunting to Menzies, 19 October 1965, A1209/80, 1966/7203, NAA; Johnston to London, 25 November 1965, PREM13/889, PRO.

61 As early as 1963 the British had assessed Gorton thus: 'Though personally friendly to us and to United Kingdom generally Senator Gorton is very strongly in favour of equipping Navy and other services with American equipment'. His American wife was thought to be anti-British. British High Commission in Canberra to London, 6 February 1963, DO169/76, PRO.

62 Richardson, 'Australian strategic and defence policies', p. 244.

63 Cabinet decision 517, 'Use of the word "British" on Australian passports', 22 August 1967, A5840, NAA; Cabinet submission 285, 'Appeals to the Privy Council', May 1967, A5842/2, vol. 10, NAA; Holt to Wilson, 24 August 1967, and Commonwealth Office (that is, the newly renamed CRO) to Johnston, 5 September 1967, both in PREM13/1320, PRO.

Conclusion

1 Darwin, 'The Pacific and decolonization', p. 410.

2 Subritzky, *Confronting Sukarno*, p. 203.

3 Lowe, 'Introduction', p. 3.

Bibliography

Government archives (Australia)

National Archives of Australia, Canberra

Prime Minister's Department and Cabinet Office

A1209   Correspondence files, 1957–
A4909   Cabinet decisions, 1951–54
A4910   Cabinet and Cabinet committee decisions, 1954–58
A4940   Cabinet files, 1949–67
A4943   Cabinet and Cabinet committee decisions, 1958–63
A5818   Cabinet submissions, 1958–63
A5819   Cabinet submissions and decisions, 1961–63
A5839   Cabinet and Cabinet committee decisions, 1966
A5840   Cabinet and Cabinet committee decisions, 1966–67
A5842   Cabinet submissions, 1966–67

Department of External Affairs

A1838   Correspondence files, 1948–

Department of Defence

A816   Correspondence files, 1928–58

Miscellaneous

A5954   Shedden Collection

National Archives of Australia, Melbourne

Department of Civil Aviation

MP464   Correspondence files, 1948–59

Department of Foreign Affairs and Trade

Tange Papers

National Library of Australia

Menzies Papers, MS4936

Government archives (United Kingdom)

Public Record Office, London

Prime Minister's Office

CAB128	Cabinet minutes, 1945–64
CAB129	Cabinet memoranda, 1945–64
CAB134	Cabinet committee files, 1945–74
PREM11	Prime Minister's correspondence and papers, 1951–64
PREM13	Prime Minister's correspondence and papers, 1964–70

Commonwealth Relations Office

DO35	Correspondence files, 1915–71
DO161	Includes Australia files, 1961–63
DO164	Includes Australia files, 1960–64
DO169	Far East and Pacific Department files, 1960–66

Foreign Office

FO371	Correspondence files, 1906–66

Colonial Office

CO1030	Far East Department files, 1948–67
CO1036	Pacific Department files, 1952–67

Ministry of Defence

DEFE6	Joint Planning Staff and Defence Planning Staff reports

Books, articles and theses

Aitkin, Don (ed.) *The Howson Diaries: The Life of Politics*, the Viking Press, Ringwood, 1984.

Alomes, Stephen, *A Nation at Last? The Changing Character of Australian Nationalism 1880–1988*, Angus & Robertson, Sydney, 1988.

Arnold, John, Spearritt, Peter, and Walker, David (eds), *Out of Empire: The British Dominion of Australia*, Mandarin, Melbourne, 1993.

Arnold, Lorna, *A Very Special Relationship: British Atomic Weapon Trials in Australia*, HMSO, London, 1987.

Barclay, Glen St J., *Friends in High Places: Australian-American Diplomatic Relations since 1945*, Oxford University Press, Melbourne, 1985.

Barwick, Garfield, 'Australia's foreign relations', in John Wilkes (ed.), *Australia's Defence and Foreign Policy*, Angus & Robertson, Sydney, 1964, pp. 3–44.

Beale, Howard, *This Inch of Time: Memoirs of Politics and Diplomacy*, Melbourne University Press, Carlton, 1977.

Bell, Coral, *Dependent Ally: A Study in Australian Foreign Policy*, Allen & Unwin, Sydney, 2nd edn, 1988.

Bell, Philip, and Bell, Roger, *Implicated: The United States in Australia*, Oxford University Press, Melbourne, 1993.

Bolton, Geoffrey, *The Middle Way, 1942–1988*, vol. 5 of *The Oxford History of Australia*, Oxford University Press, Melbourne, 1st edn, 1993.

——, 'The United Kingdom', in W. J. Hudson (ed.), *Australia in World Affairs 1971–1975*, George Allen & Unwin, Sydney, 1980, pp. 209–30.

Bridge, Carl, 'Globalisation? It's the world catching up to us', *Age*, 15 August 2001.

—— (ed.), *Munich to Vietnam: Australia's Relations with Britain and the United States since the 1930s*, Melbourne University Press, Carlton, 1991.

Cain, Frank (ed.), *Menzies in War and Peace*, Allen & Unwin, Sydney, 1997.

Carrère d'Encausse, Hélène, and Schram, Stuart, *Marxism and Asia: An Introduction with Readings*, Allen Lane, London, 1969.

Chauvel, Richard, 'Up the creek without a paddle: Australia, West New Guinea and the "great and powerful friends"', in Cain (ed.), *q.v.*, pp. 55–71.

Connors, Jane, 'Identity and history', *Australian Historical Studies*, vol. 32, 2001, pp. 132–6.

Costar, Brian, 'The politics of coalition', in S. Prasser, J. R. Nethercote and J. Warhurst (eds), *The Menzies Era: A Reappraisal of Government, Politics and Policy*, Hale & Iremonger, Sydney, 1995, pp. 93–110.

Crawford, John (ed.), *Australian Trade Policy 1942–1966: A Documentary History*, Australian National University Press, Canberra, 1968.

Crossman, Richard, *The Diaries of a Cabinet Minister*, vol. 1: *Minister of Housing 1964–66*, Hamish Hamilton and Jonathan Cape, London, 1976.

Darby, Phillip, *British Defence Policy East of Suez 1947–1968*, Oxford University Press, London, 1973.

Darwin, John, *Britain and Decolonisation: The Retreat from Empire in the Post-war World*, Macmillan, Basingstoke, 1988.

——, 'Britain's withdrawal from East of Suez', in Bridge (ed.), *q.v.*, pp. 140–58.

——, 'Decolonisation and world politics', in Lowe (ed.), *q.v.*, pp. 7–23.

——, 'Decolonization and the end of empire', in Winks (ed.), *q.v.*, pp. 541–57.

——, 'The Pacific and decolonization', in Elizalde (ed.), *q.v.*, pp. 409–19.

Davidson, Jim, 'The de-dominionisation of Australia', in John Arnold, Spearritt and Walker (eds), *q.v.*, pp. 149–69.

Day, David, 'The US alliance? Same as it ever was', *Age*, 16 October 2001.

Dee, Moreen, In Australia's Own Interests: Australian Foreign Policy During Confrontation 1963–1966, PhD thesis, University of New England, 2000.

Dennis, Peter, and Grey, Jeffrey, *Emergency and Confrontation: Australia's Military Operations in Malaya and Borneo 1950–1966*, Allen & Unwin, Sydney, 1996.

Dockrill, Michael, *British Defence since 1945*, Basil Blackwell, Oxford, 1988.

Doran, Stuart, 'Toeing the line: Australia's abandonment of "traditional" West New Guinea policy', *Journal of Pacific History*, vol. 36, 2001, pp. 5–18.

Dunn, Michael, *Australia and the Empire: From 1788 to the Present*, Fontana, Sydney, 1984.

Dyster, Barrie, and Meredith, David, *Australia in the International Economy in the Twentieth Century*, Cambridge University Press, Cambridge, 1990.

Edwards, Peter, 'Singapore and Malaysia, 1965', in Lowe (ed.), *q.v.*, pp. 187–98.

Edwards, Peter, with Gregory Pemberton, *Crises and Commitments: The Politics and Diplomacy of Australia's Involvement in Southeast Asian Conflicts, 1948–1965*, Allen & Unwin, Sydney, 1992.

Elizalde, Dolores (ed.), *Las Relaciones Internacionales en el Pacifico (Siglos XVIII-XX): Colonizacion, Descolonizacion y Encuentro Cultural*, Superior de Investigaciones Cientificas, Madrid, 1997.

Gelber, H. G., *Australia, Britain and the EEC, 1961 to 1963*, Oxford University Press, Melbourne, 1966.

Gifford, Peter, 'The Cold War across Asia', in Goldsworthy (ed.), *q.v.*, pp. 171–219.

Goldsworthy, David (ed.), *Facing North: A Century of Australian Engagement with Asia*, vol. 1: *1901 to the 1970s*, Melbourne University Press, Carlton, 2001.

Greenwood, Gordon, 'Australian foreign policy in action', in Gordon Greenwood and Norman Harper (eds), *Australia in World Affairs 1961–1965*, Cheshire, Melbourne, 1968, pp. 1–133.

Gurry, Meg, 'A tale of missed opportunities: Australia's relations with India since 1947', in Marika Vicziany (ed.), *Australia-India, the Economic Links: Past, Present and Future*, Indian Ocean Centre for Peace Studies, University of Western Australia, Perth, 1993, pp. 10–23.

——, *India: Australia's Neglected Neighbour? 1947–1966*, Centre for the Study of Australia-Asia Relations, Griffith University, Brisbane, 1996.

Hack, Karl, *Defence and Decolonisation in Southeast Asia: Britain, Malaya and Singapore 1941–1968*, Curzon, Richmond, Surrey, 2001.

Healey, Denis, *The Time of My Life*, Michael Joseph, London, 1989.

Higgott, Richard, 'Australia and Africa 1970–80: a decade of change and growth', in Colin Legum (ed.), *Africa Contemporary Record*, vol. 14, Africana, New York and London, 1981, pp. A219–A235.

Holdich, Roger, Johnson, Vivianne, and Andre, Pamela (eds), *The ANZUS Treaty 1951*, Department of Foreign Affairs and Trade, Canberra, 2001.

Holland, Robert, 'The imperial factor in British strategies from Attlee to Macmillan, 1945–63', *Journal of Imperial and Commonwealth History*, vol. 12, 1984, pp. 165–86.

——, *The Pursuit of Greatness: Britain and the World Role, 1900–1970*, Fontana, London, 1991.

Horne, Alistair, *Macmillan: 1957–86*, Macmillan, London, 1989.

Hudson, W. J., *Australia and the Colonial Question at the United Nations*, Sydney University Press, Sydney, 1970.

——, *Blind Loyalty: Australia and the Suez Crisis, 1956*, Melbourne University Press, Carlton, 1989.

——, *Casey*, Oxford University Press, Melbourne, 1986.

Hughes, Robert, 'Introduction', in Malcolm Turnbull, *The Reluctant Republic*, Heinemann, Melbourne, 1993, pp. xi–xvii.

Hyam, Ronald, 'The parting of the ways: Britain and South Africa's departure from the Commonwealth, 1951–61', *Journal of Imperial and Commonwealth History*, vol. 26, no. 2, 1998, pp. 157–75.

——, 'The primacy of geopolitics: the dynamics of British imperial policy, 1763–1963', *Journal of Imperial and Commonwealth History*, vol. 27, no. 2, 1999, pp. 27–52.

——, 'Introduction', in Hyam and Louis (eds), *q.v.*, vol. 1, pp. xxv–lxxxviii.

Hyam, Ronald, and Louis, Wm. Roger (eds), *The Conservative Government and the End of Empire 1957–1964*, vol.1: *High Policy, Political and Constitutional Change*, and vol. 2: *Economics, International Relations and the Commonwealth*, Stationery Office, London, 2000.

Jones, Matthew, 'Creating Malaysia: Singapore security, the Borneo territories, and the contours of British policy, 1961–63', *Journal of Imperial and Commonwealth History*, vol. 28, no. 2, 2000, pp. 85–109.

Kirk-Greene, Anthony, *On Crown Service: A History of HM Colonial and Overseas Civil Services 1837–1997*, I. B. Tauris, London, 1999.

Lee, David, 'The origins of the Menzies Government's policy on Indonesia's confrontation of Malaysia', in Cain (ed.), *q.v.*, pp. 72–98.

——, *Search for Security: The Political Economy of Australia's Postwar Foreign and Defence Policy*, Allen & Unwin, Sydney, 1992.

Lee, David, and Dee, Moreen, 'Southeast Asian conflicts', in Goldsworthy (ed.), *q.v.*, pp. 262–309.

Louis, Wm. Roger, 'The European colonial empires', in Michael Howard and Wm. Roger Louis (eds), *The Oxford History of the Twentieth Century*, Oxford University Press, New York, 1998, pp. 91–102.

Louis, Wm. Roger, and Robinson, R. E., 'The imperialism of decolonization', *Journal of Imperial and Commonwealth History*, vol. 22, 1994, pp. 462–511.

Lowe, David (ed.), *Australia and the End of Empires: The Impact of Decolonisation in Australia's Near North, 1945–1965*, Deakin University Press, Geelong, 1996.

——, 'Australia at the United Nations in the 1950s: the paradox of empire', *Australian Journal of International Affairs*, vol. 51, 1997, pp. 171–81.

——, 'Introduction', in Lowe (ed.), *q.v.*, pp. 1–6.

——, 'Making sense of decolonisation in the Asia-Pacific region, 1945–65: the view from Australasia', in Elizalde (ed.), *q.v.*, pp. 437–51.

McDougall, Derek, 'Australia and the British military withdrawal from East of Suez', *Australian Journal of International Affairs*, vol. 51, 1997, pp. 183–94.

Macintyre, Stuart, 'Australia and the empire', in Winks (ed.), *q.v.*, pp. 163–81.

McIntyre, W. David, 'The admission of small states to the Commonwealth ', *Journal of Imperial and Commonwealth History*, vol. 24, 1996, pp. 244–77.

Mackie, J. A. C., *Konfrontasi: The Indonesia-Malaysia Dispute 1963–1966*, Oxford University Press, Kuala Lumpur, 1974.

Mandle, W. F., *Going it Alone: Australia's National Identity in the Twentieth Century*, Allen Lane, Melbourne, 1978.

Marr, David, *Barwick*, Allen & Unwin, Sydney, 1992.

Martel, Gordon, 'Decolonisation after Suez: retreat or rationalisation?', *Australian Journal of Politics and History*, vol. 46, 2000, pp. 403–17.

Martin, A. W., *Robert Menzies: A Life*, vol. 2: *1944–1978*, Melbourne University Press, Carlton, 1999.

Meaney, Neville, 'Britishness and Australian identity: the problem of nationalism in Australian history and historiography', *Australian Historical Studies*, vol. 32, 2001, pp. 76–90.

Millar, T. B., 'Anglo-Australian partnership in defence of the Malaysian area', in A. F. Madden and W. H. Morris-Jones (eds), *Australia and Britain: Studies in a Changing Relationship*, Sydney University Press, Sydney, 1980, pp. 71–89.

—— (ed.), *Australian Foreign Minister: The Diaries of R. G. Casey*, Collins, London, 1972.

Miller, J. D. B., *Survey of Commonwealth Affairs: Problems of Expansion and Attrition 1953–1969*, Oxford University Press, London, 1974.

Nelson, Hank, 'Papua and New Guinea', in Tom Stannage, Kay Saunders and Richard Nile (eds), *Paul Hasluck in Australian History: Civic Personality and Public Life*, University of Queensland Press, St Lucia, n.d. (*c.* 1998), pp. 152–69.

Ovendale, Ritchie, *British Defence Policy since 1945*, Manchester University Press, Manchester, 1994.

Parkinson, Tony, 'America dismissed Australia's war hopes', *Age*, 12 October 2001.

Parsons, Alf, *South East Asian Days*, Centre for the Study of Australia-Asia Relations, Griffith University, Brisbane, 1998.

Pemberton, Gregory, 'An imperial imagination: explaining the post-1945 foreign policy of Robert Gordon Menzies', in Cain (ed.), *q.v.*, pp. 154–75.

Percox, David, 'Internal security and decolonization in Kenya, 1956–63', *Journal of Imperial and Commonwealth History*, vol. 29, 2001, pp. 92–116.

Pickering, Jeffrey, *Britain's Withdrawal from East of Suez: The Politics of Retrenchment*, Macmillan, Basingstoke, 1998.

Pitty, Roderic, 'The postwar expansion of trade with East Asia', in Goldsworthy (ed.), *q.v.*, pp. 220–61.

Reynolds, Wayne, *Australia's Bid for the Atomic Bomb*, Melbourne University Press, Carlton, 2000.

Richardson, J. L., 'Australian strategic and defence policies', in Gordon Greenwood and Norman Harper (eds), *Australia in World Affairs 1966–1970*, Cheshire, Melbourne, 1974, pp. 233–69.

Rickard, John, 'Imagining the unimaginable?', *Australian Historical Studies*, vol. 32, 2001, pp. 128–31.

Spender, Percy, *Exercises in Diplomacy: The ANZUS Treaty and the Colombo Plan*, Sydney University Press, Sydney, 1969.

Stockwell, A. J., 'Malaysia: the making of a neo-colony?', *Journal of Imperial and Commonwealth History*, vol. 26, no. 2, 1998, pp. 138–56.

Subritzky, John, *Confronting Sukarno: British, American, Australian and New Zealand Diplomacy in the Malaysian-Indonesian Confrontation, 1961–5*, Macmillan, Basingstoke, 2000.

Thompson, Roger, *Australian Imperialism in the Pacific: The Expansionist Era 1820–1920*, Melbourne University Press, Carlton, 1980.

——, 'Winds of change in the South Pacific', in Lowe (ed.), *q.v.*, pp. 161–71.

Tothill, David, 'Australian diplomatic reporting from South Africa 1946–1970, paper presented to the 24th annual conference of the African Studies Association of Australasia and the Pacific, Melbourne, 2001.

Tsokhas, Kosmas, *Making a Nation State: Cultural Identity, Economic Nationalism and Sexuality in Australian History*, Melbourne University Press, Carlton, 2001.

Ward, Stuart, *Australia and the British Embrace: The Demise of the Imperial Ideal*, Melbourne University Press, Carlton, 2001.

——, 'Sentiment and self-interest: the imperial ideal in Anglo-Australian commercial culture', *Australian Historical Studies*, vol. 32, 2001, pp. 91–108.

Waters, Christopher, 'The Menzies Government and de Gaulle's proposal for the neutralisation of Southeast Asia: 1963–1965', in Cain (ed.), *q.v.*, pp. 138–53.

——, 'War, decolonisation and postwar security', in Goldsworthy (ed.), *q.v.*, pp. 97–133.

Watt, Alan, *Australian Diplomat: Memoirs of Sir Alan Watt*, Angus and Robertson, Sydney, 1972.

Wilson, Harold, *The Labour Government 1964–70*, Weidenfeld & Nicolson and Michael Joseph, London, 1971.

Winks, Robin (ed.), *Historiography*, vol. 5 of Wm. Roger Louis (editor-in-chief), *Oxford History of the British Empire*, Oxford University Press, Oxford, 1999.

Woodard, Garry, 'Best practice in Australia's foreign policy: "Konfrontasi" (1963–66)', *Australian Journal of Political Science*, vol. 33, 1998, pp. 85–99.

Index

Acheson, Dean, 97, 98
Africa: Australian policy towards, 28–9, 73–92; British Empire in, 5; decolonisation, 44, 96; Menzies' detachment from, 22
Algeria, 42, 80
Allen, M. E., 42
Amery, Julian, 39
Anglo-Malaya Defence Agreement, 148
ANZAM: agreement of 1948, 26, 53; Australian, British and New Zealand military planning, 95, 140; and Britain's withdrawal from Southeast Asia, 159; and Christmas Island transfer, 60; and Cocos Islands transfer, 54; and defence of New Hebrides and Solomon Islands, 70; *see also* Southeast Asian defence
ANZUS: applicability to Malaysia, 148, 150–1; Australian obligations in Southeast Asia, 157; Australian policy in Africa, 82; British attitude to, 18, 101; South Pacific study group, 71; treaty negotiations, 14, 16, 17; *see also* Australia; United States
apartheid, 89, 90, 114; *see also* race issues
Attlee, Clement, 54
Attlee Government, 18
Australia: and Africa, 14, 73–92; aid programs, 71, 82, 86–8, 108; Britain, closeness of ties with, 1, 13, 18–21, 52; Britain, loosening of ties with, 1–3, 6–9, 14, 100–2, 115–16, 118–19, 155–6, 157–8, 170–2, 177; and Britain's approach to Europe, 7, 120–38; and Britain's withdrawal from Southeast Asia, 8, 157–72; British Empire, attitudes towards, 21–5, 36–7; British Empire, interests in, 5, 25–31, 174–5; Britishness, 2, 8–9, 15–16, 20–1, 49–50; Britishness,

decline of, 1–3; colonial governor in the Pacific, 32–3; and; colonial issues at the United Nations, 40–3; colonial policy, 34, 44–6; and the Commonwealth, 103–19; and decolonisation *see* end of empire; de-dominionisation, 3, 14; disagreements with Britain on colonial policy, 37, 40–3, 50; and Indonesia, 8, 24, 37, 59, 139, 146, 149, 150, 156; and Malaysia, 8, 142–56; and nuclear weapons, 19, 20, 100; and Southeast Asian defence, 18, 23, 26–8, 31, 139–41, 142–56, 157–72; and the South Pacific, 70–2; territorial transfers, 51–70; and the United States, economic relations, 2, 16; and the United States, strategic relations, 14, 15, 16–17, 18, 140–1, 158; *see also* ANZUS; Britain; Southeast Asian defence
Australia, New Zealand and Malaya *see* ANZAM
Australia, New Zealand and the United States *see* ANZUS
Australian Labor Party, 23–4, 27

Ball, George, 130, 131
Barwick, Garfield: favours South Pacific study group, 71; policy towards Malaysia, 144–51; on Southern African problems, 90–1; West New Guinea switch, 47–9
Beale, Howard, 104, 146
Belgium, as a colonial power, 5, 42, 44, 80, 85, 95
Bell, Coral, 161
Black, Robert, 62
Blakeney, F. J., 80
Bolton, Geoffrey, 46